RELIGIOUS LITERATURE
OF THE WEST

RELIGIOUS

LITERATURE
OF THE WEST

JOHN R. WHITNEY
AND
SUSAN W. HOWE

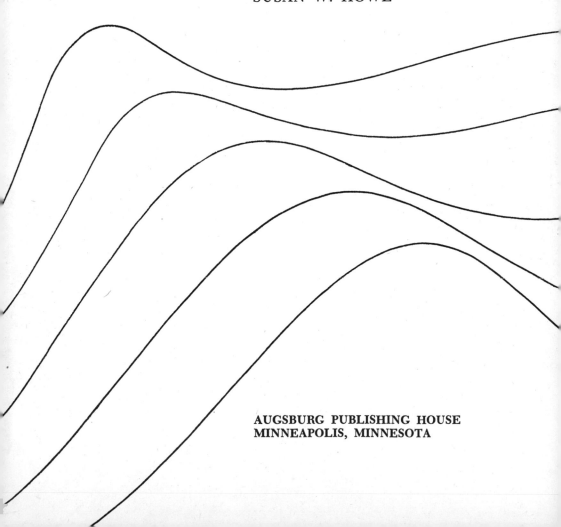

AUGSBURG PUBLISHING HOUSE
MINNEAPOLIS, MINNESOTA

RELIGIOUS LITERATURE OF THE WEST

Manufactured in the United States of America.

CONTENTS

SECTION THREE: THE QUR'AN

ACKNOWLEDGMENTS

The list of those who helped in the development of this course includes teachers, staff, consultants, committees, and advisers. The list does not mention the administrators of schools in the field study, the hundreds of students in our pilot classes, and the countless interested citizens who contributed suggestions. All help given by named and unnamed persons is gratefully acknowledged.

THE TEACHERS—

Miss Barbara E. Alberts, Rochester Area Jr.-Sr. High, Rochester; Mrs. Lois Beam, Trafford High School, Trafford; Mrs. Frances L. Black, Penn Joint High School, Claridge; Mr. John C. Chamberlain, Elmer L. Meyers High School, Wilkes-Barre; Mr. Thomas J. Collins, Spring-Ford Sr. High School, Royersford; Miss Janet L. Curtis, Mt. Lebanon Sr. High School, Pittsburgh; Mr. John S. Diehl, Pennridge High School, Perkasie; Mrs. Ruth W. Elder, Littlestown Joint High School, Littlestown; Miss Ethel E. Ewing, Donora Sr. High School, Donora; Mr. Timothy J. Ference, West Hazleton Sr. High School, West Hazleton; Miss Lois Fitzgerald, North High School, West Mifflin; Mr. Richard H. Gibboney, Lewistown-Granville High School, Lewistown; Mrs. June L. Gwyn, Exeter High School, Reading; Miss Dorothy M. Hill, Peabody High School, Pittsburgh; Miss Betty D. Keesey, Kiskie Area Sr. High School, Vandergrift; Mr. Jacob G. Kuhns, Mechanicsburg Area Sr. High School, Mechanicsburg; Mrs. Isobel E. Kulich, Southern Columbia Area High School, Catawissa; Mr. Ralph G. Kurtz, Ligonier Valley High School, Ligonier; Mrs. Inez G. Long, McCaskey High School, Lancaster; Mrs. Esther Madciff, Hershey Sr. High School, Hershey; Mr. I. Richard Martin, Central Bucks High School, Doylestown; Mrs. Mary M. McConnell, Academy Sr. High School, Erie; Mr. Ralph G. McConnell, Upper Darby Sr. High School, Upper Darby; Mrs. Lucille P. Metzger, Williamsport High School, Williamsport; Mrs. Norma Michaelson, Marple-Newtown High School, Newtown Square; Miss Marsha A. Musick, Norwin High School, Irwin; Mrs. Allene F. Poulson and Mr. Walter Vogelsong, Cedar Cliff High School, Camp Hill; Mrs. Dorothy Price, Cedar Crest High School, Lebanon; Mr. Draper P. Read, State College Area High School, State College; Mr. Robert L. Rodgers, Hanover Sr. High School, Hanover; Mr. Delmarwade Rosemergey, Tunkhannock Area High School, Tunkhannock; Mr. Joseph Sabo, Jr., Altoona Area Sr. High School, Altoona; Mr. Bernard J. Schimmel, Louis E. Dieruff High School, Allentown; Mr. Irwin Schmuckler, Springfield High School, Springfield; Mrs. Elzear L. Schoch, Bradford Area Sr. High School, Bradford; Mr. George S. Scoufalos, Fleetwood Area High School, Fleetwood; Mrs. Sally A. Shaffer, Lincoln High School, Ellwood City: Miss Jean Louis Stellfox, Shamokin High School, Shamokin; Mr. John H. Trojanowski, Jersey Shore Sr. High School, Jersey Shore; Miss Linda K. Warman, Easton Area High School, Easton; Miss Diane Weissberger, Germantown High School, Philadelphia; Mr. John M. Witherspoon, Chambersburg Area Sr. High School, Chambersburg; Mrs. Ruth C. Wright, Swarthmore High School, Swarthmore: Miss Judith Ann Ziegenfus, Abington Heights High School, Clarks Summit.

PENNSYLVANIA STATE UNIVERSITY STAFF—

Project Staff:

Dr. Luther Harshbarger, Chairman, Department of Religious Studies; Dr. John R. Whitney, Religious Literature Project Director, Assistant Professor of Religious Studies, Department of Religious Studies; Mrs. Susan Howe, Research Assistant.

Working Committee:

Dr. William E. Babcock, Superintendent, State College Area School District; Dr. Gordon C. Godbey, Associate Dean for Continuing Education, The Pennsylvania State University; Mr. Norman H. Lampman, Coordinator of English and Humanities, State College Area High School; Mr. Draper P. Read, Guidance Director and teacher of experimental class, State College Area High School.

English Consultants:

Dr. S. Leonard Rubinstein, Professor of English, Dr. Edgar K. Knapp, Professor of English Education, and Dr. W. Douglas Macneal, Instructor in English.

Field Study Staff:

The late Dr. Hugh M. Davison, initial Field Study Director; Dr. John W. Kohl, Field Study Director and Director of the Center for Cooperative Research with Schools; Dr. Robert B. Patrick, Consultant to the Field Study; Mr. George Nye, Research Assistant; Mr. Howard Newson, Graduate Assistant.

Resource Assistants:

Mrs. Ethel Ewing, Donora School District; Mr. Richard Gibboney, Mifflin County School District; Mr. Ralph Kurtz, Ligonier Valley School District; Mrs. Inez Long, Lancaster City School District; Mrs. Norma Michaelson, Marple-Newtown School District; and Mrs. Ruth Wright, Swarthmore School District.

CONSULTANTS ON COURSE READINGS—

THE HEBREW BIBLE—Dr. Bernhard Anderson, Professor of Biblical Theology, Drew University; THE NEW TESTAMENT—Dr. Krister Stendahl, Professor of New Testament Theology, Harvard Divinity School; Dr. Samuel Sandmel, Distinguished Services Professor of Bible and Hellenistic Literature, Hebrew Union College-Jewish Institute of Religion; Dr. Walter Ong, S.J., Professor of English, St. Louis University; THE RABBINIC WORKS—Dr. Joseph Blau, Chairman of the Department of Religion, Columbia University; Dr. Nahum Glatzer, Director of the Golding Center for Judaic Studies, Brandeis University; THE KORAN— Dr. Abdel Kader, Director of the Islamic Center, Washington, D.C.; Dr. El Biali, Assistant to Dr. Kader, Islamic Center.

SUMMER SCHOOL CONSULTANTS—

Dr. Lou Silberman, Professor of Religious Studies, Vanderbilt University (THE TALMUD); Dr. Kalrfried Froelich, Professor of New Testament and Church History, Drew University (THE NEW TESTAMENT); Dr. Abdel El-Baili; Assistant to the Director of the Islamic Center, Washington, D.C. (THE KORAN); Dr. Samuel Sandmel, Distinguished Services Professor of Bible and Hellenistic Literature, Hebrew Union College (THE HEBREW BIBLE); Dr. Henry Sams, Head of the Department of English at Pennsylvania State University (SACRED WRITING AND LITERARY STUDIES); and Mr. Robert Hogan, Executive Secretary of National Council of Teachers of English (LITERATURE AND THE BIBLE).

OTHER CONSULTANTS—

Mr. Henry J. Aschenbrenner, Assistant Director, Pennsylvania Catholic Conference, and his advisors, Harrisburg; Dr. Helen R. Burchell, Assistant Professor of Education, University of Pennsylvania, Philadelphia; Mr. Alvin D. Chernin, Executive Director, Jewish Community Relations Council of Greater Philadelphia, and the members of his committee; Rabbi Arthur Gilbert, Dean, Reconstructionist Rabbinical College, Philadelphia; Reverend Robert Hammer, Bovina Center, New York; Mr. Bernhard E. Olson, National Director of Interreligious Affairs, National Conference of Christians and Jews, New York; Mr. William J. Peterson, Executive Editor, *Eternity Magazine*, Philadelphia; and Reverend Richard T. Purchase, Executive Secretary, Division of Education, Pennsylvania Council of Churches, Harrisburg.

STATE ADVISORY PANEL—

Dr. John Dunlap, Supt., Susquehanna Twp. School District; Mr. Rees J. Frescoln, Director of the Humanities, Neshaminy School District; Dr. Roland M. Frye, Professor of English, University of Pennsylvania; Mr. F. Gardner Gillen, Principal, Schenley High School; Dr. Lawrence Hugo, Professor of Sociology, Duquesne University; Dr. Dorothy Miller, Associate Professor of English, University of Pittsburgh; Dr. William M. Potter, Member of the Council of Basic Education, State Board of Education; Dr. Leonard Swidler, Professor of Religion, Temple University; Dr. Claude Welch, Associate Dean, College of Arts and Sciences, The University of Pennsylvania; Mr. Earl Welch, former Editor, Silver-Burdett Co.; and ex-officio, Dr. David Engel, Professor of Foundations of Education, University of Pittsburgh; and Dr. John S. Rouch, Director, Department of Education, Gannon College, Erie.

DEPARTMENT OF EDUCATION STAFF—

Dr. David H. Kurtzman, Secretary; Dr. Neal V. Musmanno, Deputy Secretary; Dr. B. Anton Hess, Commissioner for Basic Education; Mr. Donald M. Carroll, Jr., Assistant Commissioner for Basic Education; Dr. John E. Kosoloski, Director, Bureau of General and Academic Education; Mr. David T. Chestnut, Coordinator, Division of Languages; Mr. John L. Meehan and Mr. David W. Miller, English Education Advisors, Division of Languages; Mrs. Linda Jovanelly, Secretary, Division of Languages; Mr. Patrick Toole, then Curriculum

11

Development Specialist, Bureau of Curriculum Development and Evaluation; and Dr. Carroll Curtis, Research Associate, Bureau of Research.

In addition to the generous help of all who have contributed their time and ideas for this project, we acknowledge the work of the authors and editors, who are responsible for the text of this book.

JOHN E. KOSOLOSKI,
Director, Bureau of General and Academic Education
Pennsylvania Department of Education

PREFACE

THE ORIGINS OF THE COURSE

The genesis of this course of study was the Supreme Court's decision in re Abington vs. Schempp in which Mr. Justice Clark wrote that

> . . . it might well be said that one's education is not complete without a study of comparative religion or the history of religion and its relationship to the advancement of civilization. It certainly may be said that the Bible is worthy of study for its literary and historic qualities . . . .

The general Assembly of the Commonwealth of Pennsylvania responded to those options by passing Act 442 which was signed into law by Governor William W. Scranton on December 22, 1965. It reads:

> Section 1515. Religious Literature.— (a) Courses in the literature of the Bible and other religions writings may be introduced and studied as regular courses in the literature branch of education by all pupils in the secondary public schools. Such courses shall be elective only and not required of any student.

THE DESIGN OF THE COURSE

In September 1966, the Department of Public Instruction contracted with the Pennsylvania State University to assist in producing a course which would fulfill the mandate of Act 442. Project staff decided that the first course to be developed should be one dealing with the literature of the major religious traditions of the West.

A survey of the religious literature courses available found most of them both sketchy and non-systematic. A review of the literature anthologies used regularly in secondary schools revealed that the selections were limited to readings from the Bible, and that these readings consisted of only two or three selections, usually excerpts. It was clear that these great and seminal works of literature had long been and were still being neglected.

Decisions had to be made concerning content and course design. It was first decided that the readings for this course be limited to the classical writings of the three major religions which came out of the Middle East: Judaism, Christianity, and Islam. Since the students could not be expected to read all of the writings appropriate for such a course, selections from the classical writings of these religions had to be made. Staff from Pennsylvania State University in consultation with nationally known scholars in the field of religious studies made the selections of readings on the basis of the following criteria:

(1) That they best express the heart of the ethos of the religious traditions involved.

(2) That they have had the most extensive influence in subsequent Western literature.

13

The first year of the project was planned in three phases. In the first phase the program was organized and procedures developed. In the second, readings were assembled, specific units and lessons were written, and the materials were tested in the State College Area Senior High School, Centre County. Its proximity to the Pennsylvania State University allowed for immediate output and feedback. The third phase involved the preparation of teachers to field test the course during the 1967-68 school year.

A special training institute to prepare teachers for the field testing was conducted at Pennsylvania State University during the summers of 1968 and 1969 by members of the Department of Religious Studies. During the institute participants met each morning in regular classroom sessions. In the afternoon they met in seminar groups to plan units of instruction. During the first Institute, special consultants visited and talked with the participants.

The 1967-68 field testing program was designed to obtain both student and teacher reactions to the course structure and materials as developed by Pennsylvania State University. The study was designed to measure favorable and unfavorable student responses to each passage from the literature and its accompanying commentary. The field test also incorporated methods for measuring any change in student attitudes toward the literature as they studied and became more familiar with it.

The field testing program measured teachers' responses toward each literary passage and its commentary. Regional conferences were held during the year so that teachers might share and develop more successful methods and materials for teaching the course. The results of the field testing program were an influential factor in determining the direction for the revision of the course materials.

Letters were sent out to all county and district superintendents explaining the project and asking them to nominate schools and teachers for participation in the field test. Over 70 school districts responded the first year. Some 40 additional school districts wrote in and indicated their interest in the project without applying.

The department sent out applications to each high school and again explained the conditions for participating in the field testing project. They were as follows:

1. That the school agree to offer the course to students in the 11th and/or 12th grades.
2. That the school assure a minimum enrollment of 15 students.
3. That no students be enrolled who did not freely elect to do so.
4. That the teacher selected to teach the course be a certified teacher of English with at least three years of teaching experience.
5. That teachers selected attend a special summer institute at Pennsylvania State University prior to teaching in the field testing program.

Teachers selected by their school district completed an application which included their experience, their academic background, and a short essay explaining their reasons for wanting to participate in the project.

The 31 schools selected for the first year's field test in 1967-68 ranged from large to small and were located in rural, suburban, and urban areas. A total of 725 senior high school students took the course in the first year.

During the year of the field test the department was also seeking the advice of groups such as the State Religious Literature Advisory Committee, and various concerned organizations such as the Pennsylvania Council of Churches, the Pennsylvania Catholic Conference, the Anti-Defamation League.

The results of the 1967-68 field test led to a revision of the materials and expansion of the study to involve 43 schools and more than 1300 students for the 1968-69 school year. The 1968-69 field study included on-site visits by trained research assistants, interviews with teachers and students, periodic regional meetings with project consultants, and a final report which documented the information gathered, listed the inferences drawn about the strengths and weaknesses of the course materials, and outlined the assistance teachers needed in teaching the course.

RESPONSES TO THE COURSE

The great majority of the students said they like the course for the following reasons:

- they learned new things which gave them an understanding and appreciation of the religious traditions other than their own;
- they found the readings from the literature not only inspiring but also helpful in the development of their intellectual powers;
- they had an opportunity to discuss human issues with a variety of people without undue censorship or "the answers" being provided.

Most teachers are enthusiastic about the course and the experiences they have had in teaching it. They found their students to be more ignorant of the basic facts of their own traditions, more curious and tolerant about divergent feelings and opinions, and more understanding about human issues and concerned about human feelings than the teachers had expected. The teachers found the course an excellent vehicle for responding to these conditions. Many teachers spoke of the opportunity for dialogue and the elective nature of the course as major factors in determining its success.

THE ROLE OF THE TEACHER

Extensive observations of and discussions with those in the field led to a definition of the role of the teacher of this course. The teacher's job is:

- to provide time, space, and an atmosphere where open inquiry can go on and the pressure to supply or find "the answers" is reduced;
- to assist students in the messy, almost chaotic, business of finding out what they want or need to know, and then helping them look for it;
- to train students in the basic skills and understandings necessary to their becoming independent learners;
- to help students find meaning in the years of human experience they bring into the classroom and the further experience of the literature and history student and teacher read together;
- to teach about religion objectively.

FURTHER DEVELOPMENT

Outside interest in the course varied with each school. In some schools there was none; when there was some reaction it was consistently enthusiastic and supportive. Parents, teachers, administrators, and supervisors visited the classrooms. Teachers were asked to explain the course of study to various organizations; included among them were Parent-Teacher Associations, School Boards, Ministeria, and Women's Clubs.

THE OBJECTIVES OF THE COURSE

The aim of this course of study is the development in both teachers and students of an understanding of and continuing interest in religious literature and the traditions from which it springs. To develop these attitudes both teacher and student should:

- be aware that there are various interpretive approaches to the reading of religious literature;
- be able to read and explicate on the literal level, as well as the metaphorical and symbolic levels where appropriate, the religious literature included in the course
- be able to describe the form and content of the various course readings and demonstrate an understanding of how form and content interact to generate meaning;
- be able to identify, compare, and contrast ideas, concepts, and themes from the course readings;
- be able to identify, compare, and contrast ideas, concepts, and themes from the course readings with those of other literature;
- be aware of the influence religious literature has had on the styles, forms, contents, and themes found in American, English, and World Literature;
- be able to describe the cultural development of the individual traditions: the basic modes of expression, the identifying events, beliefs, and world views;
- be able to describe the historical interrelationships of the religious literature included in the course;
- be able to communicate ideas about literature and basic human experiences, values, and beliefs;
- experience and be able to analyze the process of creation, whether it be in the realm of ideas, human relationships, or art.

UNIT ONE:

INTRODUCTION
TO THE COURSE

A MATTER OF QUESTIONS AND ANSWERS

Most people agree that we learn by asking questions. It might even be said that every known thing in the world exists as an answer to somebody's question. But not everything is known in the same way, and not every question can be stopped by a single answer.

A child begins to learn when he starts to ask questions about the things immediately around him. He wants to know the names of things. "What is this?" "What is that?" His questions demand one answer. They are questions of fact.

He begins to learn more when he puts together a new kind of question from the answers people give him to the simple questions he asked in the first place. "If this is such-and-such, and if that is so-and-so, then what have the two of them to do with each other?" By asking questions about the relationships between simple facts, he has begun to build a world in his mind with connections between the facts, connections he can understand. His questions demand answers that make sense to him, and just anyone's answer will no longer do.

A person learns much more, however, when he discovers he can ask questions not only about facts and the relationships between them, but also about questions themselves, and about the people who ask and answer them. He discovers that different people frequently give him different answers to the same questions. Questions, he discovers, come not from questions, and answers come not from answers, but from people. Busy at building a world himself, he becomes aware that other people are building worlds also. He quickly senses that the worlds people build differ from each other in varying degrees. "Why do I ask him, 'What is this?' " "Why do I believe him when he says, 'That is so'?"

By questioning the validity of others' answers, by discovering that answers come out of people and not out of questions, a person is discerning something beyond the mere relationships in his own world and in others' worlds; he is discerning meaning. The difference between my world and your world arises out of what you and I build with the facts—out of the way we make the connections. It is the meaning we seek in life that determines the shape we give our worlds. Some of those worlds are quite similar. Some, almost literally, are worlds apart. My world may be very much like your world. Nevertheless, our worlds may be very unlike their worlds, whoever they may be.

But as soon as a person begins asking questions about people, he moves beyond the recognition of differences between them to an awareness of the unity that binds all men. From being a wide learner he becomes a great learner. He finds that people grow increasingly concerned with searching out the deeper questions behind the questions they ask, and behind the answers they give. They take a searching interest in the inner experience of other human beings —in what they think and how they feel. He learns that to search out the inner experience of other people and communities is to recognize that men and women in all times and places build worlds as answers to certain questions that confront us all. He begins to realize that it is only because people share the same unspoken questions that they can understand each other, however different their answers. These generally unspoken questions that unite all people—these universal questions—suggest their answers in the ways people act out their lives. Human lives may be united or separated by the answers men propose, but all men everywhere are bound together by the same fundamental questions.

To understand the power of universal questions is to realize one's own experience in all of its depth of meaning. The richest of all learning occurs when people dare to move on from the mental mechanics of simply learning the answers to questions of fact—on, that is, to search out, within the answering worlds men build, those questions of meaning that never consent to be dispensed with, disposed of, or forgotten.

We do not, of course, outgrow one level of questions by moving on to the next. We never leave behind our need for questions of fact, because facts are the material upon which we operate in our quest for meaning. Without facts we would quietly float away. Nor can we do without questions of relationship, because the connections we make between facts hold the shape of the impress of meaning upon our worlds. Without putting things together, we cannot know where we are. But neither can we live out satisfactory lives without passing beyond facts to questions of meaning—questions whose spoken answers reveal the differences between people and opinions in all their rich variety, and at the same time hint at unspoken, deeper, universal questions whose sameness for all people is the common reference against which our differences can be measured. However people's lives may be united or separated by the answers in which we agree or disagree, we learn well and we learn much if we experience how inevitably all human lives are bound together by the same ultimate questions.

A course in good literature leads the ready reader to this kind of adventure into the meaning of human experiences. In such a course we do not entertain questions for the purpose of finding the factual answers that will dispose of them. Instead, we read existing answers, already couched in a rich variety of storied events which lead us back to discover and rediscover the great universal questions. The universal questions we answer with our own lives are the same questions men faced and lived when writing was new—indeed before men knew how to write, when stories were handed done by word of mouth from father to son. Good literature does not dispose of the questions it raises just because it presents dramatic and profound answers to them. Instead, it redoubles the fullness of their meaning, and turns them upon the reader to challenge the facts of his own life.

In this course in religious literature you will be reading a variety of agreeing and conflicting answers to these questions of human experience and its depth of meaning. You will find them in the forms of stories, teachings, laws, and poetries of various sorts. The universal questions of meaning hover above, lurk beneath, and move within the accounts, charging them with meaning. It's up to you to search out the questions and to reflect on their meaning as you become involved in the experience of these people through the medium of the written word.

Religious literature reminds us that we cannot really participate in the full meaning of human experience if we do not consider the serious answers that other people and other groups of people propose to such questions as these:

> Who are we?
> What's really happening?
> What does it all mean?

As your involvement in this literature and the universal questions it responds to deepens it is especially important that you realize and maintain an objective point of view. The following key questions might help you do so:

Do you understand that you are dealing with more than just "facts"; that thoughtful interpretation of them is an inherent part of the process of being a learner?

Can you say that you listen openly to other readings of the materials than your own? Are you willing to apply other modes of reading to find out how they operate and where they lead you?

Are you able to deal with this literature without insisting that others agree with your reading of it?

Are you able to suspend judgment about the ideas and customs of other times and cultures, and expend some energy to get inside them and find something of the meaning they provide for the human beings who hold and practice them?

Is your study of this literature disciplined? Are you approaching it systematically, always searching for evidence to confirm your feelings and support your ideas? Can you, when you have read a selection, say clearly what it says to you, something about how it says what it does with the effect it has, and finally, how well it says it? If you can read for what the selection says rather than for what you want to hear, analyze to understand how the work works (rather than dissect the life out of it), and evaluate its worth to you (so you possess the work rather than it possessing you), then you have gone a long way towards finding those fuller meanings for which we all search.

THE LITERATURE INCLUDED IN THE COURSE

The bodies of literature with which the course is concerned are the Hebrew Bible (or Old Testament), the New Testament, the Apocryphal Writings (Apocrypha and Pseudepigrapha), the Rabbinic Writings, and the Qur'an. Time would not begin to permit you in this course to read all of these writings. Therefore, we have selected portions of these books that scholars and students have agreed are typical, readable, and influential. Even so, some intensely interesting parts have had to be omitted. We hope you will continue your reading in these books long after you have completed this course.

At first glance, some of the readings may seem quite familiar. Most people know something about Abraham and Isaac, or Moses and the Red Sea, or the birth of Jesus, or the inspiration of Muhammad. Nevertheless, one can be amazed sometimes, when he gets down to more searching and reflective study, to find how unfamiliar he really has been with the depth of meaning that wells up through some of these factually familiar stories.

This book is divided into three major sections. Section One comprises readings from books of the Hebrew Bible. It contains nine units. Section Two comprises readings from the Apocryphal Writings, the Rabbinic Writings, and the New Testament. It contains six units. Section Three contains readings from the Qur'an, and consists of three units.

WHERE THE ACTION TAKES PLACE

The literature you will be reading involves for the most part real people and communities. Their affairs take place in a certain geographical scene of action. The scene is the Near East. In terms of latitude and longitude, the world of early Judaism, Christianity, and Islam developed in the lands bounded by the 15th and 45th parallels, North Latitude, and by the 25th and 60 meridians, East Longitude. As you read this geographical description, it will be helpful to refer to the map on page 23.

The greater bodies of water in this area, beginning in the north, are the Black Sea, the Caspian Sea, and Mediterranean Sea, the Persian Gulf, the Red Sea, and the Arabian Sea. As for the continents, one can see Eurasia to the west, north, and east, and Africa toward the southwest. Dominating the center of the scene is the Arabian Peninsula that juts down out of Eurasia something like a hatchet head with its blade cutting southeast into the Arabian Sea.

The center of the scene of action occupies a rough arc across the top of the Arabian Peninsula. It stretches from the northern shore of the Persian Gulf north and west to the Mediterranean and then south down the coast to the north end of the Red Sea.

To the north and east of that arc rugged mountain ranges largely isolate it from the northern seas and from the high plateau to the east. South of that arc, known as the Fertile Crescent, the great Arabian Desert permits some human infiltration but defies any mass invasions.

Inasmuch as the origins of civilization correspond with the invention of agriculture and writing, the scene of the literature of this course is also the place— or the two places—where civilization was born. Men first developed the recording of thoughts and their transmission by means other than the spoken word in the bottom lands of the Tigris and Euphrates Rivers that feed the Persian Gulf and in the valley of the Nile River in North Africa.

All place cues included in this book are within this general area. The literature itself will take on additional meaning if you take time as you go along to detail your knowledge of where the action is taking place.

THE COMMUNITIES OF PEOPLE INVOLVED

Of the three main religious communities of people (Jews, Christians, and Muslims) who produced this literature, the first on the scene were the Jews. Their tribal and cultural ancestors were the Hebrews, who had migrated in much earlier times from the valleys of the Tigris and Euphrates along the Fertile Crescent and down into the Palestinian hill country rising inland from the eastern coast of the Mediterranean. (Please see the time line on page 25.) Later these Hebrews migrated southward into the delta of the Nile. Subsequently, they returned dramatically to Palestine, moving across the Sinai Peninsula, and then northward to cross from east to west through the Jordan River back again into the hill country. The descendants of these migrating Hebrews many centuries later knew themselves as Israelites and then as Jews, with a high civilization centered in Palestine and the city of Jerusalem.

The earliest Christians were tribal members of the Jewish community, and all Christians, then and now, have been their descendants with respect to religious culture. The Christian community, however, rapidly became separated from its Jewish background, and acquired adherents from a large variety of other cultural groups, largely Greco-Roman.

The third of the religious communities that produced the literature dealt with in this course was Islam. These people originally were native to the western regions of the Arabian Peninsula along the Red Sea. Arising in the Arab world

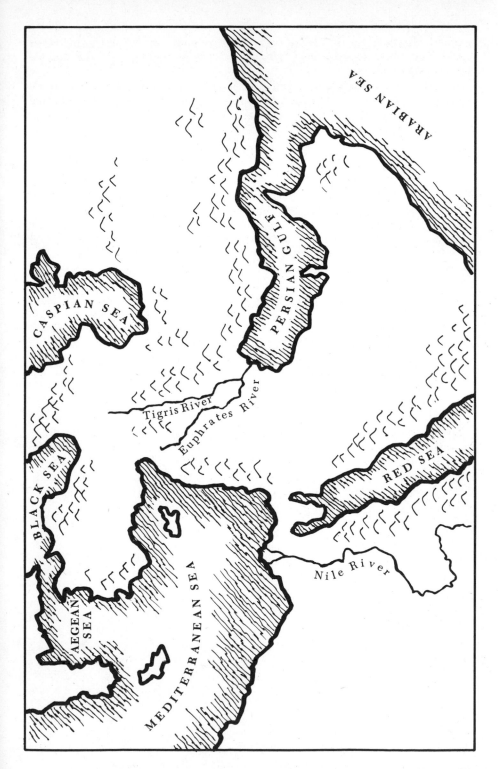

ARABIAN SEA

PERSIAN GULF

CASPIAN SEA

Tigris River

Euphrates River

RED SEA

BLACK SEA

Nile River

AEGEAN
SEA

MEDITERRANEAN SEA

centuries after the rise of Christianity, the community of Islam traced its religious roots back through the Christian and Jewish traditions to the original Hebrew community.

The literature you will be reading is an expression of the internal experience of each of these three communities. It also reflects the relationships between the three, and between each of them and other communities with which they came in contact, both in war and in peace.

HOW AND WHEN THIS LITERATURE WAS WRITTEN

If you look at the time line on page 25, you will see that the approximate dates for the beginnings of the three communities precede the beginnings of their writings by varying spans of time. Perhaps 250 years went by after the beginning of the Israelite community before men began systematically to write down material that would be included later in the Hebrew Bible. Twenty years went by after the beginning of the Christian community before the content of the New Testament began to take written form. As for the Qur'an, we know that it was recited verbally in its original form and straightway either was written down by those who heard it, or else was memorized and written later. The important thing to understand at the start is that in all three cases, a large majority of the material was passed along and handed down verbally as oral tradition or recitation before anyone put it to writing.

None of the communities that produced this literature has come to an end. Nevertheless, each of the bodies of literature dealt with in this course was declared complete by a certain point in time, as you can see on the time line. The subsequent literature of the communities does not bear the stamp of "sacred," "classical," or "original" the way these do.

The works known as Apocryphal Writings (Apocrypha and Pseudepigrapha) are variously regarded as sacred or as interesting and valuable expressions of the thought of their times. The Rabbinic Writings, while not a part of the Hebrew Bible, nevertheless exercise great authority in the Jewish community as a body of interpretation and teaching oriented to the Bible and to the oral tradition of Judaism.

TIME LINE

	B.C.	
	2000-	
Beginning of the Hebrew tradition	c. 1800	
Beginning of the Israelite Community	c. 1250	
	c. 1000	Beginning of the Hebrew Bible writing
	c. 200	Beginning of the Apocryphal writing
	c. 165	End of the Hebrew Bible writing
	c. 30	Beginning of the Rabbinic writing
	A.D.	
Beginning of the Christian Community	c. 30	
	c. 50	Beginning of the New Testament writing
	c. 100	End of the Apocryphal writing
	c. 150	End of the New Testament writing
	c. 500	End of the Rabbinic writing
Beginning of the Muslim Community	c. 610	Beginning of the Qur'anic writing
	c. 655	End of the Qur'anic writing

THE
HEBREW
BIBLE

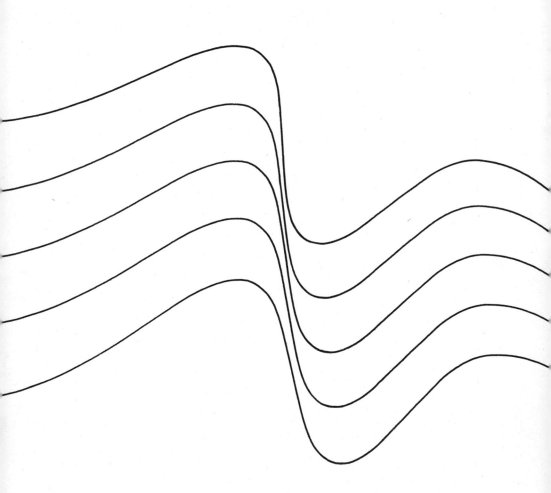

ISRAEL REMEMBERS WHO SHE IS

Part 1:

AT SINAI
GOD NEGOTIATES
HIS COVENANT WITH ISRAEL

The long history of Israel contains many good stories that are important episodes in the drama of Israel. The story of the establishment of a covenant between God and Israel, led by Moses, is one of these. We read it first because it confronts us all at once with so much of what Israel means. Both here and in the readings to follow, we seek not simply to catch the highlight events in Israel's life, but to move through these events into a greater understanding of the experience of her people.

This story recounts an important transition for the people of Israel. You will not understand all of what is happening, and what it means, all at once. Read first for main ideas. While you read raise questions that will bring you closer to what the events meant to the people who enacted them and wrote about them.

The *Search Cues* will help you to seek out action that has significance beyond the story itself. Such action bears meaning for the people who were originally involved and also for you, as you search your way into the mind and heart of their experience and compare it with your own.

Search Cues are meant to help you in your *depth search for meaning* while you read.

SEARCH CUES

1. the meaning of the mountain, and the appearance of God
2. the ten words
3. gods of silver and gods of gold
4. covenant and steadfast love, and the practical results of obedience

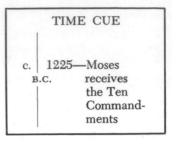

TIME CUE

c. | 1225—Moses
B.C.   receives
       the Ten
       Command-
       ments

NOW READ: EXODUS 19:1—20:26; DEUTERONOMY 6:1—7:26

COMMENTARY

Motifs and Metaphors

In the story of God's covenant with Israel at Mount Sinai, we observe the motif of the mountain as the place of great events of revelation in the life of God's people. Biblical literature contains many symbols and metaphors that express the appearance and presence of God. In the Sinai story the presence of God is represented by a cloud, by a storm, and by fire and smoke. In the language of biblical scholars, the appearance of God to his people is a *theophany*.

Fear of the Holiness of God

Exodus 19 portrays the motif that man cannot look on God and live. In the awed reverence of the Israelite we find a vivid example of human response to the sacred, or holy. The place of God is a life and death place to the eyes of the faithful. For a person to misuse the sacred place, or for someone who is not sanctified through religious rites to trespass there, is to offend the holiness of God and to court instant death.

Israel's fear of the Lord was no sentimental fear. The Israelites did not view God as a genial father who never does anybody any harm. Their fear of him was real. It included both awe at his holy power and a fear of what he could do with it. This fear of punishment may have served to promote obedience and to encourage right conduct. God made Israel fear in order to save her from the consequences of disobedience. Fearful obedience to the terms of the covenant would bring security to the people.

God promised that he would make of his people a royal order of priests, a sacred people acting for God. Israel is destined to be a mediator of the interaction between God and man. Israel is to be a holy nation, a nation elected to perform a special and supreme function within the providence of God's action in history. This awesome responsibility may bring to Israel suffering and sorrow, as well as joy and peace.

The Decalog

People often refer to the Ten Commandments as the Decalog, "the Ten Words." The commandments in Exodus 20:1-11 refer to the relationship between a person and God, whereas those in Exodus 20:12-17 are directed toward how a person should relate to his community or society. Especially controversial is the commandment in verse 13. Some people believe that this applied to the taking of any life whatsoever, since all flesh and blood life is sacred to God. Others believe, from the biblical context, that this meant that no man can kill except in those cases where God authorizes it: for food, for ritual animal sacrifice, for punishment, and for the conduct of war against the enemies of God.

Didactic Literature

Most of the book of Deuteronomy is an address by Moses to the Israelites before they entered the promised land. It is called one of the "Five Books of Moses" (Pentateuch), and many believe Moses was the author. Others, however, believe that Deuteronomy was written down in its present form in the seventh century B.C., with the substance of the book reaching back to the Mosaic period.

A large part of the book of Deuteronomy, including the two chapters you have read, is didactic literature. Didactic literature may be identified by the following five marks:

1. For the faithful, it derives its authority and finds its source not primarily in the accumulated insights of human experience, but in the will and word of God spoken in the voices of prophetic personalities in specific historical situations.

2. It instructs the reader about moral conduct and religious practice.

3. It takes the form of commands and their explanations.

4. Its teachings apply universally and forever to the people to whom it is addressed.

5. The conduct it requires fulfills the terms of a covenant between God and these people.

In a sense, we could say that all the literature of the Judeo-Christian-Islamic tradition is didactic because it teaches people what to do and why in response to what God does.

While didactic literature can involve detailed and minute instructions, Deuteronomy and other didactic literature of this tradition describe the meaning of the covenant of love and loyalty between God and Israel, revealed in the experience of Israel in their wilderness migration from oppression in Egypt.

The Shema

The Shema is considered to contain the principles of the Ten Commandments and is Judaism's highest confession of faith. Originally, the Shema was only Deuteronomy 6:4, which expresses God's uniqueness and oneness. According to Judaic tradition, Deuteronomy 5-9 later was added to the Shema, and still later, Deuteronomy 11:13-21 and Numbers 15:37-41.

God's Relationship to His People

Israel lived a family life. Throughout her literature we find her people expressing their experience primarily in terms of family relationships. This understanding of experience also affected Israel's interpretation of her life with God. We find two such metaphorical family relationships in Deuteronomy 7.

REFLECTION QUESTIONS

When we read literature primarily for entertainment, we do so with an uncritical openness to the events and their obvious meanings. We do not concern ourselves with searching out facts to remember after finishing the story.

Religious literature, however, confronts us with more than just entertainment. Its value lies in its power to produce more and more meaning for us as we remember its content and reflect on it.

The reflection questions that follow accentuate the concerns we share with the people of the literature. By such questions, we reflect on the meaning of reading we've done.

1. How effective would you say the educational system of the Israelites was?
2. What do holy places, holy things, and holy people seem to have in common?
3. Did God at Sinai appear to love everybody in the world? Cite your evidence from the text. How would you interpret your findings to the class?
4. Do you regard the covenant between God and Israel as a relationship of law? Of love? In such a relationship, would you interpret law and love as interchangeable terms? Why?
5. Consider the Ten Commandments one by one. Do they apply as well in the circumstances of your life as they did in those of the Israelites in the wilderness?

Part 2

GOD CALLS MOSES
TO BE THE LEADER
OF ISRAEL

How had these people come to be in the midst of the desert, led by Moses, agreeing to a covenant with God? To understand let us go back to the beginning of the Exodus story, to the earlier days of Israel's slavery in Egypt. There we see the birth and youth of the man through whom God gave Israel her original hope and freedom as a national people.

SEARCH CUES

1. the oppression of the Israelites
2. the voice from the fire
3. the assignment and promise given Moses
4. fear and humility of Moses

NOW READ: EXODUS 1:1-3:22

COMMENTARY

The Israelites in Egypt

When Moses was born, the Israelites had been living in Egypt for about 400 years. They had come into Egypt when a Semitic dynasty, the Hyksos, was in control of the land. Being Semitic people themselves, the Hyksos readily accepted the Israelites, who settled in the Goshen region of the Nile delta, where they prospered and multiplied. Later, however, the Egyptians expelled the Hyksos from their land and reduced the Israelites to a semi-slave status.

About 50 years before the Exodus an Egyptian pharaoh, Ramses II, came to the throne. He ruled vigorously and inaugurated an extensive building program. He required the Israelites to provide the necessary labor. The pharaoh also had another reason for initiating the policy of Israelite enslavement. The population of the Israelites had grown so large that the pharaoh began to see the Israelites as a foreign community within his borders and a threat to Egypt's national security. Later he inaugurated a program of genocide under which the Egyptians set about to reduce the numbers of the Israelites by systematically killing their sons.

The Figure of Moses

The story of Moses' birth in Exodus 2 is similar to other birth stories of famous leaders found in the ancient literature of the Near East. For example, in Mesopotamia an early king by the name of Sargon of Akkad records that after his birth his mother concealed him in a basket of rushes covered with bitumen. The basket floating in the river was found by an irrigator who reared Sargon as his own son.

With Moses' first encounter with God, in the third chapter, we reach the heart of one of the great efforts to show a man taking his identity from his response to God. The event is depicted as occurring on Mount Horeb. As you go further in your reading, you will find that biblical authors typically describe events of great significance as taking place in high places, or on mountains. Another motif frequently occurring in biblical writing is fire, symbolizing the presence of God.

In Moses, we see the figure of the first and greatest of Israel's prophets. Yet Moses was more than a prophet. He was also the founder of his people as a nation. He would mediate to his people God's original Torah or Teaching, in terms of which God's covenant with Israel was to be fulfilled.

The whole account of Moses demonstrates that the drama of Israel's history is always the drama of God's own continuing judgment and guidance, rather than that of a succession of human heroes.

REFLECTION QUESTIONS

1. What problems are there in naming the one speaking from the burning bush? Is *God* a proper name, like Henry or Alice?
2. What sort of person does Moses seem to be?
3. How would you describe the character of the Israelites from your reading thus far?
4. What sort of person do you seem to be thus far in your life? How would you describe the character of your own people?

Part 3:

THE LORD'S PASSOVER PLAN
BY WHICH
HE RESCUES HIS PEOPLE
FROM PHARAOH

After Moses returned to Egypt as God commanded him at Mount Horeb, God used him as his agent and spokesman while he visited nine grotesque plagues on the Egyptians. Moses' brother, Aaron, helped Moses in his task. As we begin our reading, God is about to deliver a tenth and final blow against the Egyptians so that, "compelled by a mighty hand," they will let the Israelites leave Egypt to travel the wilderness toward the land of promise.

SEARCH CUES

1. the reputation of Moses in Egypt
2. the nature of the tenth plague
3. the Passover of the Lord
4. the law of the Passover

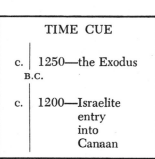

TIME CUE

c. | 1250—the Exodus
B.C.

c. | 1200—Israelite
entry
into
Canaan

NOW READ: EXODUS 11:1-12:51

COMMENTARY

The Plagues

Many of the plague stories recorded in Exodus reflect natural conditions and hazards of life in Egypt at that time. The ninth plague was especially pertinent to the beliefs of the Egyptian people. That plague, in which God imposed a thick darkness on the Egyptians, came as a symbolic forecast of death and destruction to Egypt, the people of the sun-god. To the Egyptians, that deep darkness represented an eclipse of the power of their god by the power of the God of the Israelites.

In the tenth plague God destroyed the strength and spirit of the Egyptians by destroying the firstborn offspring of every Egyptian. According to Hebrew understanding, in which all first fruits belonged symbolically to God and represented God's rule over all things, God took the symbolic God's-share of everything Egyptian and destroyed it. By this culminating act God destroyed all the powers of the Egyptians.

The Passover

We have read how God arranged that the Israelites be spared the effect of his wrath as it swept through Egypt. The Israelites slew young male lambs, which were referred to later as Passover lambs, or paschal lambs. They sprinkled the symbolically innocent blood of these lambs on the lintels (horizontal top-pieces) and doorposts of their doors. Seeing this blood at the doorway, God, in his destroying wrath, would pass over and not enter there. Thus God was a god of death and violence against the nations that threatened the destiny of his people. At the same time, he acted as the savior of his people. In chapter 12 Moses instructs the people regarding the ways in which they should remember their deliverance from Egypt in their family worship.

In this story, we also note a symbol which occurs frequently in biblical literature. *Blood,* in this literature, represents the vital essence of life and is considered to be symbolic of the very principle of life itself.

Conclusion

Having been rescued by God from Egypt by means of the plagues, the Passover, and the parting of the sea (Exodus 14), the tribes of Israel moved eastward into the wilderness with Moses leading them.

Eventually they came to the region of Mount Sinai, after having struggled with hunger, enemy tribesmen, internal quarrels, and doubts about the wisdom of Moses. The promised land seemed far away as they encamped near the foot of the mountain and Moses went up to hear the will of God.

Think back over the events you have been reading, from the birth of Moses to his descent from Mount Sinai bearing God's commandments and covenant. Consider the experience of Moses and his people through the following reflection questions.

REFLECTION QUESTIONS

1. How would you describe the life of the Israelites in the wilderness, or of any group of people in a wilderness, as a practical and emotional experience?
2. Why do you suppose the Sinai story puts an emphasis on the fearsome qualities of God?

3. From your reading thus far, how do you account for the fact that the Israelites were both afraid of God and trusted him?
4. In the wilderness situation, what did the Israelites remember when they looked back, what did they observe when they looked around, and what did they anticipate as they looked ahead?
5. Why was it so important that the Israelites remember the details of the Exodus?
6. Does the story of the Exodus suggest to you why the study of history is important to a sense of national identity?

THE EMERGENCE
OF
THE KINGDOM

Part 1

MOSES
GOES UP THE MOUNTAIN
OF DEATH
AND PROMISE

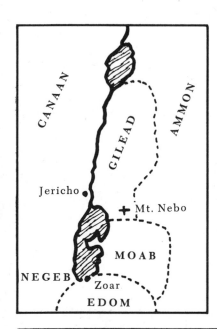

After the long years of pilgrimage across the wilderness, Moses and his people reached the highlands of Moab, just east of the Jordan. God told Moses that he would not live to enter the promised land, for Moses, even as leader of his people, had broken faith with God in the wilderness (Deuteronomy 32:48-52). But Moses would go up on the mountain at the end of the wilderness journey. There he would see the land of milk and honey that soon would become the possession of his people in fulfillment of God's promise.

SEARCH CUES

1. Moses' punishment and reward
2. sharp-eyed and virile to the end
3. the succession of leadership

NOW READ: DEUTERONOMY 31:1-8; 32:48-52; 34

COMMENTARY

Looking Back

We began the reading in this unit with the entry of the Israelites into the promised land, and with the gathering at Shechem where the people reconsidered who they were. We now have looked back into Israel's past to the Passover and to Sinai and have returned to the time just prior to that entry into Canaan.

With the death of Moses, the first great adventure of the nation was complete. The Exodus from Egypt through the wilderness to the very threshold of the promised land is the *original identifying event* that Joshua and the tribesmen would dramatize at the assembly at Shechem, about which you will read next. Remembering the Exodus, Joshua and his people would know who they were, what was really happening, and what it meant to serve the Lord.

Torah

The literature we have read from Exodus and Deuteronomy is part of the first section of the Hebrew Bible, known to Judaism as the Torah. This section contains the first five books of the Bible: Genesis, Exodus, Leviticus, Numbers, and Deuteronomy. "Torah" means Law. The writings of these first five books are thus the law for the community of Israel. But law is not used here in the restricted sense of something judicial or legalistic. Rather, Torah is used in the broader sense of teaching or instruction. Torah, then, expresses the meaning of God's covenant relationship with Israel as he taught it to them.

REFLECTION QUESTIONS

1. What does the death of Moses say about the relationship of the leader to the law of God that the leader gives to the people?
2. If you think the story of Moses is a story of human greatness, then what is human greatness?
3. Can you describe some event in American history that dramatizes the meaning of Moses on Mount Nebo?

Part 2:

THE TRIBES OF ISRAEL
ENTER CANAAN
AND RECONSIDER WHO THEY ARE

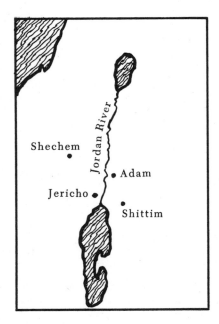

The story of the entry into the promised land under the leadership of Joshua recounts a violent transition for the people of Israel.

SEARCH CUES

1. Rahab and the part she plays

2. circumcision of the men

3. purpose of the assembly at Shechem

4. Joshua's description of God

NOW READ: JOSHUA 1:1-6:27; 24:1-33

COMMENTARY

The following information may be helpful to you as you consider the story of Joshua.

1. The only *written* record of these events is the biblical accounts you have read.

2. Archaeological evidence provides us with these historical facts:

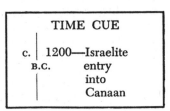

TIME CUE	
c.	1200—Israelite
B.C.	entry
	into
	Canaan

45

a. The Israelites entered Canaan sometime around 1200 B.C.

b. The ruins from the city of Jericho show that it was destroyed at about the same time.

c. For many centuries Shechem was an important religious center.

Holy War

The last verses of Joshua 6 tell us that Joshua and his forces destroyed the entire city of Jericho, with the exception of Rahab and her household. Everything else, except for certain metallic vessels, was put to the ban. Everything, including men, women, children, animals, buildings, and treasures, was destroyed. All were declared *cherem*, which is to say, sacred or set aside for the Lord's destruction. Using the Israelites themselves, God destroyed an alien culture that threatened the Israelites as they moved to establish themselves in the territory God had promised to Moses and the patriarchs.

We cannot understand this story without understanding the principle of holy war, which we find expressed in such biblical verses as Deuteronomy 7:2, 13:15, and Joshua 6:17. The principle of holy war, and that of *cherem*, or the ban, represent a universal tendency for people of one culture to live in anxious fear of a strong foreign culture. The only way the threatening foreigner can be made safe is to destroy him. He is taboo in his attractiveness as well as in his apparent defiance of God's will. Only his total destruction removes the hostile or seductive "otherness" which he radiates. Encounter with him must mean, under the principles of holy war and *cherem*, total victory for the people of God and total annihilation of the people counted as God's enemies. To stop short of this is to court disaster—punishment from God or corruption or destruction by the stranger.

The Tribal Confederacy

The Israelite assembly at Shechem raises several questions: How were the Israelites organized? What kind of leadership did they have? How did the Israelite tribes relate to each other?

A confederacy is a group of semi-independent states in league with each other. In some cases, these states may be bound together by a common deity whom they all worship at a common shrine.

The tribal league expressed in Joshua's assembly at Shechem was similar, yet different. First, the people were family tribes and not states. Second, while they were bound together by their common obligation to God, they also were bound together by their consanguinity (blood relationship). They were a people comprised of families combined in clans and tribes. They knew their family relationships. Genealogy, or carefully traced family background, was important to them. They were a birthright people, and theirs was a birthright religion. One could *belong* to Israel by circumcision, but one *became* an Israelite by birth from an Israelite mother. Thus Israel was a confederacy of family, clan, and tribal units at the time of the Shechem assembly.

After their gathering at Shechem, the tribes fanned out from their beachhead in the promised land. Tribe by tribe, by military campaign as well as by less warlike infiltration, they permeated the hills and valleys, the towns and the country places, which a century-and-a-half later would change dramatically, becoming the empire of King David.

Questions and Answers

With their entry into the promised land, the Israelites arrived at a decision point in their history. They could look back to their past, as Joshua related it to the assembly at Shechem. They could also look forward to their future in an unknown land. Here the people were challenged with the question of their identity and the meaning of their current situation in relation to their past and future: Who are we? What's really happening? What does it all mean?

These questions are implicit in Joshua's challenge to the assembly, "Choose this day whom you will serve." The response of the Israelites to Joshua's challenge was a reflection of how they were answering these questions in the light of their past and in their hope for the future.

As you read the Hebrew Bible, you will see through the actions and words of the Israelites how they continued to answer these questions of identity and meaning.

REFLECTION QUESTIONS

1. What seems to be the difference between God's attitude toward Israel and his attitude toward the people of Jericho?
2. If you don't know the meaning of the word *anthropomorphism*, look it up in the dictionary. How might a person use the word in thinking about this story?
3. Do you find any events in the Joshua story that one might call miracles?
4. Who would you rather be, Moses or Joshua, and why?

Part 3:

A HEROINE-JUDGE
BOASTS A VICTORY
WITH A SONG

At Shechem the Israelites had recalled the story of their Exodus out of Egypt and through the wilderness in such a way that the story became a challenge which they had to accept or reject. The promised land turned out to be an alien and often violent frontier—two frontiers, in fact—dangerous both militarily and religiously. The land to which Moses had led them was not vacant either of peoples or of ways of living. The culture there was full of seductive new ideas and gods. Having conquered Jericho under the command of Joshua, the tribes rededicated themselves at Shechem to their faith in who they were and in the meaning of what they were doing. They chose to honor the debt they had incurred to God by their rescue in the past, and to continue the conquest of the promised land in that light.

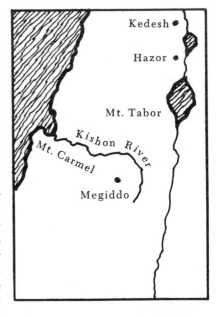

Their invasion varied between peaceful settlement among the people they found there and war with them. The tribes of Israel were loosely associated and not yet well-organized as a nation. When danger threatened, heroic personalities arose to call the tribes together, revitalizing their internal loyalty to God as at Shechem, and marshalling their efforts against the common foe. These frontier heroes were the judges.

SEARCH CUES

1. Deborah the prophetess and Barak
2. the song of triumph
3. the role of nature in the victory
4. the mother of Sisera

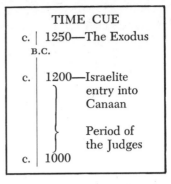

TIME CUE

c. | 1250—The Exodus
B.C.

c. | 1200—Israelite
entry into
Canaan

Period of
the Judges

c. | 1000

NOW READ: JUDGES 4:1-5:31

COMMENTARY

The Period of the Judges

After the Israelites' entry into central and southern Canaan from Shechem in the late 13th century B.C., the twelve tribes of Israel encountered a variety of disconnected adventures. Throughout these events we find a common theme. Here was an aggressive, disorganized confederacy of people bent upon establishing their own rule in a promised, yet alien, land. Only a relatively small number of the Canaanites had been eliminated under the initial successes of Joshua. After that, the problems of the Israelites were the problems of invaders trying to find a way to live in a land already occupied by people with a different and conflicting way of life.

The period of the judges was one of uneven cultural consolidation and halting political integration among the Israelites. Like all ambitious nations, they lived with leaders who could identify both the enemy without and the enemy within. For Israel, the enemy without was the threatening aggressor from the cities and regions beyond Israelite control. The enemy within was the domestic religious culture of the Canaanites.

This domestic religion centered itself on El, the father of a whole company of gods, and his consort, Asherah. More familiarly, the Canaanites worshiped one of the offspring of these two, Baal, who personified the forces and events of nature which were important to the survival of the Canaanite agricultural economy.

To the Israelites, the frequent Canaanite rites of sacred prostitution and child sacrifice in the name of love and fertility were abhorrent to the God of a seminomadic people for whom harlotry spelled social decay, and for whom human sacrifice violated the image of God himself. Thus, in the period of the judges, the fundamental battle, as the Israelites saw it, was a two dimensional struggle. On the one hand, it was a struggle against being assimilated into Canaanite culture. On the other hand, it was a military

49

battle against the unconquered Canaanite and foreign kings who held out or swarmed in against them.

Poetry and Prose

We find in Judges 4 and 5 not two stories, but one event expressed in two different ways. Judges 5, usually called the Song of Deborah, tells in poetic form substantially the same story we have read in chapter 4.

Archaeological evidence from the city of Megiddo suggests that the battle between Deborah's forces and the Canaanites took place in the late 12th or early 11th century B.C. The prose account of the battle in chapter 4 according to some scholars was written down several centuries later. The Song of Deborah, however, is thought to be one of the oldest poems in the literature of Israel, written possibly by an eye witness to the battle.

The prose story relates the facts of the experience in a historical narrative. If you were a reporter, you easily could answer the questions a reporter uses—who, what, when, where, why and how—by reading Judges 4. On the other hand, the poetic narrative gives the reader an emotional feeling for the events that occurred; the author seems to be involved with the action rather than detached from it.

The Song of Deborah

If we could read this poetry in Hebrew, we would find a wealth of rhythm, but no rhyme. The rhythm of Hebrew poetry is found not only in the sounds of the words and in the way they flow, but also in the way the authors skillfully blend and balance the sequence of thoughts the poetry expresses. To do this, the poets frequently use the techniques of parallelism.

Basically, we can find three kinds of parallelism. We shall refer to them as paraphrastic, comparative, and cumulative parallelism.

A *paraphrastic* parallelism simply puts the same thought in two successive lines, with each line expressing the thought, but in different words. That is, each is a paraphrase of the other. Verse 28 in the Song of Deborah shows the effective use of this kind of parallelism, in lines 1 and 2 and again in lines 3 and 4.

A *comparative* parallelism expresses one thought in one line and then expresses a vividly contrasting thought in the next line. The contrasting thought reveals a sharp comparison between the thought in the first line and the thought in the second. The last verse of Judges 5 uses this method of contrasting thoughts.

A *cumulative* parallelism uses a certain pattern of words in one line and then repeats the pattern in one or more lines that follow, each time adding new words to the original pattern. Thus each line adds something of its own to an original thought which is carried on from line to line. This kind of parallelism is used in verse 27 of Judges 5.

If you slowly read through the Song of Deborah again, you can locate more of these parallelisms. You may want to consider what function parallelism has in expressing the drama and emotion of Hebrew poetry.

REFLECTION QUESTIONS

1. Scan Judges 2 and see if you then can define the cycle of events typical of the affairs of the judges. How does the cycle apply to the story of Deborah?

2. Do you think the peg and hammer technique was justified?

3. What kind of woman would you say Sisera's mother was? Should you feel sorry for her? How would you apply the term 'irony' to the situation of Sisera's mother?

4. If the Song of Deborah had been written in paragraphs, would you have called it poetry? Why?

5. How does the Song of Deborah express the attitude of nationalism?

6. If you were a cultural anthropologist, how might you describe the relationship between Israel and her neighbors in Canaan?

Part 4:

GIDEON THE JUDGE DOES BATTLE AGAINST THE BAAL AND THE BEDOUIN

Another of the famous judges, Gideon, reminds us of Moses in the way he responded to his call to leadership. He also reminds us of Joshua in his strategy of war. Unlike the enemies of Joshua, however, Gideon's Midianite enemies were on the attack and came from another direction. They were a bedouin people from the east and south beyond the Jordan. Again, the story begins with the assertion that "the people of Israel did what was evil in the sight of the Lord." By this refrain the writer who assembled the heroic tales of the individual judges reminds us that Israel's choice at Shechem made *being* Israel a demanding ideal.

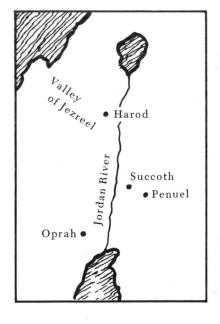

SEARCH CUES

1. the doubts of Gideon
2. the dew and the fleece
3. Jerubaal
4. the men of Succoth and the men of Penuel

NOW READ: JUDGES 6:1-8:35

COMMENTARY

Enemies of the Community

The story of Gideon, many scholars believe, was passed down from generation to generation by oral transmission before it was recorded in writing. We find again in this narrative the two-dimensional theme discussed in Part 2 of this unit: resistance to the corrupting neighbor and war against the foreign aggressor. The Midianite raids were especially effective because they confronted the Israelites with a factor unknown before this time, the strategical use of the camel. As a matter of fact, the story of Gideon records the first organized camel raid known to history.

Blood Revenge

In routing the Midianites, Gideon acted as an effective leader of the Israelite community. He carried through this leadership with the execution of the Midianite kings, Zebah and Zalmunna. In addition to his obligation to God's covenant community, however, Gideon had a particular obligation to his own family in relation to the kings. As we see in Judges 8:18-19, the men whom Zebah and Zalmunna killed at Tabor were Gideon's blood brothers. In Israel, as well as in other societies, a relative of the victim had to execute, or take blood revenge on, the victim's killers; there could be no exemption from this rule.

REFLECTION QUESTIONS

1. What indications do you find in the story of Gideon that the economic way of life of the Israelites had changed since the wilderness days?
2. How might the Midianites have reminded the Israelites of their own past?
3. How would you explain the fact that Gideon was hated for what he did to the holy place of Baal and Asherah?
4. How would you evaluate Gideon's skill in psychological warfare?
5. What do descriptions of Israel as "playing the harlot" refer to in terms of her relationship with God?
6. Why did Gideon reject the offer of the kingship made to him by the Israelites?

Part 5:

THE TRIBESMEN
DEMAND
A KING

As the Israelites became more firmly established in Canaan and more accustomed to a settled life, they no longer wanted to live like nomads of the wilderness, but securely as a nation of cities and towns engaged in trade and agriculture. Increasingly they felt the need to be organized for national defense against their adventuring enemies to the east and west. The frontier situation was fading into history and legend, and the judges grew more and more judicial and less and less heroic in their exercise of office. In Samuel we find the last of the effective judges, and among the people of his day we find the first effective demand for a fundamental change in Israel's life—from the ways of tribe and patriarch to the ways of court and king.

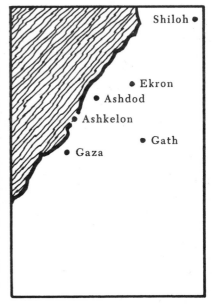

SEARCH CUES

1. the sons of Samuel
2. give us a king to govern us
3. the ways of the king
4. the verdict of God

NOW READ: 1 SAMUEL 8:1-22

COMMENTARY

New Invaders in Canaan

At about the same time that Gideon was driving off the Midianite camel-eers (c. 1100 B.C.), sea people from the islands of Greece were colonizing the Mediterranean coasts of Palestine. The most significant of these groups were the Philistines, from whom Palestine later derived its name. Just as the bedouin Midianites came with their camels from the desert to plunder Canaan's eastern valleys, the Philistines came from the sea to raid and settle the coast along the west side of the Promised Land. The Philistines, by the beginning of the 11th century, had established a network of five cities on the coastal lowland. These cities, from south to north, were: Gaza, Ashkelon, Ashdod, Ekron, and Gath.

Like the Israelites, these people were new in Canaan and were bent on expanding their beachhead. The Philistine cities were related to each other in a manner similar to the tribal confederacy of the Israelites. Unlike the Israelites, however, they apparently worshiped at no common shrine, and they formed an association of city states rather than of tribes. These cities banded together politically and militarily to face the threat of their common enemies.

The Philistines brought with them into Canaan the advantage of iron weapons, which they used against the bronze of the Israelites. It was largely pressure from these Philistines during the period of the judges which moved the tribal confederacy toward a united government and military leadership.

The Last Judge

In the history of Israel, Samuel and his career mark the dividing line between Israel as a tribal confederacy and Israel as a political monarchy. He also marks the watershed between the older days of the rough and ready judges, and the period when the prophets would become the conservative conscience of Israel. In most cases, those prophets would strive to conserve and recover in the minds and behavior of their people not the man-centered ways of the political monarchy, but the God-centered ways of the patriarchal and Mosaic commonwealth of tribes.

Samuel had been brought up by a priest of Shiloh named Eli. While in the temple service of Eli, Samuel had heard the voice of God calling him to be a prophet, and so he was understood to be by Eli and the people. In his old age, Eli had wanted to establish his two sons to succeed him as priests at Shiloh, the central sanctuary of the Israelites. It was a tragic effort, however, since the two sons were worthless fellows and were killed in a battle with the Philistines. The battle was a disastrous defeat in which the ark of the Lord was taken as spoils by the enemy. The shock of the event killed Eli.

Samuel grew to be a recognized judge and prophet in Israel. His judge-ship took the form of judgment and mediation as we know it today, rather than the form of heroic deeds such as those performed by Deborah and Gideon.

55

REFLECTION QUESTIONS

1. How did Joel and Abijah become judges, how did this differ from the way former judges had been chosen, and in what sense was this already similar to the ways of monarchy?
2. In what ways do you think the people's expectations of what a king would do were correct, and in what ways incorrect?
3. What do you think was happening to the people of Israel as evidenced by their demand for a king?
4. In what profound sense was the demand for a king a renunciation of the king? How did Samuel's and Gideon's responses to this demand differ?
5. Compare the "ways of the king" as Samuel described them with the ways of national governments in your own day.

Part 6:

THE GREAT KING STEALS A WIFE

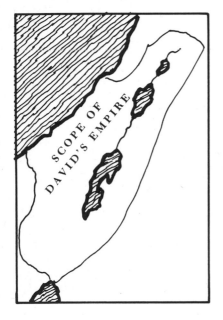

SCOPE OF DAVID'S EMPIRE

The people of Israel were granted their national wish and their anointed king. The first was Saul, who bore in his tragic personality many of the qualities of the judges as well as the aspirations of monarchy. His successor, David, led Israel to her golden age as an imperial kingdom. Under his initiative, she became a nation feared and respected by her neighbors, who paid her tribute in wealth and servitude. David the king also was David the man. This story points to the king, but speaks most eloquently of the man.

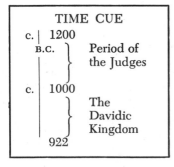

TIME CUE

c. | 1200
B.C. } Period of the Judges

c. | 1000
} The Davidic Kingdom
922

SEARCH CUES

1. David's plight and plot
2. the character of Uriah
3. the motives of Joab
4. the role of Nathan
5. David's confession and character

NOW READ: 2 SAMUEL 11:1-12:25

COMMENTARY

The History of the Monarchy

In the story of Samuel, we heard the voice of resistance to the monarchial development—a denial that Israel would be fulfilled in her covenant relationship with God when she became like the nations and had a king. Other voices, however, favored the monarchy. That monarchy, beginning with Samuel anointing Saul as king (c. 1020 B.C.), continued with but one brief interruption after Saul's death for almost a century as a kingdom of united tribes, built into an empire by David and consolidated by his son, Solomon. Nevertheless, it promptly separated into two parts after Solomon's death (c. 926 B.C.). Israel never again would be a monarchy, free and dominant in her own land.

The northern kingdom, Israel, lasted precariously until 722 B.C., when the Assyrians overwhelmed it under Sargon II. Judah, the southern kingdom, continued in various circumstances of struggle and vassalage until 598 B.C., when Nebuchadnezzar, the Babylonian, subjugated it. A decade later, in 587 B.C., Nebuchadnezzar laid a second siege on Jerusalem, Judah's capital, and completely demolished it. He systematically killed off the leadership of Jerusalem and exiled the bulk of the population back to Babylon (Mesopotamia). This was the beginning of the Babylonian Exile.

David the King

Few kings in history are more colorful than King David of Israel. The Bible portrays him as a man of great depth and character. In the story of David and Bathsheba, the author seems interested in the personal character of the monarch, just as in modern times people take an intense interest in the ruling families of their nations. Notice the interplay of the personal qualities of the actors in this story, and the realism of the story, in which the facts speak for themselves to the experience of the reader. One should see, with the eyes of the author, the judgment of God as to which man, Uriah or David, exemplifies the ideal of a faithful and obedient Israel.

REFLECTION QUESTIONS

1. If you were to ask him, what reasons might King David have given for staying home from battle—even before having seen Bathsheba?
2. What was David's personal predicament? What was his basic plan for solving it?
3. Analyze the character of Uriah the Hittite.
4. What evidence do you find in the story to indicate that David was a man of considerable moral courage?
5. How does 2 Samuel 11:14 illustrate the principle of irony?
6. How does the Nathan episode dramatize the line, "O wad some Pow'r the giftie gie us/To see oursels as ithers see us!"
7. Compare David with Moses in his power to influence other men by example. What modern political leaders did each resemble? How important is the example a leader sets?

Part 7

KING DAVID LOSES A BELOVED AND REBELLIOUS SON

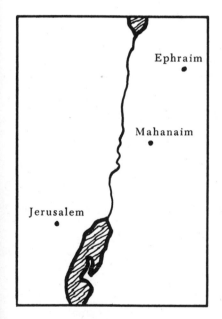

When David was in the prime of his life as king, his handsome son, Absalom, grew embittered by tragedies within the family and inflamed by ambition for the throne. He plotted a revolt against the power and pride of his father.

Thus the father and the son, who loved each other, found themselves opposed in a life and death struggle for control of Israel, a struggle marked by personal intrigue and military violence. The friends of each promoted plots and rumors to feed the ambitions and suspicions of the king and prince against each other and to bring to a climax the power struggle between them.

The tragic stage was set as Absalom, having driven David from Jerusalem, gathered his forces in the forests of Ephraim, while David mustered his army at Mahanaim, ready for the fatal battle.

SEARCH CUES

1. why the king stayed in the city
2. his orders to his departing generals
3. the way Absalom died
4. the plan to tell the king
5. the king's grief

COMMENTARY

Historic Tragedy

Research has led some scholars to conclude that this story was written by one of David's court historians. In this account of the tragic rebellion of Absalom against his father's pride and power, the writing is a straightforward chronicle. Apparently no attempt was made by the historian to soften the tragedy, or to make either David or Absalom better or worse than the facts might indicate. Instead, the historian wrote down his observations of the people and their deeds in a foreshadowing of modern documentary reporting. He let the drama and the tragedy of events cry out through his realistic account of the events themselves.

REFLECTION QUESTIONS

1. What unmentioned reason might have restrained King David from leading his army into the field?
2. How does the conduct of Joab and the "certain man" at the oak of Absalom dramatize the moral issues involved in their own careers as professional men of power?
3. What might have been the thoughts of Absalom at the time, assuming he could hear their conversation prior to his death?
4. Do you think David meant what he said as he wept in the chamber over the gate? Make a case for your answer.
5. Explain the significance of the announcement to the people, "Behold the king is sitting in the gate."
6. In this story, in what sense does tragedy consist in a man's not being able to change his mind?

ISRAEL REMEMBERS THE PATRIARCHS AND THE OLD TIME BEFORE THEM

Part 1:

GOD CREATES HIS WORLD

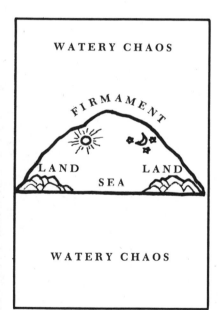

In the days of King David Israel achieved the national power to which she had aspired. Meanwhile, her storytellers continued to write down not only the record of Israel's origin and growth as a nation, but also the lore of times even more ancient. Throughout the Near East, varying accounts of the first beginnings of things abounded. The men of Israel handed down two remarkable stories that told of how the God who brought Israel into being as a nation created the world itself.

SEARCH CUES

1. in the beginning God
2. the sequence of creation
3. the image of God
4. the two trees
5. naming the animals
6. the expulsion from the garden

NOW READ: GENESIS 1:1-3:24

COMMENTARY

Stories of Creation

The passage you have just read is regarded by some biblical scholars as two different stories of the beginning of the world—the first story being found in Genesis 1:1-2:4a, and the second in Genesis 2:4b-3:24. Other scholars believe that Genesis contains only one account of creation and that this account, as part of the Torah, was revealed by God and written down by Moses.

Still others think that the two stories were recorded by different authors at different periods of time. According to this theory, the first story was written down by a person or persons belonging to the priestly writing tradition, during exilic or post-exilic times (c. 600-500 B.C.). The second story according to this theory was recorded by earlier writers living in the tenth century B.C., at the time of the Davidic kingdom. Regardless of the time in which each was recorded, many scholars agree that both stories were handed down orally for many generations before they were put into writing.

These stories were not the only narratives of creation recorded in the literature of the Near East. The Genesis stories in particular are similar to other Near Eastern creation narratives—Genesis 1:1-2:4a to the Mesopotamian *Enuma Elish* story, and Genesis 2:4b-3:24 to an early Eden saga of either Canaanite or Mesopotamian origin. There are many similarities between the Genesis stories and the Canaanite and Mesopotamian versions, especially in the descriptions of the events of creation. Some scholars believe the Israelite authors may have used creation narratives from surrounding cultures in creating their own account. According to this view the authors transformed the ancient accounts to reflect the *meaning* of creation in terms of the Israelites' conception of God and his relation to man. If the writers used the information and traditions of their day, they radically revised it to assert the primary principles of Hebraic faith.

The First Version of Creation (Genesis 1:1-2:4a)

In this account, called the priestly account by those who accept the theory of two accounts, the writers emphasized that in the beginning, before all, and supreme above all, is God. Without God, nothing came to be, not even the primordial watery chaos over which he hovered. The story then says that God created the world in orderly, almost liturgical, steps, day by day through six days. Part of the marvel of it, for the author, lay in its having been done in such a short span of time. With God the impossible task was done in only a week.

Here we see the author's vision of God's work as orderly and good. The theme of separation, the differentiating between one created thing and another, runs throughout. Each day brings God's work closer and closer to the reality of human life. Man occurs as the image of God. Man and beast alike, as originally created, are vegetarians.

If we contrast this story with the Mesopotamian *Enuma Elish* account, we find differences like these:

1. The *Enuma Elish* story portrays the creation of the world as a consequence of violent action by capricious gods, whereas the priestly version tells it as a benevolent act of the one God of the Hebrew tradition.
2. In the Genesis story, man is seen as the highest order of creation. The Mesopotamian narrative presents man as a servile instrument for the gods.
3. The *Enuma Elish* account tells of man as the object of the arbitrary forces of nature, whereas the Genesis writers show man as having dominion over these natural forces.

A further difference in the Genesis account is God's designation of the Sabbath as a holy day of rest. The celebration of the Sabbath as a day of rest and worship was an unusual event in the Near East. In fact, only the Hebrew people observed it. They traced its origin to the creation of the world itself, thus confessing their faith that it was a fundamental part of the world order, created at the very beginning of time and thus to be observed by all men.

The Garden of Eden Story (Genesis 2:4a-3:24)

The story of Adam and Eve, according to scholars who accept the two-account theory, is the earlier of the two stories. They believe that it is a faithful people's way of understanding how the world was created. Others believe that it is a historical account and that Adam and Eve were the first human beings. Both groups of interpreters accept it as a statement about the origin of man. It is told in the light of men's faith that man was created and brought into the historical world by an act of God. It affirms the theme of the first or priestly story in Genesis 1:2-2:4, that man is created with holiness and dignity, as a free creature made in the image of God.

This story also deals with problems all people must confront in this world. Why do human beings act the way they do, apparently from the very beginning of history until now? How does this behavior reflect our relationship with the God who has created us and our relationships with each other? What can we do about it? What is God doing about it?

In the Adam and Eve story we find an expression of all these problems. We may think of Adam and Eve as the first human beings. We may also think of them as everyone who has ever lived, including ourselves. The story may reflect the cultural circumstances of the man or men who wrote it, yet it speaks to every man in all his circumstances.

According to the story, in the timeless beginning before God made man, no recognizable order of nature existed. All was a watery flood of chaos. With the advent of Adam, when God put breath, the sign of living human existence for the Hebrews, into man, it seems that chaos largely ceased. The earth bloomed, and the floodwaters found their orderly way in the great rivers. This was so that man might not be alone in chaos. God gave man intelligence and freedom by which to name the other animals and appreciate the God-given order of life. But this was not enough. Man needed company for himself as a person, another like himself in which he could see himself. And the one flesh of Adam became two, the man and his wife, sexually differentiated, one flesh made two in order that the two might know themselves in knowing each other. Yet in knowing each other as man and wife, they would not forget that in the beginning and in the depths of meaning, mankind is not two or many, but one.

A theme of this story is how man is tempted to oppose the will of God by disobedience. Man eats from the tree of knowledge of good and evil, rather than from the tree of eternal life. According to Hebrew understanding, man has a quest for knowledge and a need to choose between good and evil. But, man's dilemma comes when he makes his choice separate from his awareness of the presence and purpose of God.

The Garden of Eden story also portrays God's reaction to the disobedience of Adam and Eve. His punishment, his self-restraint and mercy, his plans and provisions for them, all reflect the facts of human life, such as work, sweat, pain, and death.

REFLECTION QUESTIONS

1. If you considered choosing one or the other of these stories to tell to a person seven years old, which one would you expect to be more interesting to him, and why?
2. How would you compare the mood and style of these two creation stories, deemphasizing for the moment the details?
3. What attitudes on God's part toward man, the natural world, and man's place in the natural world, do the two stories portray?
4. Would you agree that one of the two stories tells us more about human nature than the other? Defend your position.
5. What universal matters of human morality are illustrated in the story of the Garden of Eden? What is morality?
6. Discuss the significance of the following claim: "The Garden of Eden was a Garden of Love."
7. Which of the stories would you say is more involved in modern arguments about science and religion? Why?

Part 2

THE FIRST
BROTHERHOOD
OF MAN

The story of Adam and Eve begins again in the world beyond the Garden and becomes the story of their first two sons—the first two brothers.

SEARCH CUES

1. Adam knew Eve
2. the keeper of sheep and the tiller of the ground
3. the sin and punishment of Cain

NOW READ: GENESIS 4:1-16

COMMENTARY

A Didactic Story

This narrative makes some statements about the nature of men's relationships with God and with one another. Reading this story with imagination and an eye for symbols which say more than they seem at first to say, you will find a model of how the author viewed some of the basic practical and personal tensions in human experience.

We read in the first verse how human beings find sexual intercourse as a means of mutual personal knowledge and common effort toward the production of children. "And Adam knew Eve his wife . . ." means that he had sexual intercourse with her.

In the fact that Abel was a shepherd and Cain was a tiller of the soil we see a human division of labor, and a human division into two culturally different ways of life. Cain and Abel each built an altar. Here was a competitive division of worship. In these divisions of work-ways and worship-ways, we find also the division of man against man, and the division of man against God.

In this story the question of human brotherhood arises, and the question of the right use of superior power. It shows how the seed of envious malice and murder lies within each of us. It confronts each of us with the question Cain asked of God, "Am I my brother's keeper?"

This story shows how God regards the killing of one human being by another. Here again we encounter the use of blood as the symbolic representation of life. All human killing is fratricide, or brother-killing, the story implies. Human killing also is an offense against God himself, the giver of life. This story affirms that God does not let murder go unpunished. However, it also affirms that the God who punishes is the God who shows mercy.

Cultural Implications

According to one way of thinking, many of the characters in the Genesis stories represent not only individuals but also groups of people. In examining the stories from this point of view, we need to know the cultural setting of the stories and the relationship between the Israelites and other peoples around them.

The story of Cain and Abel may have been written down by the same writer or writers who recorded the Adam and Eve story, possibly during the tenth century B.C. Before that time the Israelites, as pastoral nomads, had moved into the land of Canaan and had taken control of the area from the Canaanites. Some scholars believe that the story of Cain and Abel was told to affirm the nomadic life of the Israelites under Moses, against the agricultural life of the Canaanites.

About the time the story was written down, enmity existed between Israel and a neighboring group of people called the Amalekites. Hebrew tradition considers Cain to be the founder of the Kenites, who were part of the Amalekite group. Thus, one of the purposes of the storyteller may have been to explain, through the characters of Cain and Abel, why the Israelites and the Amelekites were enemies.

REFLECTION QUESTIONS

1. How might one explain why God looked with favor on the offering of Abel and with disfavor, or less favor, on the offering of Cain?
2. In terms of this story, of whom was Cain jealous and whom did he envy? (Look up the definitions of *jealous* and *envy* in a dictionary.)
3. What does it mean to say, "sin is couching (not crouching) at the door"?
4. How did killing promise to solve Cain's problem with God and Abel?
5. To what do you suppose the mark of Cain refers? Was it meant to do him good or ill?

Part 3:

GOD
FLOODS
AN EVIL EARTH

In the days of Israel the Near East listened not only to lore of how the world began, but also to accounts of the primeval flood. The writers of Israel ascribed to Moses the first writing of Israel's story of the flood, as part of the Pentateuch, the original Torah, the first five books of the Hebrew Bible. Here is yet another portrayal of the ways of God with a disobedient creation and with the faithful few.

SEARCH CUES

1. why God chooses Noah
2. the sons of Noah
3. the covenant with Noah and all flesh
4. God's bow in the clouds

NOW READ: GENESIS 6:5-9:17

COMMENTARY

Stories of the Flood

The civilization of the Near East, which in the long centuries following was to spread its formative influence throughout the Mediterranean world and into Europe and America, had its own roots in the irrigation cultures of the Nile Valley in Egypt and in the Mesopotamian valley of the Tigris and Euphrates rivers north of the Persian Gulf. The Hebrews, dwelling in the land of Palestine astride the trade routes between Egypt and Mesopotamia, shared the ancient stories of that general region by which the people explained who they were and why they lived the way they did. They did this by recounting ancient tales of how things were in the first days, ages prior to the longest memories of their own generations. One pervading motif in those ancient stories was the vision of the pre-primeval watery chaos. We met that motif in the creation stories, and now we meet it again, dramatically, in the story of Noah.

According to some interpreters, the flood story may have been based on a Mesopotamian version of the great flood, called the Gilgamesh epic. This story also told of a flood that destroyed all life on the earth with the exception of one man, Utnapishtim, and the animals he saved in his ark. Like Noah, Utnapishtim sent out three birds after the flood to find dry land. He released a dove and a swallow, and both returned to the ark. The third bird, a raven, did not return, indicating to Utnapishtim that the waters were receding.

If the biblical writers used the Gilgamesh epic, they retold the flood story in a way which expressed the central tenets of the Hebrews' faith in God. In comparing the epic and Genesis, we see differences such as these:

1. In the Gilgamesh epic, the gods caused the flood to destroy the earth out of malicious caprice, whereas the Noah story teaches that the act was the result of God's judgment on the corruption of the peoples of the earth.

2. Utnapishtim survived because he was the favorite of one of the Mesopotamian gods. Noah, on the other hand, was picked because he was a righteous man.

3. In the Mesopotamian flood story Utnapishtim alone was rewarded with immortal life. The Noah story, however, ends with God making a universal covenant with all of mankind.

God's Judgment

The biblical tradition describes man as created in the image of God. It also describes God in terms of human experience. The story of the flood is an account of God's earliest and profoundest judgment on his creation. God looked and saw social injustice and moral corruption. Because of it, God decided to restore the pre-primordial chaos of flood water to do away with this corruption of man and beast. This way of referring to God as though God felt, thought, and acted like a human being, called *anthropomorphism*, does not occur in the story as a moral judgment or evaluation of God. On the contrary, the story describes the nature of human life in its relationship with a God whom all his people understood to be their creator, their ruler, their judge, and their guide. Human joy and sorrow, pain and pleasure, whether resulting directly from men's own doing or from the phenomena of nature, all reflected to the Hebrew mind the result of a divine judgment, whether favorable or unfavorable, as God kept a patriarchal eye on the free conduct of his human creatures from generation to generation.

70

The Motif of the Righteous Remnant

The destructive judgment of God did not fall at the time of the flood on all men and all beasts. Before the flood came, God showed Noah a way to escape, because Noah had walked righteously with God. God would preserve Noah and his family with a representative group of animals. After the flood, this family and these animals would become the forebears of a new world economy. A remnant would be saved, and this remnant would become a new beginning.

The righteousness of Noah and his being saved by an act of God introduces another great motif in religious literature, the idea of the righteous remnant. According to this motif, out of death and destruction which come to the corrupt majorities in the world, God chooses in his own mysterious way those he regards as righteous, and he provides that their kind shall endure. The story tells how Noah and his people survived by building the ark. In other times, other peoples have done other things by which a righteous remnant might survive.

The Animals

In biblical literature little things often have great symbolic importance. They bear a living significance for the informed person far beyond their literal commonsense meanings.

The story at one point can be interpreted to describe the clean animals as entering the ark in sevens (Genesis 7:2). That is, some scholars believe an editor took out "in sevens" and inserted "seven pairs" instead. Here the original author may have been thinking of three pairs for breeding, plus one male for use as a sacrificial victim after the landing of the ark. In speaking of clean and unclean animals, the author no doubt was referring to the fact that animals had to fulfill certain physical requirements to be eligible to be eaten by the people, or in order to be offered at the altar in behalf of all the people, when the animals' lifeblood was sprinkled on the ground (Leviticus 11:1ff).

If you look at Genesis 6:19 and then at Genesis 7:2, you will notice that God gives Noah two different sets of instructions at two different times. In the first verse, God tells Noah to bring into the ark one pair, male and female, of every living creature. In the latter verse, Noah is to bring seven pairs (or animals "in sevens") of all clean creatures, and one pair of all the unclean ones. For some scholars this discrepancy is an indication that the story was written down by an early author, presumably the same writer or writers of the second creation story, and later revised and expanded by a different author or authors of the literary tradition from which the first creation story came.

The Noachide Laws and Covenant

Chapter 9 of Genesis tells of three laws God gave to Noah, and a covenant which God made with all the creatures of the earth. The laws are natural, fundamental ones. That is, they apply to the basic relationships which are to be between man and man, and man and all other animals. You will find these laws in Genesis 9:2, 9:3-4, and 9:5-6. The people of the Hebrew tradition believed that these laws had been put forth at the very beginning of history and thus applied to all of mankind.

Likewise, the covenant God made after the flood was universally applicable. It was a very special covenant in that it was an unconditional one. God promised to keep this covenant forever, no matter how men behaved in the future.

REFLECTION QUESTIONS

1. Trace the theme of God's responses to his creatures through the stories of Adam and Eve, Cain and Abel, and Noah. In each case, what basically made God sorrowful and angry?
2. Trace the theme of God's self-restraint through the same three stories.
3. Reference to the *image of God* appears again in the Noah story. Some say man makes God in the *image of man*. Can these two claims be reconciled?
4. Show how the motifs of breath and blood occur in the story of the flood. Again, how do they symbolize life and death? How realistic do you think they are as symbols? Which one has to do more with acts of God in the story? Which has more to do with acts of man?

Part 4

ABRAHAM
BECOMES THE FATHER
OF GOD'S PEOPLE

To Israel (and centuries later to Christianity and to Islam as well), the experience of Abraham was the first example of what the life of faith in God might be expected to involve. Abraham's deeds showed how faith in God's good will, complete power, and right purpose was the substance of every act by which a faithful Israel might know herself. Indeed, the story of Abraham tells how a man learns to trust God's love by doing God's will. In these passages, we follow the story of Abraham in biographical fashion, reading in it, however, not only the faith of a man but also the faith of a people.

SEARCH CUES

1. a command and a promise to Abram
2. the oaks of Mamre
3. the barrenness of Sarai and the arrangement for an heir
4. God's covenant with Abraham and the meaning of circumcision
5. Sarah laughs at a promise

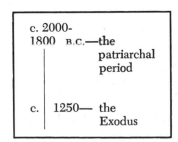

c. 2000-
1800 B.C.—the
patriarchal
period

c. 1250— the
Exodus

6. the birth of Isaac
7. thrice uttered "Here am I"
8. Isaac's question

NOW READ: GENESIS 12:1-13:18; 16:1-19:38; 21:1-21; 22:1-19

COMMENTARY

The Patriarchs

As Israel looked back into her past, she remembered not only the narratives of the beginnings of the world, but also the epics and stories of the earliest ruling fathers of the Hebrew tribes.

There are a number of reasons why the stories of the patriarchs were important to the Israelite community. First, these stories showed the Israelites that their existence as a people was deep rooted in a long tradition of faith in, and obedience to, the God of Israel. The narratives demonstrated that God's relationship with the Hebrew people began long before they became conscious of themselves as the Israelite community of Moses or David.

Second, the patriarchal stories expressed the universalism of Israel's God, as did the stories of creation and the flood. The God of Israel was the God of all the world. For example, in these stories you have read of the blessings of all peoples through the lineage of Abraham. Other religious traditions have seen these same universal elements in the patriarchal stories. You will read later in this course how both Christianity and Islam look back to Abraham as the founding father of their tradition of faith in God.

Third, these stories established the connection between the chosen people and the holy land which they possessed. In the centuries of the monarchy, the Israelites looked around and saw the very places which were believed to have become sacred to the Hebrews in the time of Abraham, Isaac, and Jacob. The Israelites, in the later days of the storytellers, could thus feel that the land into which Joshua had brought them had already been possessed by their patriarchal ancestors and dedicated to their God.

God's Call and Abraham's Response

For all the members of the Judeo-Christian-Islamic tradition, Abraham remains an *archetype* of what the faith relationship between man and God is supposed to be. These traditions look on Abraham not only as a man of faith but also as a man who demonstrated his faith by the righteousness of his behavior. Abraham exemplified such a faith through his own conduct when he heeded the call of God to abandon his personal security to journey to a distant undesignated place which God would provide for his people.

The first eight verses of Genesis 12 tell about the command and the threefold promise which God addressed to Abraham. In the light of the promise,

Abraham obeyed God's command and set out on the long pilgrimage to the land of promise. Only when Abraham had arrived in the mountainous hinterlands of Canaan did God let him know that this very land, where now the agriculturalist Canaanites lived, was destined to be the place of the promise, where Israel, his people, would find her historic fulfillment. You will notice that this narrative expresses all three significant features of the patriarchal stories.

Hagar and Ishmael

Children are always important in the human family. However, their importance varies in form from one cultural situation to another. In the seminomadic world of Abraham and Sarah, children were especially important for extending the influence of the parents. In a pastoral and patriarchal society, where the father ruled the extended household, the larger the family the greater his prestige and sphere of influence. In such a situation the need for children warranted the practice of polygamy.

Since the senior wife had her own stake in the growth of the family, we read in Genesis 16 that Sarah, being barren, gave one of her maids, Hagar, to Abraham as a second wife. Hagar, while referred to as an Egyptian, perhaps is better understood as a vigorous bedouin woman of the desert, spirited and proud.

The story illustrates the domestic problems in a polygamous household and the power structure in the patriarchal Hebrew family. When Hagar became contemptuous of Sarah for her failure to conceive, Sarah took her complaint to the head of the household. Only with Abraham's permission did she act harshly toward Hagar, both before and after the birth of Hagar's son (Genesis 16 and 21). In making Hagar and Ishmael leave Abraham's tribal community, Sarah was well within her rights, for, according to the laws of the times, Abraham either had to make the son of Hagar an heir or else give Hagar her freedom.

Angels

A number of stories in this part have referred to angels. We may define angels in the world of the Hebrew Bible as God's supernatural messengers, a means by which God could be present to human beings without actually being present himself, thus sparing them the deathly shock of a direct confrontation.

Circumcision as a Sign of the Covenant

The 17th chapter of Genesis is divided into four major sections: (1) the covenant which God made with Abraham; (2) circumcision established as the sign of the covenant; (3) the promise to Abraham of a son; and (4) the fulfillment of the divine command by circumcision.

The act of circumcision, that is, the severing of the loose skin at the end of the penis, was not unique among the Hebrew people. Many of the Semitic peoples of the Near East practiced this rite. In the Hebrew tradition, however, instead of being a puberty rite related to adult sexuality, circumcision became a rite of initiation into the covenant, to be performed when the child was eight days old. With the divine authority given to circumcision in Genesis 17, it became one of the characteristic marks of the Hebrew people.

Toward the end of chapter 17 God rules out Ishmael as the child of Abraham who will inherit the covenant, even though he is circumcised according to God's command. Instead, God will continue his covenant through Isaac, as yet unborn.

Sodom and Gomorrah

In the story of Sodom and Gomorrah we again find the motif of the righteous remnant, as we did in the story of Noah and the flood. In this case, the plea is that if there are any righteous people at all, the city should be saved. At the end of the story is an account of Lot and his daughters. Some scholars believe that this was a local story, originating in Canaan, which was incorporated into the Hebrew literary tradition centuries later to explain the origins of the Moabites and the Ammonites. In its original form, the story quite likely came after a flood story, in which the human race was destroyed, except for Lot and his daughters. In this instance, it would have been heroic for the daughters of Lot to attempt to repopulate the earth with Lot's offspring. However, as it was incorporated into the Hebrew tradition, the story was used to pass negative judgment on the origins of the Ammonites and the Moabites, neighboring enemies of the Israelites.

The Offering of Isaac

In Genesis 22 the biblical author introduces dramatic evidence concerning the faithfulness of God to the agreement into which he had entered with the Hebrews. God had promised Abraham that through his son, Isaac, God would build a great people. If Abraham had been allowed to carry his obedience to God's command to the point where he had actually killed Isaac as a religious sacrifice, he would have destroyed the only living possibility that the promise might be fulfilled. Thus, this story not only dramatized the faith of Abraham, but it also served as an inspiring explanation for later Hebrews of their own national identity, and how they owed their existence to a trustworthy God.

This story is also a protest against human sacrifice, a common practice among the Hebrew's neighbors. The biblical narrative makes the point that the God of Israel does not desire human sacrifice.

REFLECTION QUESTIONS

1. Using a map, trace the migration of Abraham from Haran to the place where he and his nephew parted company. Using your imagination, consider the conditions of that migrant life. How do you account for the economic circumstances of Abraham and Lot at the time of their separation?

2. What are the elements of the covenant which God made with Abraham? Why were these elements important to the Hebrew community?

3. Consider each of the stories in this part. What literary devices and techniques are used to make the stories effective?

4. Does the episode involving Abraham, Sarah, and the Pharaoh express a moral judgment about the relative integrity of Abraham and Pharaoh? Why?

5. When the land where Abraham and Lot settled in Canaan became too crowded to support them both, the two peoples separated. What options do people have where the land is over-populated today?

6. In the story of the conception of Ishmael, what seems to be the difference between planned parenthood in those days and today? Why the difference?

7. Suppose, centuries later, you are a famous storyteller who understands himself to be a descendant of Ishmael and his Egyptian wife. Tell your tribe an imaginative story that dramatizes how important Abraham, Hagar, and Ishmael are to you.

8. What attitudes toward city life and city people does the story of Lot, from the time he separated from Abraham until he fled to Zoar, seem to imply?

9. What was the sin of the men of Sodom?

10. Why, finally, did Sarah drive Hagar and Ishmael into the wilderness, and why did God save them and promise Ishmael a future similar to that of Isaac?

11. Do you find any indication that Isaac was aware that he was going to be sacrificed? If he were aware of this, why might he have gone along with the idea?

12. Can you describe the forms that human sacrifice takes in the modern world? What are the gods that require it? Are rams provided?

Part 5:

ABRAHAM
ACQUIRES A WIFE
FOR ISAAC

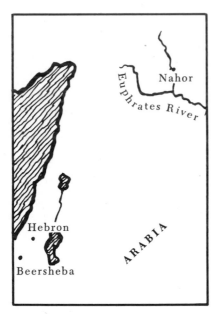

The story of how the marriage of Isaac and Rebekah was negotiated reflects the ways of Israel as a family-centered people. It also presents insights into the economic calculations in marriage prospects, but also into the subtle workings of genuine human affection and good will.

SEARCH CUES

1. the daughters of the Canaanites
2. Abraham's thigh
3. the role of Abraham's servant
4. Rebekah's attitude
5. Laban's attitude
6. the mother of thousands and ten thousands
7. an evening meditation is interrupted

NOW READ: GENESIS 24:1-67

COMMENTARY

In the Time of Abraham

Many stories in the Hebrew Bible reveal the customs of the Hebrews and other Near Eastern peoples, as individuals and as communities. This story gives us insights into Abraham's faith relationship with God and into the life of the people of the Near East in Abraham's time.

In this narrative, we find Abraham an old man, filled with the concerns of his final years. He saw the integrity of his faith and family both dependent on the marriage arrangements he might be able to make for Isaac his son. God had blessed Abraham by giving him long life and material prosperity. Now Abraham was concerned for the purity and integrity of his family faith and genealogical line.

In the eyes of the Hebrews, the Canaanites were an alien people among whom the Hebrews were sojourners. They were pagan idol worshipers who one day would be supplanted as the masters of the land by the people of the promise.

Abraham's faithfulness to God's promise of an inheritance in Canaan would not permit him to send his son back to the homeland of Haran for a wife. Isaac might settle down there and not return. Therefore Abraham sent a trusted servant to Haran to find a wife for Isaac, taking care that she be of good stock and the proper degree of family relationship. The servant would bring the bride back to Canaan.

Abraham required an oath from the servant. The journey would be long, and Abraham might not be alive when the servant returned. The form of the oath, in which the servant's hand was put under the old man's thigh, reflects an ancient custom of swearing by the genital powers of the father.

The ten-camel caravan which Abraham sent back to Mesopotamia with the servant was an indication of his considerable wealth. The fact that Bethuel had straw and feed enough for the camels, plus room for all the men to lodge, indicates that this was a negotiation between two prosperous families.

REFLECTION QUESTIONS

1. What was the long-range purpose of the marriage?
2. Whom did the actors in this story understand to be the one above all who arranged the marriage?
3. Why did Isaac seem to be a good prospect for a son-in-law, sight unseen?
4. What do you think the story assumes about "family arrangements" and "falling in love" as necessary conditions for a solid marriage? What are your assumptions about such a matter?

Part 6:

ISAAC
SUFFERS AS A HUSBAND
AND FATHER

Isaac, the second of the patriarchs of Israel, looms in the literature as a man of faith more steady and less volatile than either Abraham his father or Jacob his son. It must have been interesting to be the son of an adventuring Abraham, the husband of a self-confident Rebekah, and the father of two such contending twins as Jacob and Esau. We have learned much already about Isaac through his experience with his father. Now we learn more of the man and his personal qualities as we turn to affairs involving his wife and sons, and the later tribes they prefigure.

SEARCH CUES

1. two nations in one woman's womb
2. father's boy and mother's boy
3. the man of the moment vs. the man of the future
4. the blind Isaac
5. the paternal blessing, and the plot to deceive
6. Isaac's shock

NOW READ: GENESIS 25:19-34; 27:1-45

COMMENTARY

Etiological Stories

According to some scholars, many of the stories you have been reading served two purposes at the time they were written: they described past events and explained present conditions. In this theory such stories are called *etiological*. An example is the story of Isaac's marriage. It clearly describes a past event—Isaac's marriage. But it also explains, for its hearers, the relationship between the Israelites and the Arameans.

According to this theory, the passages you have read for this part are also *etiological*. The story shows how Jacob took Esau's birthright. But for its hearers at the time it was told, the story could also explain why the Israelites felt superior to the Edomites, who lived south of Palestine. They were nomads, believed to be descendants of Esau. But if they were descendants of Esau, they were also descendants of Isaac and Abraham. Why didn't they prosper like the Israelites? Because Jacob, one of the fathers of Israel, stole Esau's birthright. Thus the story, in this theory, serves two purposes.

The Birthright and the Blessing

In this account, the writer shows how Jacob (Israel) cleverly outsmarted his brother twice, with regard to both Esau's (Edom's) birthright and his inheritance. The birthright which Esau possessed was held normally by the eldest son in a family. This custom entitled him to a position of honor as the next head of the family, and it gave him a double share of the inheritance at the death of his father.

Equally important to the eldest son was the father's blessing, granting him his inheritance. The people of Israel believed that prophetic powers and the power to bless increased greatly in the period of a man's old age. In those days old age meant not senility, but venerability and an increasing wealth of offspring. A man exercised his powers legally and personally until his dying day. They were powers retained in him by God, and no offspring could directly deny them or take them away. Thus Isaac wasn't going to be easily fooled.

Also, we should understand the belief that an old man's blessing, once bestowed, possessed a certain virtue or power of itself which was quite independent of the person who bestowed it. The old man's final blessing could not be wrested from him. Because the blessing did possess a power in itself, once the old man gave it, he could not take it back again. The blessing spoken was a deed irrevocably done.

The Character of Isaac

You have been reading several stories that describe the personalities of the patriarchs and the people around them. If you were to describe Abraham, Sarah, Rebekah, Jacob, or Esau, you probably would have very little difficulty in painting a lively picture of a flesh-and-blood figure.

Oddly enough, however, relatively little information has come to us from the Genesis stories concerning Isaac. He appears as a rather shadowy and passive figure, the favorite of his mother, the near-victim of his zealously faithful father, and the unwitting object of a scheme planned by his wife and younger son.

Isaac's passiveness, however, is also his strength. We find in Isaac a steadfast person who remains in the land promised to his father Abraham. Isaac endures there despite all his hardships, sinking his roots deep into the land.

In living out the faith of his father in this way, Isaac becomes the patriarch who gives strength and endurance to that faith.

REFLECTION QUESTIONS

1. What custom appears to be contradicted in the phrase, "the elder shall serve the younger"?
2. What seems to be the peculiar quality of a paternal blessing on which this story hinges?
3. If Jacob and Esau symbolized Israel and Edom in this narrative, who might Isaac represent?
4. From reading the story of Esau's sale of his birthright, how would you describe the relationship between Edom and the tribes of Israel?
5. Write a paragraph on Jacob and Esau, describing them both as individuals and as communities of people.
6. Compare the rules of inheritance and the way the prospective heirs dealt with them in this story with the rules of inheritance and the way people deal with them today.

Part 7:

JACOB BECOMES ISRAEL AND ENCOUNTERS ESAU AFTER YEARS OF SEPARATION

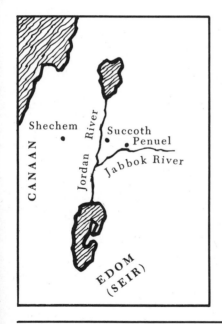

After fleeing to Paddan-aram to escape the wrath of Esau, Jacob worked for 14 years to earn the right to marry Rachel, the daughter of Laban, his mother's brother. Meanwhile, Esau had moved into Edom, and there he took as a wife one of the daughters of Ishmael. The passage we now read tells of the extraordinary experience of Jacob in receiving the name Israel, and of the precautions he took when he sought out his long separated twin brother.

SEARCH CUES

1. Jacob's fear of Esau
2. What is your name?
3. Esau's reaction
4. Jacob sends Esau on ahead

NOW READ: GENESIS 32:1-33:20

COMMENTARY

Jacob's Return

In this passage we find another expression of the intimate relationship between the chosen people and the promised land. Jacob *had* to return to

83

Canaan, because his father's blessing was meaningless unless he possessed the land on which God's promise was to be fulfilled. In reading how Jacob arranged his return to the land of the promise, we see again the shrewdness and caution with which Jacob dealt with Esau.

Jacob Becomes Israel

The stories of Jacob in the Hebrew Bible present him in several different lights. On the one hand, Jacob seems to be a scheming and wily man who, in outsmarting his brother, does not seem to be morally very attractive. On the other hand, Jacob receives God's favor and, in the present story, prevails against one of God's messengers.

One explanation for these differing characteristics of Jacob's personality is that Jacob was a man maturing in his faith who eventually became worthy of being a patriarch. If this is the case, then the story of Jacob's wrestling with the angel marks the occasion of the change in Jacob's personality, symbolized by the new name Israel.

REFLECTION QUESTIONS

1. How do you account for the acute anxiety Jacob felt at the prospect of meeting Esau again?
2. Obviously Jacob's experience at Penuel was more than "just a wrestling match." What would it mean after that to be one of the "children of Israel"?
3. Compare the attitude of Jacob and the attitude of Esau concerning Jacob's gift.
4. Was Jacob freed of his anxiety concerning Esau when they continued on their way? Explain.
5. How might an Israelite of a later day, with this story in his tradition, feel about Israel's relationship with Edom?

THE SONS OF ISRAEL
GO DOWN
INTO EGYPT

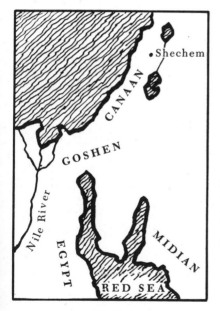

The stories about the patriarchs describe them both as individuals and as tribes. To tell about the ancestor was also to describe the people called by his name. The story of the man became the story of the people. Thus the story of Joseph and his brothers became both a dramatic series of events in the family life of a father and his sons, and also the story that explained how Israel came to be "way down in Egypt land." Settled in Goshen, the tribes of Israel dwelt there for generations before the later days of slavery when Moses would be born to confront the pharaoh "who did not know Joseph."

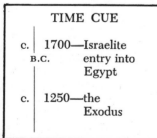

TIME CUE

c. 1700—Israelite
B.C.   entry into
       Egypt

c. 1250—the
       Exodus

SEARCH CUES

1. Joseph's robe and Joseph's dream
2. Potiphar's wife
3. the pharaoh's dream
4. Joseph tests his brothers

COMMENTARY

The Genesis Stories and the God of History

The stories of Adam and Eve, of Cain and Abel, of Noah, and of Abraham, Isaac, and Jacob add up to a long sequence of events by which the Hebrew people understood their origins. This account of a people's origin and sense of destiny reveals a vigorous tribal society bound together by ties of common faith in God and by ties of blood. Here was a people who accepted its existence as a life derived from one God and one blood.

The long story of Joseph tells us, in terms of a personal history, how the patriarchal tribes of Israel found their way south from Canaan to begin their long sojourn in Egypt. Out of that long stay in the delta of the Nile, the Exodus experience would be born. Through the leadership of Moses, God would mold the twelve tribes, all descendants of the sons of Jacob, into unity as a national commonwealth.

The Joseph story points to one of the most important principles of faith expressed in the Hebrew Bible: the God of Israel is a God who acts in and through history. That is, God is ultimately the author of history, and whatever men do, it is God who will use history for good or for evil. The Joseph story makes explicit this concept in Genesis 45:5-7 and also Genesis 50:20, by stating that God can use evil for the sake of good.

The Literary Quality of the Joseph Cycle

The Joseph story is one of the most effective narratives in the book of Genesis. In reading the story, no doubt you have discerned the dramatic plot and the ways in which the characters are brought to life as flesh-and-blood people.

Some scholars believe that the Joseph cycle was formulated in part from several independent and unrelated Near Eastern narratives, such as the Egyptian "Story of the Two Brothers," in which one brother rejects the advances of the other's wife, but is accused of seducing her anyway. Whether or not the story is a composite of earlier episodes, however, the literary genius of the Joseph cycle stands as a tribute to the skill of its Hebrew author.

Some Details of the Story

Both the *Ishmaelites* and the *Midianites* are associated with the movement of Joseph from Canaan to Egypt. The term *Ishmaelite* is used both for the descendants of Ishmael, son of Abraham and Hagar, and also as a general name for any of the nomadic peoples dwelling in the desert to the south and east of Canaan. *Midianite* also refers to a group of nomads, but it is more specific. The Midianites were a group that lived in northwest Arabia, on the eastern shore of the Red Sea's Gulf of Aqabah.

By interpreting correctly the pharaoh's dreams, Joseph rose to the position of *grand vizier,* that is, the pharaoh's own personal representative, second in power only to the pharaoh himself. It was possible for a foreigner to rise to such power in the pharaoh's court, since it is quite likely that the Hebrews came into Egypt when the Hyksos, the Hebrews' fellow Semites, controlled the land.

When Jacob talks about going to *Sheol* in sorrow over the loss of his children, he is referring to the underworld, beneath the earth, to which many peoples of the Near East thought the spirits of the dead went. The whole idea of a place for the dead was not fully developed in Hebraic thought, and at no time did it take on the concept of a place of punishment, such as the later idea of hell. Rather, the dead were thought to carry on a shadowy and insignificant existence in Sheol, separated from the presence of God.

Later in the story, Joseph's wife bears him two sons, *Manasseh* and *Ephraim.* These names represent the ancestors of two of the twelve tribes of Israel. Both of these tribes occupied territory in the northern part of Palestine at the time of the divided kingdom. Note that the whole story of Joseph has an emphasis on the people and places of the northern kingdom. For example, the story presents Joseph as a person from the area of the northern kingdom who obtained success and wealth for himself and his family. The narrative also relates that the family of Jacob lived near Shechem, an important assembly place in the north for the Israelites in the time of their early history in Palestine.

Because of these various elements in the story that emphasize the background of the northern kingdom, scholars who follow the documentary theory think that in part the Joseph story was written down by an author or authors who lived in the northern kingdom during the time of the divided monarchy (c. 800-700 B.C.).

Family Relationships

In this story, we see again the persistent sense of family which is so central to all the patriarchal stories. Joseph is at least as concerned to be reunited with his father as he is to be reunited with his brothers. For him, family is not simply a matter of relationship with one's own generation. Family is the heritage which comes down in time through all the generations of the family, from the fathers to the sons. Out of the Hebrew's intense awareness of his own involvement in the generations of the past and future, and out of his equal awareness of the presence of God to all the generations of the people, was born the unique sense of history that marks the Judeo-Christian-Islamic traditions.

As a result of the reunion, Jacob and his entire family moved into Egypt to live in honor under the sponsorship of Joseph and a benign pharaoh. Jacob and Joseph both would die in Egypt. Both would remember that Palestine, not Egypt, was the promised land. For this reason, the body of Jacob would be embalmed and buried in the old ancestral burial place in Machpelah, where lay the bones of Abraham, Isaac, Sarah, and Rebekah.

87

Long years after his own death, the descendants of Joseph would carry his bones to Shechem, and bury them there in the soil of the promised land.

REFLECTION QUESTIONS

1. How do you evaluate the story of Joseph for its presentation of human characters and its dramatic development?
2. How innocent, do you suppose, were Joseph's dreams about his family?
3. Why was Potiphar's wife the wrong woman for Joseph to make love to, as Joseph saw it? You might compare the experience of Joseph with Potiphar the Egyptian and that of David with Uriah the Hittite.
4. Show, in Joseph's case, how it paid to be a good administrator.
5. How did Joseph combine shrewdness, honesty, imagination, self-interest, and generosity in his dealings with the Egyptians?
6. What weaknesses of character, if any, do you find in Joseph?
7. Would you say that Joseph loved his father more than Judah did? Why?
8. How does the Joseph story portray the action of God?

HYMNS
OF
ISRAEL'S COVENANT
AND KINGDOM

POEMS
OF ISRAEL

The psalms, whatever else they may be, are poetry of Israel's covenant with God. Although scholars debate the period of their authorship, it is clear that the psalms reflect the Davidic monarchy. We have already seen how, during that period, writers were beginning to write down the stories in Israel's oral tradition of the patriarchs and of even more ancient times. It was at that time that different forms of worship were coming into use. Much of the poetry in the Book of Psalms probably was set to music for the Israelites' worship ceremonies.

Our intent in this unit is to take an opportunity to share the emotional heart and the thinking mind of the Israelites who wrote down these songs they sang to God about their human situation. All of them evidence a common loyalty and faith in the God who made the people what they were by giving them his Torah.

Unit Five has only one part. We enter through these readings into the emotional thought world of Israel, comparing it with our own most serious emotions and our own profoundest thoughts about who we are, what is happening to us, and what it means.

SEARCH CUES

1. God's majesty and glory
2. the glory of God's creation
3. Israel's joy at being God's people
4. loneliness, sorrow, and despair
5. self-doubt, confession, patience, and hope

NOW READ THESE PSALMS:

1	15	19	22	23	24	27	42	46	51
73	90	96	103	104	127	130	139	145	150

COMMENTARY

Hebrew Poetry

We may define *poetry* in general as any writing which inspires an unusually emotional response in the reader, both to the message and to the form in which it is expressed, whether in prose or verse. As you have found from studying the Song of Deborah, Hebrew poems, while fitting this general definition of poetry, also have characteristics of their own.

Each line of the poem is divided into two parts. The rhythm is derived from the two to four stressed words in each line.

Second, the most dominant characteristic of Hebrew poetry is its use of paraphrastic, comparative, and cumulative parallelisms, which you have studied in connection with the Song of Deborah. If you look again at some of the psalms you have read in this unit, you will find that they are filled with these kinds of parallelisms.

Third, the Hebrew poets often, but not always, grouped the lines of their poems into stanzas. They appear to have had no rigid rules about this, since frequently the stanzas vary in length even within a single poem.

Fourth, some Hebrew poetry is characterized by having an acrostic structure. That is, each line of the poem begins with a different, succeeding letter of the alphabet. In English, the lines thus would begin with A, then B, then C, and so on. Psalm 145 uses an acrostic structure in the original Hebrew. Many scholars believe that the use of the acrostic structure in some Hebrew poems was a literary fad, lasting for a short period of time and then dying out.

The Structure of the Book of Psalms

Included in the Book of Psalms are 150 poems. Unlike many of the books of the Hebrew Bible, the psalms generally present the words of individuals or groups of men directed toward God, rather than the words of God directed toward men or nations. The poems are divided into five smaller books: Psalms 1-41, 42-72, 73-89, 90-106, and 107-150. There seems to be no particular reason for the divisions to occur where they do. A number of scholars think that this was done in imitation of the five books of the Pentateuch. The divisions relate to no formal literary structure, and the various types of poems are scattered throughout the entire Psalter, as the psalms are often called.

The Authorship of the Psalms

The question of who wrote the psalms, and when, has been debated by scholars for many years. Early Jewish and later Christian and Islamic traditions attributed authorship of many or all of the psalms to King David, in line with the belief that he was a poet and a musician. It is not unreasonable to assume that David did have considerable influence on the development of the formal worship in which the psalms played such an important part. The psalms also reflect in form and content the older non-Israelite worship music of the Near East. They resemble especially the psalms and hymns of Egypt and Mesopotamia. Scholars believe that many of the psalms actually were written over a number of centuries by temple personnel associated with the music of the worship service. Other psalms may have been composed by individual poets offering their thoughts to God.

Most authorities agree that the Psalter is a compilation of a number of psalm collections from a variety of different sources. Beyond that, however, there is disagreement as to just when the psalms were written. Some scholars think that while many of the psalms are pre-Exilic (before 587 B.C.), reflecting a tradition continuing back to the early days of the monarchy, nevertheless, the majority of psalms probably were composed during the period 400-100 B.C. Others believe that most of the psalms were written in the days of the monarchy (1020-587 B.C.), and then collected and compiled in post-exilic times. Regardless of the precise date of authorship, the compilation (i.e., gathering together) of former collections of psalms most probably was completed by the beginning of the first century B.C. However, variations in the final collection are known to have existed down to the fourth century A.D.

Types of Psalms

In general, the psalms embody the concept of one God. They remain intensely personal, and dwell on the vast distinction between the greatness of God and the frailty of man. The psalmists took note of the moral dimensions of human experience, and they often asked God to forgive them their offenses and to protect them from their enemies.

As you have noticed in your reading, however, the individual psalms vary a great deal in content. This reflects the fact that the different psalms were written to be used in different ways. Many of the psalms probably were sung as congregational hymns or used in other worship procedures in the temple of Jerusalem, and later employed in similar ways in smaller synagogues throughout Palestine and the Near East. Others appear to have been written by individuals as devotional poetry to be used in the home and have no formal liturgical purpose. One of the problems scholars have had in studying and interpreting the psalms is the idea that the poems that appear to be individualistic may in fact be representative of the corporate personality of Israel as a nation. That is, a psalm which seems to be addressed to God by an individual may actually refer to Israel as a whole addressing God.

To understand the psalms more fully, scholars have classified them into various types of poems that reflect their original settings. Although there are many different classifications, one of the most widely used schemes is by a scholar named Gunkel. He suggested five main types of Psalms, and offered a sixth category of several minor or sub-types. His five main types are as follows:

1. *Hymns.* (See Psalm 19) These psalms were written for congregational use in the temple, and they offer praise to God.
2. *Laments of the community.* (See Psalm 79) These were written most probably during times of national disturbances and dangers. They seek God's intervention on behalf of the nation Israel.

3. *Royal Psalms.* (See Psalm 2) The psalms of this type were associated with various Israelite kings and used in the temple ceremonies. These psalms most likely were composed before 587 B.C., since the monarchy ceased to exist after the exile.
4. *Individual laments.* (See Psalm 22) These are apparently the most common kind of psalm, and they parallel the laments of the community, asking for God's intervention in times of trouble.
5. *Individual songs of thanksgiving.* (See Psalm 103) These are similar to the community hymns, and probably were used by individuals during the temple ceremonies.

REFLECTION QUESTIONS

1. In what respects does the God of the psalms appear to have attitudes like a human being? In what respects does he seem to have different attitudes?
2. Explain what attitudes in the psalms seem most agreeable to your own attitudes and which seem least agreeable.
3. In what respects would you describe the psalms as out of date? In what respects would you call them up to date?
4. Read the hymns, "America," "America the Beautiful," and "The Star Spangled Banner." Compare them with the psalms. How is their meaning similar? How is it different?
5. What songs of your own times seem to you best to reflect the emotional climate of the psalms?
6. Write a psalm of praise for the reality you believe in most. Then consider how adequately your psalm accounts for the experience of yourself, your family, your enemies, and your friends.

THE PROPHETS SPEAK WHILE MONARCHY DECLINES

Part 1:

AMOS
DRAWS A CIRCLE
OF DOOM

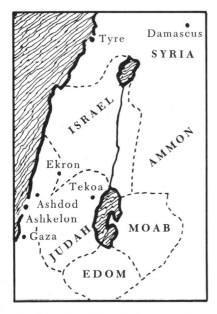

In the understanding of Jews, Christians, and Muslims, prophecy occurred when men inspired directly by God spoke in criticism of the ways and conditions of the people. The words of the prophet were understood as the words of God himself.

The kingdom that Saul had started, that David had built into an empire, and that Solomon had exploited, had split in two by the time of Amos. Now one monarchy in the north called itself Israel, while the Davidic dynasty remaining in the south took the name Judah. In both cases the old pastoral ways had been modified by settled agriculture, urbanization, and accommodation to the religion of the Canaanites.

Amos, one of the great prophets of the period of the divided kingdom, saw in all this the fall of the people, especially the rich and powerful, into indolence, cruelty, and corruption. He also saw the wrath of God hovering over this kind of decline and sensed the coming of an inescapable punishment. A shepherd from Tekoa, in Judah, he spoke to the people of the northern kingdom.

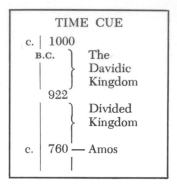

TIME CUE

c. | 1000 B.C. } The Davidic Kingdom

922 } Divided Kingdom

c. | 760 — Amos

NOW READ: AMOS 1:1-2:16

COMMENTARY

What Is Prophecy?

Prophecy occurs when men speak with the power of God's inspiration in criticism of the ways and conditions of the people. These utterances may foreshadow the future through the prophet's interpretation of contemporary events. In the understanding of the prophet and his believing listeners, the words of the prophecy express the active will of God. In effect, as the prophet speaks, God speaks. "Thus says the Lord," on the lips of the prophet, means, "God is saying, here and now. . . ."

Inspiration, Ecstasy, and Possession

To understand the prophet's influence among the people, we need to understand what words like *inspiration, ecstasy,* and *possession* mean in relation to prophecy. The prophet who spoke to the people was inspired by God. This means that, according to Jewish, Christian, and Muslim understanding, the prophet pronounced God's vital will and judgment.

Another way of describing this is to say that the prophet was in ecstasy, or that his utterances were ecstatic. This means that the prophet was "beside himself," or "displaced from himself." To some, this means that God directed the prophet toward a particular thought or word. To others, this means that God verbally inspired the prophets, dictating word for word what the prophet was to say.

Still another way of describing the dynamics of prophecy is to speak of the prophet as being possessed. He was possessed in the sense that his mind and body were "taken over" by a spirit other than his own, in this case, by that of God himself. Prophetic possession was a special instance of a widespread experience of Near Eastern people in biblical times which we call spirit possession. The people understood that the prophet was

98

possessed by the spirit of God. However, a person might also be possessed by demons, or evil spirits of irrational suffering, anxiety, and violence.

Inspiration and ecstasy still occur in modern language. People speak of inspired art, inspired patriotism, inspired mercy. People also refer to being in ecstasy. In modern language, however, the source of inspiration and ecstasy is not always seen as God, or, in the negative cases, evil spirits. More often than not, modern inspiration is ascribed to "natural" or "human" causes.

The Development of the Prophetic Movement in Israel

Prophetic groups in the history of Israel go back to the 11th and 10th centuries B.C. At that time, groups of prophets lived near the various Israelite sanctuaries. They were called ecstatic prophets, because, like the Canaanite prophets, they prophesied in a state of frenzy that may have been stimulated by rhythmical music and bodily movements. However, they differed from the prophets of the Canaanites in that they spoke with the authority of the God of Israel to oppose the practices of the Canaanite Baal worship and to express the will of God in the shaping of history.

During the monarchy, in the tenth and ninth centuries B.C., the ecstatic element in these prophetic groups subsided. But, the groups, then known as the "sons of the prophets," continued to defend the religion of the God of Israel against Baalism.

During those early days of the monarchy, there existed another group of prophets, the official prophets of the king. They tended to tell the king just what he wanted to hear, whether it brought evil or good to the Israelite people. In doing this, the official prophets were more the prophets of the king, reflecting his wishes and desires, than they were the prophets of the God of Israel.

In the ninth and eighth centuries B.C., when the kings of Israel and Judah became more selfish in the making of their royal policies, and when the people of the two kingdoms became more and more lax in keeping their covenant with God, individual prophets began to make themselves heard apart from the prophetic groups. They sought to bring the people back to the ways of the covenant. Scholars divide these men, known as the classical prophets, into two types: (1) the preliterary classical prophets, and (2) the literary classical prophets.

The preliterary prophets included those men, such as Elijah and Elisha, who spoke the will of God during the ninth century B.C. These prophets are called preliterary because we do not have written records of their prophetic messages; the biblical accounts of them come to us in story form.

The literary classical prophets began with Amos in the eighth century B.C. and continued down through the sixth century B.C. into post-exilic times. The words of these men are recorded primarily as direct addresses by the prophets to their listeners.

Israel and the Classical Prophets

The decline of the monarchy in Israel can be traced back to the end of Solomon's reign when, in 922 B.C., the great united kingdom of Saul, David,

99

and Solomon became divided into two smaller kingdoms, Israel in the north and Judah in the south. This decline ended in 587 B.C. with the fall of Jerusalem. After this, Israel never again set an earthly king on the throne to rule over her people. Those centuries of monarchy's decline were also the centuries when the classical prophets began to speak.

In the brief periods of prosperity during the long decline of the monarchy, both in Israel and in Judah the prophets seldom represented the popular point of view. They proclaimed bad news when the people saw the times as good. Monarchy itself was not necessarily the element of culture which the prophets singled out as evidence of disobedience to God.

What they criticized most was the transfer of the people's loyalty, in whatever form it took, from the kingship of God to the kingship of powerful men.

The prophets criticized the self-satisfaction of the rich, who saw in their wealth evidence of their own virtue and lived in luxury at the expense of others who lived in bondage and poverty. They deplored the popular abandonment of the old tribal moral standards handed down by God to Moses. Sharp dealing in business, irresponsible sex life, the idleness of men and the laziness of women, the abandonment of obedience to God and his torah, all appalled the prophets and opened their minds and lips to think and speak the judgment of God. Often the prophet protested against the urban corruption of the people, and especially of the rich and powerful who gained an oppressive advantage by it.

With the protest came expressions of hope to the poor, to the oppressed, and to those who persevered in keeping the ways of God. During acutely bad times, and especially during the exile in Babylon, the prophets often played a role of encouragement to the demoralized people. They would recall the glories of David and Jerusalem and would look forward to a day when God would restore Israel to integrity and favor.

In general, when times were relatively prosperous, and influential people were cruel, soft, and corrupt, the prophets spoke in figures of wrath and doom. In times of suffering and oppression from foreign powers, the voices of the prophets often would sound alone in telling the people that their punishment would come to an end, and that God would deliver them to better times.

As you study the classical prophets of Israel, keep the following summary in mind.

1. The prophets always arose in response to some historical situation in the life of Israel. The prophetic passages you are studying should be read with an eye to the historical and political situation of the time in which, and to which, the prophet spoke.

2. The messages of the prophets can be classified either as prophecies of doom or as prophecies of consolation. The type of message the prophet utters depends to a large extent on the historical and political situation of the time.

3. Each of the prophets looked back to a period in Israel's past which he considered to be an ideal time in the relationship between God and

his covenant people. Some of the prophets looked back to the days of Israel's wilderness wanderings during the Exodus from Egypt. Others looked back to the time of the Davidic kingdom and the establishment of Jerusalem as the holy city of Israel. Each of these two ideal periods of prophetic remembrance usually is associated with one of the two types of prophecies noted above. You may wish to see if you can tell from your readings which type of prophecy is related to which ideal vision and why.

How the Classical Prophets Prophesied

In dealing with prophets like Amos we deal with individuals whose expressions of inspiration were rational and instructive. They were men bent not on achieving a kind of union with God, but on delivering to the people messages which they knew God was giving them.

We do not understand these men as being possessed or in ecstasy in some wild and irrational way. We do, however, want to understand that they believed they were speaking and acting under the direct influence of the spirit of God.

Keep in mind that the prophet, even though he may be described as a writing or literary prophet, was first and foremost a speaker. As speakers, the prophets expressed God and themselves to their believing listeners in the most primitive and dynamic mode of human verbal communication. Telling and listening between human beings is a moment of personal communication of which writing and reading are only a lingering reflection. The prophets expressed their thoughts, then, out of a situation of immediate and vocal communication with their listeners and with God.

The Prophecy of Amos

Amos, in addition to being a shepherd, was also a trimmer of sycamore trees in the southern kingdom of Judah. When he received his call to prophecy, he went north to Israel. He was a model prophet of doom, and an example for his later counterparts. Amos spoke about the year 760 B.C.

The words of Amos, in the two chapters you have read as well as in the rest of the book, expressed a strong monotheism in which he understood God as the only god. For Amos, God's concern and control was not limited just to Israel, but encompassed all of the nations. Amos reflected a God who is insistent upon social justice and who discounts formal rites and sacrifices where they appear to be a substitute for obedience to God's covenant.

The outlook of Amos was so sharply critical that he did not incorporate into his speeches any appreciable element of hope, or any constructive suggestion for correcting the corruption that he saw. It was too late for that. His series of condemning oracles, or dire predictions against Israel's neighbors, contained a clever strategy in which he played on the nationalistic animosities of the people of the northern kingdom to lead them to agree to the rightness of God's judgment and punishment. Then, in the climax of the series of judgments, he laid out the two last oracles against Judah and Israel herself.

The people to whom he spoke the Lord's judgment in the eighth century B.C. did not accept his message as the word of God. Amos' prophecy was rejected at the time, but later circumstances led many to recall the shepherd who had pronounced such a harsh judgment and to acknowledge him as a prophet of God.

REFLECTION QUESTIONS

1. Why is a map showing the locations of cities and kingdoms cited necessary to understand Amos' strategy for making the prophecy against the northern kingdom dramatic?
2. Amos spoke repeatedly of "transgressions." What does the word generally refer to in the reading, that is "transgressions" against what?
3. Reviewing these two chapters, list some of the specific social practices that the prophet deplored. Of what practices would you say he approved in light of what he disapproved?
4. Would you identify these two chapters as poetry? Why?
5. How do Amos' observations compare with your own evaluation of city life?

Part 2

HOSEA ACTS OUT THE MEANING OF GOD'S COVENANT WITH A FAITHLESS ISRAEL

A second prophet announcing doom to the northern kingdom was Hosea. He reinforced his words by acting out in his own marriage the relationship between God and an unfaithful Israel. If Amos found a lesson in looking at the surrounding nations, Hosea found one by looking into the significance of his own marriage.

SEARCH CUES

1. Gomer, the harlot, and her lovers

2. renewal in the wilderness

3. a change of metaphor from wife to son

4. God and not man

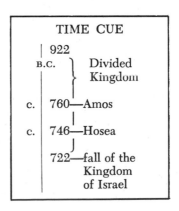

TIME CUE		
	922	
B.C.		Divided Kingdom
c.	760—Amos	
c.	746—Hosea	
	722—fall of the Kingdom of Israel	

NOW READ: HOSEA 1:1-4:19; 11:1-11

COMMENTARY

In the Time of Hosea

About fifteen years after Amos prophesied, Hosea began to speak the words of the Lord's judgment to the Israelites of the northern kingdom. At that time, the kingdom of Israel was ruled by a member of the Jehu dynasty called Jeroboam II. The house of Jehu had taken control of the northern kingdom about 842 B.C. by a gory bloodbath at Jezreel which included the murder of the reigning king of Israel and all of his seventy sons. After the death of Jeroboam II in 746 B.C., the northern kingdom underwent a period of political instability that lasted until the fall of Israel to the Assyrians in 722 B.C. Four of the six kings who ruled during this period were murdered by their successors.

During this period, shortly after 745 B.C., Assyria rose to power in the Near East. The Assyrians eventually took control of the entire Fertile Crescent, from Egypt through Mesopotamia to the Persian Gulf. Some of the nations over which Assyria asserted her control paid heavy tribute to her, and for this were allowed to continue with their own forms of government. This was true of the southern kingdom of Judah, less wealthy and less politically and economically important than Israel. One of the northern kings also appeased Assyria with tributes during this time of political change and intrigue. He was very unpopular with the rich people of his kingdom, however, because he imposed heavy taxes to pay the tribute. After his rule, the northern kingdom revolted against Assyria, eventually being utterly defeated in 722 B.C. by the powerful Assyrian army. Much of Israel's population then was deported to Persia to prevent further uprisings, and the area was repopulated with people from several other lands, including Babylonia and Syria.

A Prophecy of Doom and Hope

It was to this turbulent setting of political unrest and social corruption that Hosea prophesied, probably from shortly before 746 B.C. to about 734 B.C. Like Amos, he was a prophet of doom. He condemned the social evils of the times, the idolatry and the fertility cults which had become associated with Israelite worship, and the political alliances the monarchs formed instead of relying on God for deliverance from the oppressive enemy.

Unlike Amos, however, Hosea also offered a message of hope. He pointed to the steadfast love, or covenant love, which God had for his people. Even though Israel would suffer a just punishment for her unfaithfulness to the covenant agreement, God would still restore and renew her because of his steadfast love for her.

Hosea's Marriage

Chapters 1 to 3 in Hosea have presented difficult problems of interpretation for scholars. One interpretation is that Gomer was not actually an adulteress when Hosea married her, but that she had a tendency toward adultery at that time. If this is the case, then Hosea, is reflecting on the development of his own marriage, used it as a symbol to express the unfaithful behavior of Israel toward God.

A second common interpretation is that Hosea did in fact marry a prostitute, perhaps a temple prostitute for Baal, to act out his prophecy. In this case, Hosea wanted to display to the people of the northern kingdom, by means of his own life, a real, concrete representation of what they were doing in their relationship to God.

In either case, Hosea's own personal life portrayed his prophetic message to the kingdom of Israel. His message spoke of Israel's unfaithfulness to the covenant forged in the wilderness, and of God's judgment and redemptive love in light of that unfaithfulness. It represented the relationship between God and his people as that between a husband and his wife. You already have considered this type of metaphorical relationship in your study of Deuteronomy 7, in which the marriage covenant is expressed as a permanent and exclusive mutual relationship. Amos was the first Israelite prophet to use the marriage relationship as a symbol for the bond between God and Israel.

Another Metaphor of God and His People

As you have seen in Deuteronomy 7 and here again in Hosea 1-3, biblical writers sometimes used these family relationships between husband and wife, or master and servant, as metaphors for the relationship between God and Israel. They also frequently used another type of metaphorical family relationship, which we see expressed in Hosea 11. Here the relationship used as a model is that between a father and his son.

The relationship between father and son contained something of the quality of the husband and wife relationship and also something of the quality of the lord and servant relationship. Throughout the literature of Israel, the father valued his son not only as an *object* of his love but also as an *agent* of his will. The father lived not only *for the sake of* his son but also *by means of* his son as the father's heir and successor.

The Israelites always understood their relationship with God, no matter what the model being employed, in covenantal terms. Their relationship with God was a binding agreement, initiated by God, agreed to by Israel, and binding on both.

REFLECTION QUESTIONS

1. Does Amos or Hosea portray a more merciful God? Why?

2. What indications do you find in the reading that Hosea valued the ways of the wilderness life?

3. How do the names of Hosea's children relate to the covenant relationship between God and Israel?

4. The Canaanite Baal cults of fertility involved temple prostitution. The prophets make it clear why Israel considered such an institution evil. From available reference sources, search out the reasons why the Canaanites thought otherwise.

5. Assume that Hosea loved Gomer, and then discuss the role of happiness and sorrow in his life.

6. Do you think that the family relationships used as metaphors in Hosea are effective in expressing his prophecy? Why?

7. How does the phrase, "for I am God and not man," (Hosea 11:9) summarize the meaning of the whole chapter?

Part 3:

THE TEMPLE CITY FALLS
AND A POET SINGS
THE PEOPLE'S GRIEF

During the long decline of monarchy between the reign of David and the fall of Judah, rural prophets like Amos, Hosea, and Micah extolled the ways of the wilderness morality represented by Israel's Exodus pilgrimage. Others, like Isaiah, had been more urban in their values and had upheld the restoration of the Davidic kingdom as the great hope for Israel's future. But with the destruction of Jerusalem in 587 B.C. the hopes of both kinds of prophets seemed dashed to pieces.

In 2 Kings, which is not prophecy in the usual sense but a historical account, we read a history of the destruction of Jerusalem. In Lamentations, we read a poem of grief and despair expressing Israel's reaction to that cruel event.

SEARCH CUES

1. Nebuchadnezzar and Babylon
2. the house of the Lord and its furnishings
3. the Lord has destroyed
4. the law is no more

TIME CUE

922	
B.C.	Divided Kingdom
722	Fall of Israel
587	Fall of Judah; Babylonian Exile begins

NOW READ: 2 KINGS 25:1-30; LAMENTATIONS 2:1-22

COMMENTARY

The Fall of the Monarchy

In 2 Kings 25, we contemplate the violent death of the faded Judean monarchy. The twelve tribes, as we have seen, had become united centuries before as one political nation under David and Solomon. Subsequently, the one kingdom had divided against itself when Solomon died, forming two nations: Israel, the northern kingdom and Judah, the southern kingdom. Then, as Israel fell, only the shadow kingdom of Judah remained. This last remnant of the great imperial adventure finally met destruction when Jerusalem, the urban heart of Judah, fell under the blows of the Chaldeans (Babylonians).

Thus, according to the witness of history, did God deal with his people's dream of being like the nations, with a destiny of kings and empire. Never again would the Israelites place on their throne a human monarch. Significantly, Israel continued her existence after the fall of Jerusalem as a *religious* community, rather than as one of the many *political* entities of the Near East. Whether in Babylon, or back in Palestine after the exile, or dispersed throughout the other nations of the Near East, Israel would survive primarily as the covenant people of God. She would find her freedom in loyal obedience to the torah, rather than in political triumph as a nation among the nations.

Israel's Grief

The second chapter of Lamentations shows the same events through the eyes of a poet who puts in the form of a dirge and a prayer the anguish of his people. This is more than a description of the destruction of Jerusalem —it is a deep expression of the meaning of God's severe punishment of his people, carried out through Nebuchadnezzar and his Chaldean army.

REFLECTION QUESTIONS

1. In a sense, 2 Kings, 25:1-30 provided you with an objective description of the fall of Jerusalem, while Lamentations 2:1-22 shared a subjective description of it with you. Compare your reactions to the two accounts.
2. Lamentations 2:2 says, "The Lord has destroyed without mercy all the habitations of Jacob. . . ." What method does this imply that God used for punishing his people?
3. What sort of man did King Nebuchadnezzar seem to be from what you read of him in 2 Kings 25? Can you list some of his more obvious personality traits?
4. What was the strategic significance of the way in which Nebuchadnezzar disposed of the various classes of people he found in Jerusalem?

5. From these accounts, and from what you have read previously, what seems to have been the relationship between religion and politics in Israel and throughout the Near East in Hebrew Bible times?

6. Does the author of Lamentations appear to you to have been an eye-witness to the fall of Jerusalem, or does he appear only to have heard about it? Why?

7. Describe how you would feel if your country were overrun by an enemy, your nation's capital destroyed, and you and your family taken forceably to live in the land of the conquerors.

PROPHETS
OF
THE EXILE

Part 1

A PROPHET
SPEAKS WORDS OF HOPE
TO THE DESPAIRING EXILES

For a generation before the fall of Jerusalem the prophet Jeremiah had been warning the people to mend their ways and return to obedience to God. When Nebuchadnezzar approached, Jeremiah advised the people not to resist, since the Chaldean king, he said, was an instrument of God's punishment. Such advice scarcely made him popular.

However, when Jerusalem in fact had been destroyed and her surviving people exiled, Jeremiah's prophecy changed from doom to encouragement and hope.

SEARCH CUES

1. again I will build you, and you shall be built
2. the remnant of Israel
3. Rachel weeping for her children
4. the city shall be rebuilt for the Lord

NOW READ: JEREMIAH 31:1-40

COMMENTARY

The Prophet Speaks to the History of Israel

We turn again to the terrible year of 587 B.C., when King Nebuchadnezzar and his Chaldean army destroyed Jerusalem, murdered Judah's king and all her outstanding leaders, leveled the city to the ground, and took the cream of her remaining citizenry away to Babylon. By that year Jeremiah the prophet had been speaking in Jerusalem for almost a generation.

In 587 B.C., Jeremiah could look back on the long struggle between Assyria and the Babylonian Chaldeans and Medes, which ended when the Assyrian capital Nineveh fell, and all the Assyrian power with it, in 609 B.C. Now, in this dark year for Israel Jeremiah was witness to the final destruction of Jerusalem by that same Chaldean, King Nebuchadnezzar, and to the despair of those people of the southern kingdom who had been proud to call themselves the sons of Judah.

During his career Jeremiah had seen the hand of God's judgment in the struggles between the nations that surrounded Judah. He had looked on the Chaldean empire as a power God had appointed to rule the world. He had spoken against the Judean movement to resist that power. Now that power had overwhelmed and destroyed Judah and Jerusalem. In the days of her pride, Jeremiah had spoken to Judah of punishment and doom. Now, when punishment and doom engulfed her, the prophet spoke of promise and hope.

A Message of Hope

Jeremiah 31 reminds the Israelites going into exile of who they are, of God's unceasing love for them, of his power to restore and to rebuild as well as to destroy. Jeremiah tells them they deserve their present punishment. Yet he gives them hope for the future by saying, in his most important teaching, that God will renew his covenant with them. He will reestablish his torah in their innermost hearts and minds.

This chapter concerns not only the people of the lately defunct southern kingdom, but also the descendants of the long defunct kingdom of the north, whom the prophet recalls when he refers to Samaria, Ephraim, and Rachel. In patriarchal history, Rachel, was the wife of Jacob, the mother of Joseph and Benjamin, and a mother-figure for the tribes of the north.

We also find in chapter 31 the recurring metaphor of the husband and wife to express the relationship between God and Israel. It reflects the Israelite conviction that God's intense concern for them was nothing casual and second hand, but basic and exclusive. It was like the love of a man for his wife, to whom he commits himself and all his powers in return for her obedient dependence on him alone forever.

REFLECTION QUESTIONS

1. Does Jeremiah seem suspicious of city life like Amos and Hosea?
2. What appears to be Jeremiah's hope regarding the relationship between the former northern and southern kingdoms in the event of a restoration of his people to their own land?
3. What reality did Jeremiah anticipate would become the very heart of the restoration?
4. What would be the outstanding architectural symbol of the restoration?
5. From your reading in this chapter, find evidence to connect the concepts of *sacred people* and *sacred place*. What does "sacred" appear to mean?

6. What do verses 29-30 have to do with the new covenant Jeremiah prophesies in verses 31-34?

7. Compare the attitude of Jeremiah speaking to the exiles with the attitudes of Amos and Hosea speaking to the people before the fall of the northern kingdom. Do you think the change in attitude was appropriate? Why?

8. Does the covenant of which Jeremiah speaks sound more to you like a *renewed* covenant or a *new* covenant? Why? Does it include the giving of a new law?

Part 2:

A PROPHET
ENCOURAGES ISRAEL
IN HER EARLY DAYS OF EXILE

Early in the period of exile in Babylon, the Israelites suffered profoundly from the shock of being torn from their home country to be marched into isolation in an enemy land. It was at this time that Ezekiel appeared. To people haunted by deadly humiliation and despair he described his vision of the valley of dry bones.

SEARCH CUES

1. the hand of the Lord
2. son of man
3. the breath
4. the spirit

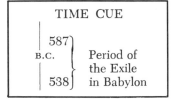

TIME CUE

587 ⎫
B.C. ⎬ Period of
538 ⎭ the Exile
in Babylon

NOW READ: EZEKIEL 37:1-14

COMMENTARY

The Prophet Ezekiel

Ezekiel, like Jeremiah, lived through the fall of Judah. He was apparently one of those exiled to Babylonia. Ezekiel, who quite likely had been a priest in Jerusalem, prophesied to the Israelites both before and after the destruction of the temple and the fall of Jerusalem in 587 B.C. In the days before the fall, Ezekiel had uttered God's message of judgment to the Judeans, pointing to their unfaithfulness to the covenant and their certain punishment, which would come through the destruction of their holy city.

After the devastation had occurred and many of the Judeans had been deported to Babylonia, Ezekiel's prophecy became a call to restoration. He offered a fresh hope to the exiled Israelites that God would renew them as a faith community and restore them to the land he once had given them.

Ezekiel was one of the prophets of Israel who communicated God's messages in a variety of ways. Frequently he would act out his prophecy, as Hosea had done centuries earlier. When he communicated his prophecies verbally, they were often in the form of allegories and visions, as we see in Ezekiel 37. Ezekiel's use of various means of prophetic expression gave dramatic force to his messages.

The Valley of Dry Bones

The prophecy of the valley of dry bones expressed to Israel a sense of God's mercy and a vision of hope for the people in the depths of their demoralizing troubles. It predicted that God would renew the vitality of the Israelites, and that he would inspire them with strength and courage to return to Palestine.

Ezekiel's prophecy foreshadowed things to come. The metaphor of the bones described the hopeless defeatism of his fellow Israelites as he saw them in exile in Babylon. But the living breath of God, the very wind itself, would breathe new life into them and bring them home. Eventually, when Cyrus the Persian conquered Babylon in 538 B.C., the Israelites were permitted to go home. This is prophecy in another sense: predictions about the future that are frequently fulfilled. Many people see in the words of the prophet, one of the initial acts of God's strategy to return the Israelites to their own land.

REFLECTION QUESTIONS

1. Whom was the Lord addressing as "son of man"? What does the term seem to mean?
2. Compare the relationship of *breath* and *bones*, *spirit* and *people*, in this vision of Ezekiel.
3. Do you think Ezekiel's prophecy spoke primarily to the Israelites as a corporate body or as individuals?
4. From this and your other reading so far, what seems to have been the relative significance of the individual and the community in the experience of Israel?

117

Part 3:

ISAIAH PROPHESIES
IN A DIFFERENT MOOD
LATE IN THE BABYLONIAN EXILE

Several decades after the prophecies of Ezekiel, the immediate shock of Israel's removal from her own land began to fade away. Taking its place was a nostalgia more characteristic of people who treasured receding memories of a better life in a former place and generation. Probably their economic and social circumstances had improved considerably since the first years of exile. During the decade before Cyrus the Persian released the Israelites, permitting them to return to Palestine if they wished, the poetic voice of Isaiah spelled out a vision of Israel's hoped-for return home.

Isaiah proclaimed a bold vision of an all-powerful and compassionate Lord decreeing for his people a triumphant procession back across the wilderness to his reestablished city of Zion.

SEARCH CUES

1. God issues a pardon and a command
2. proclamations of God's power and forgiveness
3. God's scorn for the powers of nations and idols
4. the Lord's gifts to the faithful

NOW READ: ISAIAH 40:1-31

COMMENTARY

The Book of Isaiah

Isaiah is a very complicated book in terms of its authorship. Some view it as the work of one author. A number of scholars think the book is divided into two or three parts, each written at a different time. According to this theory, chapters 1-39 are the prophecy of the "original," or First Isaiah, who was an urban citizen of Jerusalem in the southern kingdom of Judah at about the same time that Amos and Hosea were prophesying to the northern kingdom, c. 740 B.C.

The writings contained in Isaiah 40-55 according to this view, are thought to come from an unknown author who was one of the exiles living in Babylon about 540 B.C., two centuries later than the First Isaiah. This writer, called Second Isaiah, is thought to be the author of the chapter you have just read. Second Isaiah's writings expressed the hope and promise that the deliverance of the exiled Israelites from Babylonia was at hand. This author expressed his prophetic calling through the mind and heart of a poet. He envisioned God's action on the basis of what he observed, and probably expressed his searching awareness in writing more than in speech.

Scholars holding a theory that there is more than one author disagree as to whether the last portion of the book, chapters 56-66, also come from the hand of the Second Isaiah, or whether these chapters are from yet another source, called Third Isaiah. They think that this latter source may have been a disciple, or disciples, of the Second Isaiah, who wrote the concluding chapters of the book at about the beginning of the fifth century B.C.

Life Among the Exiles

Life in Babylonia for the exiled Judeans was not so difficult as it must have seemed at first. The people were permitted considerable freedom of movement, and they established themselves in business, trade, and farming. In fact, a number of them became so firmly attached to their new ways of life that they declined to return to Palestine when Cyrus the Persian conquered Babylonia and issued his edict of liberation to the Israelites in 538 B.C.

However comfortable they may have been physically, the exiles must have felt a deep personal loss at being removed from the land which had been at the very center of their religious lives. It was to this need that the priests and prophets of the exile spoke. They helped the people to understand themselves as a familial, rather than a political, community, whose traditions and memories could sustain and strengthen them in any land.

In Babylonia, even though the practices associated with the Jerusalem temple could no longer be carried out, there were other ways in which the people's faith as a community could be expressed. They could celebrate the Sabbath with the offering of prayers and the singing of their ancient hymns. They also could gather together to hear their sacred literature being read, which told of the patriarchs and the Exodus, when the covenant between God and his people was made. Although there is no concrete proof, it is quite likely that the origins of the synagogue stemmed from these gatherings of the faithful in exile.

Words of Encouragement and Triumph

In addition to the deep nostalgia for the better days in the land from which they had been taken the exiles also faced the challenge of the Babylonian prosperity around them, for which the Babylonians thanked their pagan gods. How strong was the God who could not prevent Nebuchadnezzar from carrying away his people? Or, if he was all-powerful, how much did he truly love them in permitting them to be taken to this dreary life as people powerless and dispossessed?

Chapters 40-55 of Isaiah are addressed to such a situation and to such a mental climate. They seek to rally the confidence of a scattered and exiled Israel. In outlook and content, the chapters manifest a universal monotheism, or belief in one and only one god. They greatly emphasized the creative activity of God, and look forward to a day when all the nations of the world will do honor to the one creator. At the same time they regard Israel as the original and final agency of God's all-embracing interest in the human situation.

Isaiah vividly raised the possibility of Israel's exercise of a mission to the Gentiles, that is, to the uncircumcised people beyond the original scope of God's covenant with Israel. He proclaimed that the coming restoration would redeem Israel from her sufferings and glorify her as the mediator of God's strength and wisdom to the nations. In speaking of these things, Isaiah sought to convey to his people the combination of Israel's election as God's chosen people with her mission as God's chosen agent.

In these ideas we find the seeds of a changing understanding of God's relationship to human affairs. That changing understanding would continue in the centuries following the Babylonian exile. Firmly rooted in the ancient Hebrew faith, it would affect dramatically the later views of Jews, Christians, and Muslims, as both together and against each other they expressed in their life and literature the claims and questions of their faith in God.

REFLECTION QUESTIONS

1. What seems to be the full significance of the word "comfort," with which the 40th chapter of Isaiah begins; that is, how does it appear to mean more than it does as we ordinarily use it?
2. What does this passage imply concerning the difference between God and man? Between the kingdom of God and the nations of men?
3. Can you locate in Isaiah 40 some examples of a rhetorical question? How do these differ from quiz questions?
4. Do you think Isaiah wrote good poetry in chapter 40? Defend your position.
5. Choose two consecutive verses in Isaiah 40 which you believe best summarize the meaning of the whole chapter, and explain your choice.

Part 4

THE SERVANT OF GOD
SERVES UNDER OPPRESSION,
AND TRIUMPHS BY SUFFERING

Isaiah, the same poet-prophet, has given us another vision, famous in literature, describing the suffering servant of the Lord. "Who is the suffering servant?" This question remains, and is still being studied from several religious points of view. Certainly, the idea of service through suffering bore profound meaning for the people of the exile. The situation of the suffering servant speaks to all individuals and communities who struggle to understand why some people suffer willingly, with no apparent appreciation or reward, for the sake of others.

SEARCH CUES

1. the servant's ultimate reward
2. the servant's status among men
3. the element of confession
4. the substitute victim
5. the purpose of his suffering

NOW READ: ISAIAH 52:13-53:12

COMMENTARY

Lord and Servant

This reading is the fourth of the suffering servant passages for which chapters 40-55 of Isaiah are famous. The lord and servant relationship recalls other portions of the Hebrew Bible literature. By using this model, Israel understood that God's covenant relationship with his servant was one in which the servant acted as the agent of the Lord, as his instrument in dealing with the external world.

When we appreciate Isaiah's use of the lord and servant model, we can see his strong new interpretation of the interrelationship between being chosen and being called to serve. To be the chosen one of the Lord brought with it the awesome responsibility of acting as God's instrument in history. According to the prophet's message in this passage, that responsibility would be fulfilled through suffering.

The Figure of the Suffering Servant

Scholars do not agree whether the figure of the suffering servant was meant to represent Israel corporately, to represent some individual Israelite, or both. You know from your reading that in the lord and servant metaphor, as in other family metaphors, Israel is used often in the singular, as a "corporate personality." This usage symbolized the idea that the life of each individual Israelite found fulfillment through identification with the whole community of Israel. Likewise, an individual could represent all of Israel in many cases.

Furthermore, it appears that the authors of the literature you are studying sometimes moved back and forth between these two ideas, the individual image and the corporate image, in their writings. Because of this, it is often difficult to discover, in any particular passage, just which representation is meant. In thinking about what the suffering servant image in these chapters represents, scholars have suggested different possibilities, such as Israel as a whole, the righteous remnant of Israel, a particular individual like Moses, or Isaiah himself, or the ideal individual Israelite. Many Christians have also interpreted the suffering servant songs as references to Christ.

God's Purpose for the Servant

The great significance of the figure of the suffering servant lies in the conviction that God's purpose, and the fulfillment of Israel, may come about not through military and political effort against one's neighbors, but through sacrificial human suffering by God's servant person or people. The servant suffers *on behalf of* God and *for the sake of* those hostile or indifferent people beyond the covenant relationship. In this lies the servant's eventual vindication and fulfillment.

REFLECTION QUESTIONS

1. Explain what seems to you to be the different points of view from which the suffering servant was described in this passage.
2. Assume the suffering servant to be an *individual person*. What persons today seem to resemble him?
3. Assume the suffering servant to be a *community of people*. What communities today seem to resemble it?
4. "And they made his grave with the wicked, and with a rich man in his death, . . ." If the above is an example of a paraphrastic parallelism, what does it appear to say about the relationship between wickedness and wealth?

THE LORE OF WISDOM GROWS IN THE LITERATURE OF ISRAEL

Part 1:

THE PREACHER SPEAKS
WITH WISDOM
FROM HUMAN EXPERIENCE

Wisdom sayings and wisdom literature develop out of general human experience. Human communities everywhere have produced and treasured traditions of this kind.

Usually wisdom takes the form of old sayings that tell us how to act in those situations of life which all of us must face. In literate societies wisdom often takes the form of thoughtfully organized and poetically expressed counsel of deep subtlety and great literary merit. Such wisdom literature offers an understanding of life's profoundest questions, and advice on how best to live with those questions.

Koheleth, the preacher, whose book is known in most Bibles as Ecclesiastes, was a wisdom writer of this kind.

SEARCH CUES
1. the trouble with knowledge
2. an experiment with pleasure
3. the common fate
4. the meaning of work
5. the situation in Sheol

NOW READ: ECCLESIASTES 1:1-4:3; 9:1-18

COMMENTARY

Wisdom Literature

Wisdom literature includes those writings, often in the form of ethical maxims and shrewd observations of human character, which reflect on the inevitable conditions of human experience and provide advice as to what

125

the individual can best do in the face of them. Wisdom literature often delves deeper, searching into the profound unanswered questions with which all men must deal in their lives. The wisdom literature in the Hebrew Bible includes the books of Proverbs, Ecclesiastes, Job, and the Song of Solomon.

One probable origin of wisdom literature is in collections of common sense advice provided for the young out of the experience of the elders. In some societies, such as those of the Near East, traditions of wisdom were developed also in the courts of the various nations. These traditions helped to provide the rulers of the nations with training in the wisdom with which they were to govern.

A wisdom tradition, either oral or written, occurs in all cultures. It incorporates itself in riddles, maxims, and fables, and passes down from generation to generation, and abroad from group to group, translated and refined as it goes. Thus the wisdom literature of the Hebrews is partly peculiar to the Hebrew tradition itself, but also shares themes and illustrations with the traditions of their neighbors in Canaan, Egypt, and Mesopotamia. This is called *cross-cultural diffusion,* the intercommunication and sharing of ideas and objects when cultures meet. The wisdom literature of the Judeo-Christian tradition of the last two centuries B.C. and the first century A.D. interacted increasingly with Greek philosophical thought and the highly developed mystery religions of the Near East.

The Wisdom of Koheleth

In the book of Ecclesiastes we find a kind of wisdom different from the central Jewish and Christian tradition. Some people consider it to be a good example of pessimistic wisdom literature, while others characterize it as realistic, rather than pessimistic. Scholars think that it was probably written in Jerusalem sometime during the latter half of the third century B.C.

The author of Ecclesiastes first claims to be King Solomon, but later describes himself as Koheleth, or, the preacher. The word Koheleth is perhaps better translated as the gatherer, or collector, of wisdom, and the author actually may have been a teacher of wisdom.

Some believe the point of view in Ecclesiastes is humanistic because it looks for truth fundamentally in human experience itself. It would seem that this viewpoint grew out of the search by Koheleth for an understanding of the ways of God in history. He apparently concludes that, although God has given life as a gift, his ultimate plans and purposes in giving it are unknown and unknowable. The book is an example of mature skepticism regarding "easy answers" to human problems, even in a world in which God provides and rules.

REFLECTION QUESTIONS

1. What does the word "vanity" mean in Ecclesiastes 1:2?
2. Discuss the observation that there is nothing new under the sun. Do you agree? Why?

3. How do you account for the preacher's attitude toward pleasure and success?

4. What appears to be the view in Ecclesiastes concerning the idea that people generally get what they deserve, a reward or a punishment?

5. Compare the viewpoint of Amos the prophet with that of Koheleth the preacher in doubting the value of luxurious living.

6. How do you suppose Koheleth would respond to the statement, "The God of Israel is a God who reveals himself to his people through his actions in history"?

7. How does Koheleth's general message compare with one you would expect to hear in a typical commencement address in your school?

Part 2:

A RIGHTEOUS MAN ARGUES HIS CASE WITH GOD

One of the concerns in Near Eastern wisdom tradition was the question of apparently undeserved suffering. A well-behaved and faithful man might find himself caught in a seemingly permanent situation of pain and bad fortune. Could such a person realistically count on being relieved of his suffering and properly compensated for having been loyal to God during the period of trouble? In any case, would not even the best of men sooner or later lose faith and turn disloyal if the situation were sufficiently painful and hopeless? The story of Job moved beyond these concerns to questions yet more profound.

The book is partly narrative and partly poetry. The narrative part comprises the prolog and epilog; the poetry forms the heart and bulk of the story.

SEARCH CUES

1. a wager and a test
2. Zophar accuses Job and Job defends himself
3. Job describes the plight of man
4. God's answer from the whirlwind
5. Job's confession to God

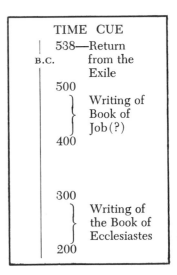

TIME CUE

B.C.

538—Return from the Exile

500

Writing of Book of Job(?)

400

300

Writing of the Book of Ecclesiastes

200

NOW READ: JOB 1:1-3:26; 11:1-14:22; 38:1-40:14; 42:1-17

COMMENTARY

The Book of Job

The book of Job begins with a prose prolog followed by an opening lament by Job. It then moves to three cycles of comments by Job's three friends alternating with Job's responses to the comments. Thus, in the first cycle, Eliphaz speaks and Job answers, then Bildad speaks and Job answers, and finally Zophar speaks and Job answers. This pattern is repeated in the second cycle and again in the third, except that in the third cycle Job's response to Zophar is interrupted by a chapter on wisdom (chapter 28), which probably is an insert, and has little to do with the movement of the poem. The speeches by Elihu in chapters 32 to 37 are considered by many scholars to be a later addition to the original poem.

These cycles of comments are followed by Job's final complaint. God's answer to Job follows, coming from a whirlwind. It occurs in two speeches that are for the most part a battery of rebuking questions. Each of God's speeches evokes from Job a confession of guilt and ignorance. The prose epilog then tells a story of Job's vindication by God. It describes the correction of his friends and the restoration to Job of all that he had lost.

Prose and Poetry in Job

The setting for the story apparently was Edom, and the central human figure, Job, was a prosperous Edomite sheik. The prose narrative portions of the book (chapters 1, 2, and 42:7-17) were written in the ninth or eighth century B.C., according to some scholars. They think that the poetic bulk of the book probably was written sometime after the sixth century B.C.

Interestingly, the prose narrative (prolog and epilog) seems to have a quite different meaning from the poem. In the narrative, we have a description of an ideal man of patience and humility before God. In spite of his almost unbelievable adversity, he perseveres steadfastly, bearing his suffering without any doubt or protest toward God. The outcome of the story supports the principle of *moral retribution:* in the end a man always gets what he deserves, reward for his righteousness and punishment for his sins. This was a common theme in Near Eastern wisdom literature, and it has counterparts in countries as far away as India.

In the poem, however, the concern appears to be different. It seems to portray an assumption on Job's part that he can know the rules that rule God. On the basis of this, he claims certain inalienable rights because God is bound to the principle of moral retribution. Job lays a claim on God's favor by virtue of his own knowledge and righteousness. To this claim God responds "out of the whirlwind," as you have read in 38:1-5 and 40:8-14.

In the prose and poetry of Job, we can see the two forms of wisdom writing mentioned in Part 1 of this unit. The prose sections take the form of a wisdom expression that informs the reader of the way a person should act to live successfully in the world. The prose narrative does this by affirming the idea of moral retribution. The second form of wisdom literature, dealing with attempts to understand the deepest questions in life, finds expression through the poetry in the book of Job.

But parts do not tell the whole, and no commentator's interpretation exhausts the possibilities for meaning in religious literature, especially in a work like Job. The reader should consider it with his own mind out of the depths of his own experience.

REFLECTION QUESTIONS

1. According to the prolog to Job, does it seem possible that a man can be faultless in his attitude and conduct?
2. How did Zophar respond to Job's lament about his condition? How does this compare with modern counselling methods?
3. What did Job seem to mean when he said to Zophar (chapter 12), "I am not inferior to you"?
4. What was Job complaining about when he said, "The tents of robbers are at peace. . ."?
5. What evidence do you find that Job was a courageous man?
6. What seems to be Job's thinking about life after death?
7. Who said, in effect, "Just who do you think you are?" and what were some of the illustrations he used in saying it?
8. In chapter 40 Job said, "I lay my hand on my mouth." What impression does this give you of the kind of man Job was?

Part 3:

A SONG OF LOVE
IN THE WISDOM LITERATURE

The Song of Solomon, or Song of Songs, is love poetry, said to be derived from a number of sources by those who do not credit King Solomon with its authorship. It falls within the genre of wisdom literature partly because of its association with Solomon and partly because the singers of such songs have been credited with expressing genuine wisdom about love.

We will read our selection from the Song of Solomon primarily to appreciate it as a love lyric in the style and imagery of post-exilic Israel.

SEARCH CUES

1. doves, goats, ewes, and fawns
2. a locked garden
3. I slept, but my heart was awake
4. I am sick with love

NOW READ: SONG OF SOLOMON 4:1-5:16

COMMENTARY

A Problem of Interpretation

The style and content of the Song of Solomon is so different from the other books of the Hebrew Bible that it has presented scholars with a problem: why was it included when the Council of Jamnia, about 90 A.D., decided which books belonged in the Hebrew Bible and which did not? Would it have been included if it had been understood simply as secular love poetry? If not, in what other way could the book be viewed?

Several answers have been proposed.

1. The Song in reality was ancient cultic love poetry, used originally by non-Israelites in the ceremonial observance of a marriage between the king

or the sun god and the goddess of fertility, symbolizing the renewal of life in the cycles of nature. It later was adopted by Israel for use in the ritual celebrations of fall and spring as part of the festival liturgy.

2. The Song was part of a cycle of wedding poems sung to honor a couple at the occasion of their marriage. It survived in the canon because of its place in the Hebrew wedding customs.

3. The Song actually was love poetry, but the Council of Jamnia believed it had been written by King Solomon. It was preserved because it expressed some of the king's wisdom on the topic of love.

4. The Song of Solomon in fact allegorized the ideal relationship between God and Israel through its presentation of the passionate love and loyalty between a husband and his wife. It was a poetic, emotional expression of the husband-wife metaphor used often in other portions of the Hebrew Bible.

5. The Song was simply 'secular' love poetry, included in the canon of the Hebrew Bible because it expressed beautifully one aspect of the experience of human beings in life. The goodness of God's creation could be found and appreciated in this expression of love between human beings, just as it was found in other songs and poems that portrayed love between God and man.

REFLECTION QUESTIONS

1. Find in the dictionary definitions of *nard, safron, calamus, cinnamon, frankincense, myrrh,* and *aloes.* Does more exact knowledge of these words enrich your appreciation of the poetry when you read it again?
2. Compare the vocabulary of this love song with the vocabulary of love songs today. How are the images similar? How are they different?
3. List some of the metaphors you liked best in this poetry.
4. How does this poetry, or any poetry, express the inadequacy of words?
5. Discuss how the Song of Solomon might be employed as an allegory to describe a quite different set of events. What characteristics do you think the other set of events would have to possess in common with those in the Song of Solomon for the allegory to be meaningful?

AN APOCALYPTIC VISION

Part 1:

ISRAEL'S ENEMIES AND THE POWER OF APOCALYPTIC WRITING

Daniel is different from other books in the Hebrew Bible. The book reflects an environmental background different from what you have been studying up to this point. For this reason a preparatory commentary precedes the reading from the book itself.

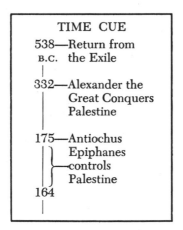

```
            TIME  CUE
      538—Return from
      B.C.  the Exile
       |
      332—Alexander the
       |     Great Conquers
       |     Palestine
       |
      175—Antiochus
       | }   Epiphanes
       | }—controls
       | }   Palestine
      164
       |
```

COMMENTARY

SOME BACKGROUND TO DANIEL

Centuries of Change

The life of the people of Israel after the restoration from exile was not a return to the circumstances of former times. Its setting was no longer the wilderness, or the Canaanite culture of the period of the monarchy. Nor was it simply the exile world brought back from Babylon. Increasingly, Palestine was becoming a crossroads of inter-regional trade and a battlefield where the fate of empires was decided. Jerusalem, at the center of it all, grew as a place where a variety of religious ideas and practices blended and contended in an urban environment.

With all these changes came a change in the Jewish understanding of God's way of involvement in human affairs. During the almost four centuries between the exile to Babylon and about 165 B.C., there were major changes in the cultural environment and inner experience of the Jewish people.

In those intervening centuries, many but by no means all of the exiled Jews returned to Palestine after the edict of liberation by Cyrus the Persian in 538 B.C. About 444 B.C., two Babylonian Jews, Ezra and Nehemiah, acted as central figures in a Jewish religious revival when they returned to Palestine. The torah was reemphasized in Palestine as the way of Jewish life. The Jews remained under the relatively tolerant rule of the Persians until Alexander the Great overcame the Persian Empire late in the fourth century B.C. Under the Persians, and later under the Greek successors to Alexander, the Jews remained a subject people. Apparently in the centuries after the religious revival under Ezra and Nehemiah, the devotion of many Jews to the torah declined again.

New and Old Ideas

The influences of Persian religion and Greek philosophy had become strong in Palestine and contributed much to the change in the thinking of the Jews. Similarly Jewish ideas became influential far beyond the Jewish community.

In the second century B.C. tension existed among the Jews between the Hellenists, who favored Greek ways, and the Hasidim, who favored adherence to the torah-centered ancient ways of Israel. On this tension, King Antiochus Epiphanes superimposed his oppressive administration. He had come to power as ruler in Palestine in 175 B.C. The Jews rioted and revolted against his humiliating regime, which included a mocking desecration of the temple at Jerusalem by offering swine's flesh in pagan rites. Under these oppressive circumstances, there was a successful revolt under Judas Maccabaeus (165 B.C.).

In those days the Near East wrestled with a welter of religious ideas arising out of the Greek, the Mesopotamian, and the Israelite backgrounds. Those ideas competed with one another and fused in the heat of intercultural trade and power struggle. This intensity of interaction diffused old ideas and gave rise to new ideas.

No one found himself more enticed and more threatened by this intellectual and religious climate than did the Palestinian Jew. He retained his faith in the continuance of God's covenant throughout this period of ferment. He believed that Israel remained God's chosen spouse and servant, who would one day be freed from oppression and vindicated before all men. God would establish himself as lord and father of the whole world, doing it all within the terms of his covenant relationship with Israel.

A New Age

However, by the second century Jewish interpretation of the way in which that final blessing was to come about was forming into a new pattern of ideas described as *apocalyptic*. The notion of the righteous remnant remained alive. Not all of Israel would be saved (i.e., enjoy the final victory and blessing), but only those who had been true to God and obedient to his torah. In a moment of final judgment on the nations, God would include the righteous Jew and exclude the disobedient from the new age he was going to inaugurate. The new age would come in unimaginable magnificence and would follow a great conflagration. That fiery holocaust would bring the old world to an end and would announce the arrival of the day of judgment and the beginning of God's new order of things. This complete transformation of the world by an act of God's judgment would be the final revelation of his purpose and the final vindication of his faithful people. This great final event, putting an end to history as men had known it, would be at the same time a great creative event ushering in the new age of God. The final end, in other words, would also be a radical new beginning for those who had remained true to God and his torah. This final destruction and new creation, which would reveal and make real the ultimate purpose of God for history, is called *the apocalypse*.

Beliefs of the Times

Dramatically involved in this developing idea of a new creation was the suffering servant as we found in Isaiah. The older belief that God marched with Israel to overcome the nations was replaced by a belief that God was watching his suffering servant Israel from on high and from the future, putting her to the test under the humiliating conditions of captivity and dispersion. With that idea was the expectation of a messiah, or anointed one, who would come at the moment of apocalypse as God's agent to bring in the new age and rule it.

There was no universally accepted, or systematically developed pattern for those apocalyptic ideas. They clashed and combined in a great variety of controversies and agreements. Yet out of that tumult would emerge the dramatic claims of Christian literature and the renewal of faith we find in the classical literature of Judaism.

Daniel's Apocalyptic Writing

While most scholars agree that the book of Daniel stands as a classic of apocalyptic writing, and use it as a model for evaluating this type of literature, they disagree about who wrote the book and when it was written. It made its first appearance in Israel during the second century B.C., and it is clearly related to the events of the time. But was it written in the second century?

One theory is that a man named Daniel (referred to in Ezekiel 14:14 and 28:3) wrote the book during the sixth century B.C. It was then hidden away with an unknown group who released it in the second century because they either recognized its relation to the events of their time or thought that the end of the world was imminent. The majority of scholars, however, reject that theory, believing that Daniel was written by an unknown author during the second century who used an ancient name as a pseudonym.

According to this theory, the author of Daniel was the product of his times. His experience was the experience of many, and he wrote out of that experience and to that experience. In a time of political oppression by an alien government, the author remained anonymous. In a period when prophetic inspiration was scarcely recognized, he ascribed the prophetic insight of his work to Daniel, a prophet-seer associated with the ancient courts of Nebuchadnezzar and Belshazzar.

The author, according to this view, wrote for his readers rather than speaking to his listeners. His method was to show that Daniel had written down a predicted history of the end of the world, to be revealed when the end of the world was at hand. Now, in the days of Antiochus Epiphanes, the end indeed was near, and the final days of history were revealed to the author in dreams and visions.

The author wrote cryptically in symbols and allegory. In a report of his dreams and visions, he loaded his writing with hidden meanings and references. He avoided direct descriptions of his own times and circumstances. Since, however, he believed the final end was at hand, the author looked to the future as all-important. The end would come at any moment. God would destroy the present order of evil and create a new order in which the persecuted people would be vindicated and their lives fulfilled according to the ageless promise of God. At the same time, God's judgment would condemn to destruction or punishment Antiochus and all the oppressors of Israel, as well as the faithless and disobedient ones from among his own people.

DANIEL INTERPRETS THE HANDWRITING ON THE WALL, AND DESCRIBES HIS VISION OF THE FOUR BEASTS

Introducing Daniel

The first six chapters of the book of Daniel contain stories of Daniel's adventures as a seer and interpreter of dreams at the Babylonian court. The account of the handwriting on Belshazzar's wall is one of these.

The remaining six chapters contain accounts of Daniel's apocalyptic dreams and visions, including that of the four beasts. The message of this allegory was understood quite well by the Jews of his time, although it remained hidden to the members of the oppressive Greek regime. It may be interesting to read the book first without commentary, simulating in some degree the situation of the Greeks who might have read it when it came into their possession.

SEARCH CUES

1. King Belshazzar and the vessels of gold and silver
2. Daniel's talents
3. *mene, tekel,* and *parsin*
4. the plot against Daniel
5. the lion's den
6. the four beasts
7. the ancient of days
8. one like a son of man
9. the judgment and destruction
10. the everlasting kingdom

NOW READ: DANIEL 5:1-7:28

THE STORIES AND VISIONS OF DANIEL

The Author's Stories

The setting of the stories in Daniel 5 and 6 is the sixth century B.C. during the Babylonian exile. The Belshazzar of whom we read shared the rule of Babylon at the close of the exilic period. The stories provide the framework for the author's message. If the book was written in the second century, the author was probably attempting to encourage his oppressed people by providing them with the example of a fellow Jew who had remained steadfast in his faith in the face of foreign rulers. The Jews of the author's time could then take heart from the strength of Daniel's loyalty to his religion and from the power of God's actions. To an outsider, the stories may have seemed to be merely tales of past glories. To the attentive Jew, however, a parallel could be found in his own situation, and he could renew his hope for the end of the present persecution under Antiochus Epiphanes.

The Vision

In contrast, the vision in Daniel 7 looked not to the past, but to the future, in which the present age of oppression would end and the new age of God would begin. In this vision, the author presents an *eschatological* picture; that is, he is concerned with a doctrine of last things, in which the old order of history is changed and a new order of things begins.

Apocalyptic writing in those days customarily employed animal-like figures to represent human kings and kingdoms. Thus, in Daniel 7 the winged lion represents the Babylonian Empire and the bear-like creature the Median Empire. The Persian Empire takes the form of the four-headed leopard, while the Greek Empire, as the author knew it under the local Palestinian regime of the Seleucids, appears as a monster more grotesque and dreadful than all the rest. The victim of all these beastly powers is Israel.

The horns of the fourth beast represent the kings or dynasties of the Greek Empire. The little horn is a symbol of Antiochus Epiphanes, the Seleucid king who was oppressing the Jews at the time of writing. Notice that God does not burn the Babylonian, Persian, and Median powers, but only reduces and constrains them. This indicates a greater respect by the author for their tolerance toward the Jews, in contrast to his complete repudiation of the harsher treatment imposed by the Greeks, as represented by the immediate cruelty of Antiochus.

The "son of man" phrase is difficult to interpret but many scholars believe that it means "like a man." Some see the figure as representing Israel. Some see it as representing a ruler of Israel and the world in God's kingdom of the new age. Increasingly, the apocalyptists saw the figure of the "son of man" to be the messiah, or anointed one, who would come from the realm of heaven, the unknowable place of God.

The above points do not exhaust the symbolism of the seventh chapter, nor are they above debate as to their meanings, but they do represent generally the findings of scholars, and they may help you in a fuller understanding of the book. They also can indicate the dramatic way in which the Jewish apocalyptists, in a language of allegory, could at once both encourage their people and damn their persecutors.

Apocalyptic literature must be read like poetry. It requires intense exercise of the imagination to picture vividly the visionary figures, both threatening and hopeful. At the same time, the reader must not neglect history. He should keep in mind the cultural circumstances in which the apocalyptic writing occurs, and with which it is concerned. Certainly he can consider the various forms which the apocalyptic attitude can take, even in his own times and in his own mind.

Hebrew, Israelite, and Jew

Note the three names, *Hebrew, Israelite,* and *Jew.* We are using these names with the understanding that each is more typically associated with particular periods of history. Thus *the Hebrew* lived as a wandering tribesman during the pre-Mosaic age of the patriarchs from Abraham to Jacob. *The Israelite* was a member of a nation struggling to establish and maintain herself in the Promised Land between the time of her exodus from Egypt and her exile to Babylon. *The Jew* is the man of God's people who has lived for the most part either in captivity or dispersion during the exile and thereafter. He looks back to his origins in the past, forward to his redemption in the future, and in the meantime, he searches the written and oral traditions of torah, coupling them to his own experience as a continuing study of the living presence of God.

REFLECTION QUESTIONS

1. What was the immediate occasion for the appearance of the handwriting on Belshazzar's wall? Why might this particular episode be especially meaningful to a Jew reading it about 165 B.C.?
2. Daniel said to the king, "Let your gifts be for yourself. . ." Does it appear that he meant it?
3. What law was Daniel opposing to the law of the Medes and Persians when he made his petitions and supplications? What does the story conclude concerning the relative power of the two laws?
4. Try drawing a sketch of each of the four beasts.
5. Having read the commentary, clarify the reasons why Daniel is considered a model of apocalyptic literature.
6. We have given explanations for several symbols used in the reading. What are some of the other symbols in the passage, and to what do you think they refer?
7. In the author's time only certain people understood the real meaning of some of his words and phrases, and his real purpose in using them. What groups do you know who use ordinary words in ways outsiders don't understand? What are their purposes?
8. If the situation between Daniel and the king's presidents and satraps was typical of human experience, how would you describe the kinds of worries that can plague a successful man?

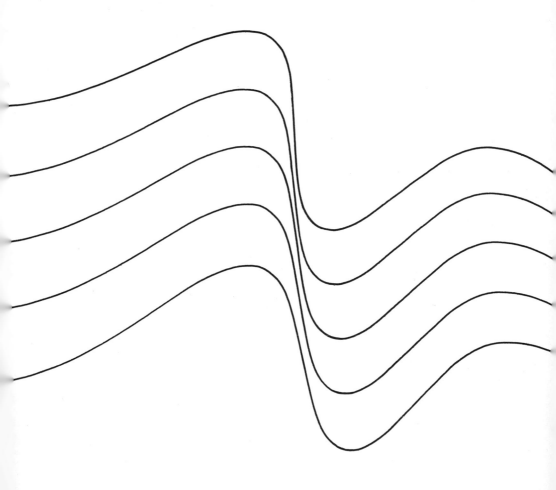

APOCRYPHAL, RABBINIC, AND NEW TESTAMENT WRITINGS

INTRODUCTION: THE TWO FIRST CENTURIES

COMPETING TRADITIONS OF THE NEAR EAST
CONVERGE ON FIRST-CENTURY PALESTINE

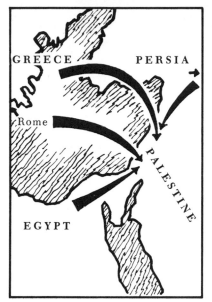

The sequence of our reading and discussion now brings us to the two first centuries, the first century B.C. and the first century A.D. This is the period of what many scholars call the classical literature of Judaism and Christianity. The literature of these two centuries expresses the experience of people who lived in a violent confusion of political interests and religious concerns.

Ever since the days of Antiochus Epiphanes, Israel had suffered the hot anger of internecine warfare among her own people, and the anguish of imperial oppression by great powers from abroad. The successive waves of alien power that swept over first-century Palestine also brought streams of conflicting religious ideas to confuse and divide the Jews. These imported ideas, whose sources lay far distant in miles and in centuries, crop up vividly in both Jewish and Christian literature. The writings of the two first centuries accurately reflect the political battlefield of the period as various factions passionately defended and rejected the same ideas.

We therefore look back to the sources of some of them, because in varying degrees they affected how people understood the covenant between God and Israel. Struggling to be himself and to build his world in that era of confusion, the first-century Jew dealt with both familiar and foreign religious ideas. Those ideas stemmed from events as far away in miles and as far back in time as Persia in the sixth century B.C., Greece in the fifth century B.C., and of course, the Sinai of Israel herself in the 13th century B.C.

THE COSMIC BATTLE BETWEEN GOOD AND EVIL: PERSIA

A thousand miles and six centuries separated the first-century Jew from the founder of the religion in which the early kings of Persia believed. The founder's name was Zarathustra, or Zoroaster, as the Greeks pronounced it. The Persian magi, the wise men of the East, traced their traditional wisdom to him. Zoroaster referred to God by the name of Ahura Mazda (Ormazd), which means "the Wise Lord." According to Zoroastrianism, all existence emanates from Ahura. He is guided by a holy spirit with a will to good. However, that holy spirit of good has a hostile twin brother, the spirit of evil, who is opposed to him at every turn. In Zoroaster's view, the world of history is a developing battle between the holy spirit on the one hand and the evil spirit on the other. The world is an ethical world, with goodness, light, and life opposed to evil, death, and darkness in all of its events. The great spiritual combatants struggle to win

145

the souls of men. A man takes sides in this battle throughout his life. When the soul of a man leaves his body at death, he stands on a bridge at the entrance to heaven. An account is rendered of the service to good and evil that appears in his record. If he has done more good than evil, he goes to paradise. Otherwise, he goes to hell. No ceremonial involvement, nor any sacrifice a man may make can alter the judgment on his record. Nor does Ahura, or Ormazd, ever intervene. The eternal law of things requires that a man standing on the bridge is utterly the victim or the beneficiary of his own former behavior in the world.

In a final apocalyptic event at the end of the world, the good spirit defeats the evil spirit forever, both in heaven and in history, and heaven and earth become a single kingdom of Ormazd (Ahura). There the faithful dwell happily forever while the faithless idol worshipers (evildoers) suffer hell with the spirit of evil. These beliefs were a powerful influence throughout the Near East into the two first centuries.

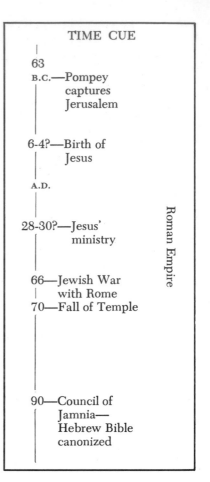

TIME CUE

63 B.C.—Pompey captures Jerusalem

6-4?—Birth of Jesus

A.D.

28-30?—Jesus' ministry

66—Jewish War with Rome
70—Fall of Temple

90—Council of Jamnia— Hebrew Bible canonized

Roman Empire

THE PERFECTIONS, HARMONIES, AND PLEASURES OF PHILOSOPHY: GREECE

Looking a thousand miles to the west of Jerusalem, and back to the fifth, fourth, and third centuries B.C., one discovers the Greek philosophers Plato, Zeno, and Epicurus. Plato was the teacher of the equally famous Aristotle, Aristotle taught Alexander the Great, and Alexander sought with great zeal to infuse the ways and wisdom of Greece throughout the Near East in the wake of his military conquest.

Plato, the touchstone for Greek philosophy, believed that ultimate reality consists of a perfect realm of pure ideas. Everything in our sensible world is a grotesque and insufficient reflection of the eternal idea it represents. The world of our experience is like a shadow of reality. Each man is an immortal soul confined by a mortal body in a material world. Men achieve self-knowledge by contemplating the realm of eternal ideas, all of which can be summed up with mathematical perfection in the ideas of the beautiful, the true, and the good. Plato's transferral of reality from the realm of experience to the realm of ideas might suggest to the first-century

146

Jew a parallel with the Persian transfer of reality from a physical to an ethical world.

The philosopher *Zeno* strolled and taught his students in the shade of the columns *(stoa)* that dominated the marketplace at Athens. His teaching took the name of stoicism. Stoics believed in the ultimate reality of the physical world. It all exists as a self-contained organic system. An indwelling world-soul, or reason, is guiding the world as it unfolds toward its final destiny. When that day comes, the evil of conflict and disorder will disappear in a full flowering of harmony in nature and brotherhood among men. When this happens, reason will bring this universe to an end, and a new cycle of destiny will begin. The stoic taught that one should live in quiet simplicity, that he should treat his fellow men with simple kindness, putting himself in tune with the world's destiny, sharing with humble joy the reality of reason's purpose unfolding in nature and the vicissitudes of human experience.

Epicurus was a sophisticated "peace of mind" philosopher. His teaching enjoyed considerable influence on upper-class Roman society in later times. He taught his prosperous young students neither in an Athenian academy like Plato's nor among the columns of the marketplace, like Zeno. His classrooms were the gardens of his own home at Athens. He taught that wealth is found in wisdom, rather than vice versa. Pleasure, like wealth, is not bad to have, but one should not become anxiously preoccupied with getting it or keeping it. Indeed, pleasure is the highest good. However, one finds it not in crude excess but in living simply and by enjoying conversation with good friends. One should avoid anxious fears of hell and ambitious hopes for heaven. One should not worry too much about the opinions of the gods, since the gods are far away and entertain scarcely any opinions at all about men and women. Moral behavior has no warrant from the gods one way or another. Instead, moral standards are wise conventions by which to estimate the effect on one's self of his behavior. Will it painfully degrade him, or will it bring him the pleasure of self-fulfillment?

THE MYSTERIES OF LIVING UNION WITH THE GODS: THE NEAR EAST

From very ancient times throughout the Near East, the mystery religions challenged the beliefs of the Hebrew nation. Greece contributed the mythology and rites of Dionysus, the god of wine. From there also came the myth of Demeter, the goddess of grain, and her daughter Persephone. From Egypt came the rites of Isis and Osiris. Men and women who believed these myths and their associated cultic rites sought not merely to understand the nature and will of the divine, but actively to participate in the very powers and experiences of the gods themselves by means of secret rituals and ceremonies. Central to these myths was the action of a semi-divine figure, often endowed with great sexual potency and the will to employ it, who suffered death and resurrection in the course of his adventures. In mystic communion with this semi-deity, the cultist participated in an experience of power and exultation at once both divine and human. These rites were often dominated by female leadership, as in the case of the

Dionysia (or Bacchanalia), and often reached orgiastic extremes of ecstatic violence.

THE PERSISTENCE OF GOD AND THE COVENANT

The first-century Jew was the object of cultural influences from distant times and places, not only from foreign peoples east and west, but also from Israel's history. Concepts and convictions characteristically held by the Jews persisted in those two first centuries, and continued to inform his thoughts and reform the conduct of his life. The past would not let him forget the Shema, "Here, O Israel, the Lord our God is one Lord." His was the same Lord who guided the patriarchs Abraham, Isaac, and Jacob. Out of the past came the experience of the covenant, the gift of the Torah, the warning and recalling voices of the prophets, and the vision of a righteous remnant Israel, to be forever the spouse and servant of God. His own past taught him that God is the God of all history, and that history is progressing toward a final destiny according to God's purposes. His tradition taught him that God always deals in particular events with particular people in normal flesh and blood experience. The Bible and the elders taught him by precept and in story the sacrificial meaning of life and death. They told him of the righteous judgment of God in human affairs, which expresses itself both in mercy and in moral retribution. From Abraham he inherited his predisposition to understand society in terms of tribe and family. His original identifying history consisted in a genealogy, in a family epic spelled out by the lips of the elders to the ears of the young.

The situation of the first-century Jew made him very much aware of his need to decide who he was in relation to God and human destiny. His decisions about God and what to do about God also involved life-and-death political choices. Antiochus Epiphanes mocked this man. The Hasmonaeans (the Maccabees) both encouraged him and deceived him. The Romans callously suppressed him. King Herod, the local vassal of Rome, cheated him and treated him with contempt. The procurators from Rome, one of whom was Pontius Pilate, encouraged him in one moment with a semblance of justice, only to disillusion him in the next by an act of treachery.

In the year 66 A.D. this representative Jew and his fellows, remembering the former success of the Maccabees, revolted anew against such cruel inconsistency. At the same time, partisan ambitions and individual fears viciously divided him from other Jews. Nero sent Vespasian and Titus, top Roman generals to crush his rebellion. After a hideous siege that pitted brother against brother within the city and Jew against Roman on the walls, Jerusalem and the second temple, built after the return from Babylonian exile, finally fell. Rome had come to bring order to Palestine, for disorder anywhere in the world was an offense against the imperial Roman peace. At first the generals tried to accomplish this by means of puppet rulers such as Herod. Finally, however, Roman arms were required to pacify the land. They did so by destroying the sacred temple and Jerusalem.

This was the situation of the first two centuries. The Jews experienced it all, in premonition, fact, or memory, whether they lived in 100 B.C. or 100 A.D. From Persia, from Babylon, from Greece and Egypt, there pressed upon them a host of ideas arrayed against their covenant tradition, all demanding their respect or outright adoption. These foreign ideas were not completely new to them. In the long tradition of their own past, these ideas had been growing and diffusing. They influenced, and were influenced by, the unique ideas revealed to the children of Abraham. But in those first two centuries, charged with a confusion of highly developed ideas, and marked by violent political change, a man's decision about God could easily be spelled out in the blood of martyrdom or battle.

Of course, it was not all violence. There were many places where at times the Jews could live dispersed but nevertheless prosperous, suppressed in one way, yet growing in another.

STUDY AS A FORM OF WORSHIP

Since as early as the Babylonian exile, the Jews developed a wealth of prayer and knowledge around their synagogues and associated schools. The synagogues may have started as gatherings in private homes where the elders told and retold Israel's epic story and ancient teachings. By the two first centuries the synagogue had become Israel's congregational gathering place. Here worshipers employed not only liturgical prayer but also vigorous study of the Torah itself as a form of worship apart from temple sacrifice.

Instrumental to this development were the scribes. These were teachers who, since Ezra and the return from exile, had devoted themselves to reading and defending the Torah, deriving rules from it for the daily conduct of Jewish life, and supplementing it with interpretations of Israel's popular wisdom in the oral tradition. The arguments and discussions in the synagogues and schools reflected in those centuries the tension of Israel's single yet divided mind. That tension took form in the development of partisan divisions within the Jewish community.

THE PARTIES AND ISSUES OF DEBATE

In the easier days of the third century B.C., many people had lent a hospitable ear to the ideas that came from Greece. These *Hellenists* could find in Greek ideas and customs the promise of enrichment for their understanding of God and for the life of their people. Urban and aristocratic individuals and families became especially receptive to the ways of Greece. Among the rural people outside Jerusalem and among the poor a conservative movement in behalf of piety, or strict loyalty to the Torah, developed. Those taking part in this movement were the *Hasidim.*

By the time of the two first centuries, the *Sadducees* had developed as a party of privilege, conservative in their view of the torah. However, religion had become for them a compartment of their lives, separated from their secular activities, which were accommodated to a concern for power and privilege. Conversely, the *Pharisees* inherited and modified the ways of the Hasidim. They remained true to the torah in a different way. Unlike the Sadducees, they did not confine their understanding of the torah strictly to the first five books of the Bible, but depended in addition on the oral tradition as a means of interpreting God's will. The Sadducees could afford to be conservative about the torah because in the first place they

149

limited it to the teaching in the books of Genesis through Deuteronomy, and in the second place they limited their concern for it by seeing it as a somewhat separate dimension of their lives. The Pharisees, on the other hand, strove to live by the torah night and day. Therefore, both by choice and necessity, they interpreted the torah more liberally to apply its authority and requirements to the whole life of the people.

Different though the Sadducees and Pharisees were, they held at least one important orientation in common. Each party involved itself in the socio-political issues of the day. But where the Sadducees attempted to take advantage of the times by a greater fraternization with foreign and domestic political power, the Pharisees stuck to a more unaccommodating attitude toward outsiders, while liberalizing Judaism. In opposition to the Sadducees, the Pharisees believed in the idea of resurrection and in the coming of the apocalyptic end of history. In this, they shared the convictions of the mass of the Jewish people.

In a third group, the *Essenes*, we find a quite different orientation. Instead of plunging themselves into the arena of current events, they isolated themselves in communalistic groups in which they shared all work and property. Their thoughts and religious observances had much in common with those of the Pharisees. Apparently they saw themselves as the righteous remnant of Israel living in the pure light of the torah until the day when God's final judgment would come. Additional insight into the ways of these people is being brought to light by modern scholars in their studies of the Dead Sea Scrolls, found in 1947 A.D. Most scholars agree that the Qumran community, associated with the Dead Sea Scrolls, was an Essene community, or one very much like those of the Essenes.

A fourth pattern of conviction that marked the divided mind of Israel in those days was represented by the *Zealots*. One scholar calls them "the heirs of the Maccabees." They were the never-say-die patriots, fanatically dedicated to resisting the Roman oppressors and to reestablishing the state of Israel.

In the classical literature of Judaism and Christianity, we find many references to these four orientations. Each group was convinced that it alone had the answers to the question, "What is Israel?" Each believed that it alone understood the torah as it was meant to be understood. The Sadducees were those who compromised with the prevailing powers to preserve the purity of the religious "side" of their lives. The Pharisees were among the intimate leaders of the people, stubbornly dedicated to living the torah in the events of history, no matter what the cost to them in suffering. The Essenes rejected society because they believed that the current process of history contained no promise of an unfolding kingdom of God. The Zealots were convinced that the fulfillment of Israel lay in the destruction of her foreign enemies and the reestablishment of her sovereign power as a national monarchy. In the Jewish and Christian literature of those two centuries we see the emergence of ideas and arguments born out of the backgrounds we have described.

We have deliberately made no distinction between Jews and Christians in our consideration of the situation in those two first centuries. In the first place, Christianity did not develop until the fourth decade of the first century A.D. In the second place, whatever the differences were—and they were considerable—between Christian disciples and Jews in general, the literatures of both emerged within the oppressive circumstances of the same Roman Empire. Their literatures developed out of a world of ideas common to both, ideas central to the Near Eastern traditions we have mentioned, ideas that both inspired and tormented the minds of Jews and Christians alike.

APOCRYPHAL WRITINGS

Part 1:

OUTSIDE BOOKS AS
WISDOM LITERATURE

In this part you will be reading some selections from two books of wisdom literature, The Wisdom of Jesus Ben Sirach (or Ecclesiasticus) and The Wisdom of Solomon. Both are examples of the *Outside Books,* or *Apocrypha* (Greek: "hidden away"). Each of them was included in the Septuagint, a translation of Hebrew Bible books into Greek, done in Egypt during the third and second centuries B.C. for Greek-speaking Jews. These two, like all the Apocrypha, were not included in the Hebrew Bible as it was authorized by the Council of Jamnia in 90 A.D.

Like many books appearing in Palestine during the last two centuries B.C., The Wisdom of Jesus Ben Sirach and The Wisdom of Solomon were written under the impact of new ideas from abroad. We can list some of those new ideas: the idea of the resurrection of the dead to a life after death; the apocalyptic end of the present world and the beginning of a new one; double destiny, or a blissful eternal life for the righteous and a horrible eternal existence for the unrighteous; the last judgment at the end of history; the idea of history as the battleground between two transcendent powers of good and evil; the Messiah, a divinely chosen human being or a divinely sent heavenly being, who would act as the herald and master of the new age; the immortality of the individual soul; preexistence not only of human souls but also of such bearers of the will of God as the Torah, the Messiah, and wisdom. All of these were elements in the thinking of the two first centuries and thereafter.

SEARCH CUES

1. the origin of wisdom
2. the way of wisdom and its benefits
3. the purpose of creation
4. wisdom's knowledge and power
5. the key of immortality

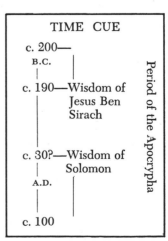

```
          TIME  CUE

 c. 200—
    B.C.   |                    P
           |                    e
 c. 190—Wisdom of               r
         Jesus Ben              i
         Sirach                 o
           |                    d
           |                    o
           |                    f
 c. 30?—Wisdom of               t
         Solomon                h
    A.D.   |                    e
           |                    A
           |                    p
 c. 100                         o
                                c
                                r
                                y
                                p
                                h
                                a
```

155

THE WISDOM OF JESUS BEN SIRACH 1:1-30

Reprinted with permission from
Glatzer, N. N. *The Judaic Tradition.*
Boston: Beacon Press, 1969, pp. 24-25.

All wisdom cometh from the Lord
    And is with Him forever.
The sand of the seas, and the drops of rain,
    And the days of eternity—who can number them?
The height of the heaven, and the breadth of the earth,
    And the deep—who can trace them out?
Before them all was Wisdom created,
    And prudent insight from everlasting.
The root of Wisdom, to whom hath it been revealed?
    And her subtle thoughts, who hath known them?
One there is, greatly to be feared,
    The Lord sitting upon His throne;
He himself created her, and saw, and numbered her,
    And poured her out upon all His works;
Upon all flesh in measure,
    But without measure doth He grant her to them that love Him.
The fear of the Lord is glory and exultation,
    And gladness, and a crown of rejoicing.
The fear of the Lord delighteth the heart,
    And giveth gladness, and joy, and length of days.
Whoso feareth the Lord, it shall go well with him at the last,
    And in the day of his death he shall be blessed.
To fear the Lord is the beginning of Wisdom,
    And with the faithful was she created in the womb.
With faithful men is she, and she hath been established from eternity;
    And with their seed shall she continue.
To fear the Lord is the fullness of Wisdom,
    And she satiateth men with her fruits.
She filleth all her house with pleasant things,
    And her garners with her produce.
The crown of Wisdom is the fear of the Lord,
    And increaseth peace and life and health.
She is a strong staff and a glorious stay,
    And everlasting honor to them that hold her fast.
To fear the Lord is the root of Wisdom,
    And her branches are length of days.

If thou desire Wisdom, keep the commandments,
   And the Lord will give her freely unto thee.
For the fear of the Lord is wisdom and instruction,
   And faith and meekness are well-pleasing unto Him.
My son, disobey not the fear of the Lord,
   And approach it not with a double heart.
Be not a hypocrite in the sight of men,
   And take good heed to thy lips.
Exalt not thyself lest thou fall,
   And bring disgrace upon thyself,
And the Lord reveal thy hidden thoughts,
   And cast thee down in the midst of the assembly,
Because thou camest not unto the fear of the Lord,
   And thy heart was full of deceit.

THE WISDOM OF SOLOMON 1:1-15; 2:23-3:9; 7:22-8:18

Reprinted with permission from
Glatzer, N. N. *The Judaic Tradition.*
Boston: Beacon Press, 1969, pp. 37-42.

Love righteousness, ye that be judges of the earth,
Thank ye the Lord with a good mind,
And in singleness of heart seek ye him;
Because he is found of them that tempt him not,
And is manifested to them that do not distrust him.
For crooked thoughts separate from God;
And the [supreme] Power, when it is brought to the proof,
   Putteth to confusion the foolish;
Because wisdom will not enter into a soul that deviseth evil,
Nor dwell in a body held in pledge by sin.
For the holy spirit of discipline will flee deceit,
And will start away from thoughts that are without understanding,
And will be scared away when unrighteousness approacheth.

For wisdom is a spirit that loveth man,
And she will not hold a blasphemer guiltless for his lips;
Because God is witness of his reins,
And is a true overseer of his heart,
And a hearer of his tongue;
Because the spirit of the Lord filleth the world,
And that which holdeth all things together hath knowledge of
   every voice.
Therefore no man that uttereth unrighteous things shall be unseen;
Neither shall justice, when it punisheth, pass him by.
For the counsels of the ungodly shall be searched out;
And the report of his words shall come unto the Lord
For the punishment of his lawless deeds:
Because there is a zealous ear that listeneth to all things,

And the noise of murmurings is not hid.
Beware then of unprofitable murmuring,
And refrain your tongue from blasphemy;
Because no secret utterance shall go forth with impunity;
And a mouth that lieth destroyeth the soul.

Court not death in the error of your life;
Neither draw upon yourselves destruction by the works of your
    hands:
Because God made not death;
Neither delighteth he when the living perish:
For he created all things that they might have being:
And the products of the world are healthsome,
And there is no poison of destruction in them:
Nor hath Hades royal dominion upon earth;
For righteousness is immortal. . . .

God created man for eternal life,
And made him an image of His own proper being;
But by the envy of Satan death entered into the world,
And they that belong to his realm experience it.
But the souls of the righteous are in the hand of God,
And no torment shall touch them.
In the eyes of fools they seemed to die;
And their departure was accounted to be their hurt,
And their going from us to be their ruin:
But they are in peace.
For though in the sight of men they be punished,
Their hope is full of immortality;
And having borne a little chastening, they shall receive great
    good;
Because God tested them, and found them worthy of Himself.
As gold on the furnace He proved them,
And as a whole burnt offering He accepted them.
And in the time of their visitation they shall shine forth,
And like sparks among stubble they shall run to and fro.
They shall judge nations, and have dominion over peoples;
And the Lord shall reign over them for evermore.
They that trust on Him shall understand truth,
And the faithful shall abide with Him in love;
Because grace and mercy are to His chosen,
And He will graciously visit His holy ones. . . .

There is in wisdom a spirit: understanding, holy,
Alone in kind, manifold,
Subtile, freely moving,
Clear in utterance, unpolluted,
Distinct, that cannot be harmed,

Loving what is good, keen, unhindered,
Beneficent, loving toward man,
Steadfast, sure, free from care,
All-powerful, all-surveying,
And penetrating through all spirits
That are quick of understanding, pure, subtile.
For wisdom is more mobile than any motion;
Yea, she pervadeth and penetrateth all things by reason of
    her pureness.
For she is a breath of the power of God,
And a clear effluence of the glory of the Almighty;
Therefore can nothing defiled find entrance into her.
For she is a radiance from everlasting light
And an unspotted mirror of the working of God,
And an image of his goodness.
And she, though but one, hath power to do all things;
And remaining in herself, reneweth all things:
And from generation to generation passing into holy souls
She maketh them friends of God and prophets.
For nothing doth God love save him that dwelleth with wisdom.
For she is fairer than the sun,
And above all the constellations of the stars:
Being compared with light, she is found to be before it;
For the light of day succeedeth night,
But against wisdom evil doth not prevail;
But she reacheth from one end of the world to the other with
    full strength,
And ordereth all things well.

Her I loved and sought out from my youth,
And I sought to take her for my bride.
And I became enamored of her beauty.
She proclaimeth her noble birth in that it is given her to live
    with God,
And the Sovereign Lord of all loved her.
For she is initiated into the knowledge of God,
And she chooseth out for him his works.
But if riches are a desired possession in life,
What is richer than wisdom, which worketh all things?
And if understanding worketh,
Who more than wisdom is an artificer of the things that are?
And if a man loveth righteousness,
The fruits of wisdom's labor are virtues,
For she teacheth self-control and understanding, righteousness,
    and courage;
And there is nothing in life for men more profitable than these.
And if a man longeth even for much experience,
She knoweth the things of old, and divineth the things to come:

She understandeth subtilties of speeches and interpretations of
    dark sayings:
She foreseeth signs and wonders, and the issues of seasons and
    times.
I determined therefore to take her unto me to live with me,
Knowing that she is one who would give me good thoughts for
    counsel,
And encourage me in cares and grief.
Because of her I shall have glory among multitudes,
And honor in the sight of elders, though I be young.
I shall be found of a quick discernment when I give judgment,
And in the presence of princes I shall be admired.
When I am silent, they shall wait for me;
And when I open my lips, they shall give heed unto me;
And if I continue speaking, they shall lay their hand upon their
    mouth.
Because of her I shall have immortality,
And leave behind an eternal memory to them that come after me.
I shall govern peoples,
And nations shall be subjected to me.
Dread princes shall fear me when they hear of me:
Among my people I shall show myself a good ruler, and in war
    courageous.
When I come into my house, I shall find rest with her;
For converse with her hath no bitterness,
And to live with her hath no pain, but gladness and joy.
When I considered these things in myself,
And took thought in my heart how that in kinship unto wisdom
    is immortality,
And in her friendship is good delight,
And in the labors of her hands is wealth that faileth not,
And in assiduous communing with her is understanding,
And great renown in having fellowship with her words,
I went about seeking how to take her unto myself.

COMMENTARY

The Books of the Hebrew and Christian Bibles

The books that constitute the Hebrew Bible were not gathered into an authoritative collection until 90 A.D., long after most of them had been written. Those constituting the Christian New Testament were not fully agreed upon by the Christians until after the middle of the fourth century A.D. In each case, the canonical (accepted as sacred) books represented selections from a large field of writings.

Many books containing the new ideas we have briefly described in the introduction were read widely during the first two centuries A.D., but were not included in either the Hebrew or the Christian Bible. Often the arguments were long and tempestuous as to whether the new ideas of the times were consistent with the ancient and accepted beliefs in God and his covenant with Israel, and whether the books that contained them were consistent with the ancient faith.

A number of these apocryphal, or outside, books were included in the Septuagint translation of the Hebrew Bible. The Council of Jamnia excluded these outside books from the final version of the Hebrew Bible canon. Therefore, the apocryphal books are not regarded by the Jewish community as sacred, but simply as interesting and valuable expressions of the times.

The Christians, on the other hand, used the Greek Septuagint translation as their Bible. Therefore, certain apocryphal books appearing in the Septuagint also were included in the authorized version of the Christian Bible. During the Reformation in the 16th century, most Protestants rejected the apocryphal books and took the Hebrew canon as the basis for their Old Testament. Thus some Christians today accept the apocryphal books; others do not.

The Wisdom of Jesus Ben Sirach

The Wisdom of Jesus Ben Sirach, otherwise called Ecclesiasticus, was put into writing in Jerusalem about 190 B.C., before the times of Antiochus and the Maccabees. Jesus Ben Sirach saw in the ways of wisdom the ways of men's rich personal fulfillment in obedient communion with God. He emphasized the belief that all wisdom begins with the mystery of God himself. One cannot live with wisdom unless he humbly understands that he cannot understand the divine depths of it. If one would live wisely, he must respect profoundly the God from whom wisdom comes. He must obey the torah which God has revealed to be the express basis for all wisdom in one's daily conduct. Jesus Ben Sirach assumed the preexistence of wisdom with God before all things, but in writing contains no apocalyptic ideas, such as a last judgment, or a resurrection to existence after death.

The Wisdom of Solomon

The Wisdom of Solomon was probably written in Alexandria, Egypt, sometime after 100 B.C. The unknown author, who ascribed his work to King Solomon, shows the influence of many of the new ideas we have mentioned. While The Wisdom of Solomon centers its thought on God, and while it uses the customary family-relationship image in describing one's relationship with wisdom, it exhibits the influence of both the idealism of Plato and the panthcism (God inhabiting everything and harmonizing it) of the stoics. The idea of personal immortality also is strong in this writing. In chapter 8:7, one can even read, as evidence of Greek influence, the four cardinal virtues of Plato and Aristotle, which the Christians centuries later were to adopt as the four natural virtues, coupling them with the three "theological virtues," faith, hope, and charity, to form the seven virtues recognized as basic by the medieval Christian church.

161

REFLECTION QUESTIONS

1. What does the Wisdom of Jesus Ben Sirach assume about the relationship between wisdom and moral retribution?
2. In the relationship between wisdom and man, which of the two seems, in these readings, to take the primary initiative? When they are united, which possesses which?
3. Show how wisdom from God and torah from God are similar, and yet different.
4. Locate the places in the reading from The Wisdom of Solomon where the author uses some form of the word *love*. Assuming you are the author, what does love mean to you?
5. What differences do you see between the message of these readings and that of your reading in Job?

Part 2:

THE APOCALYPSE APPEARS
IN THE APOCRYPHA

The book of Enoch, while included neither in the Septuagint nor in the canonical Hebrew Bible established at Jamnia, falls within the literature of the Apocrypha, or Outside Books. It has been referred to in the past as an example of writing called the *pseudepigrapha* (Greek: "false writing"), because they were not written by the persons to whom their authorship was credited. In this case, the pseudo-author was Enoch, about whom you can read in Genesis 5:18-24. The book of Enoch was probably written at the beginning of the first century B.C.

Our reading from Enoch is a vivid example of the apocalyptic writing that was widespread and contemporary with the wisdom literature of the last two centuries B.C. However, it was quite distinguishable from the wisdom literature in its attitude and content. Its author was acquainted with the new ideas that were streaming into Palestine, to be confronted there by the thoughts and ways of Israel and the covenant.

SEARCH CUES

1. the grievous fire
2. the word against you
3. wait for the day
4. what the sinners say
5. the message in the heavenly tablets

NOW READ BELOW: ENOCH 102:1-103:4

ENOCH 102:1-103:4

Reprinted with permission from
Glatzer, N. N. *The Judaic Tradition.*
Boston: Beacon Press, 1969, pp. 62-64.

In those days when He hath brought a grievous fire upon you,
Whither will ye flee, and where will ye find deliverance?

And when He launches forth His word against you
Will you not be affrighted and fear?
And all the luminaries shall be affrighted with great fear,
And all the earth shall be affrighted and tremble and be alarmed.
And all the angels shall execute their commands
And shall seek to hide themselves from the presence of the Great Glory,
And the children of earth shall tremble and quake;
And ye sinners shall be cursed for ever,
And ye shall have no peace.
Fear ye not, ye souls of the righteous,
And be hopeful ye that have died in righteousness.
And grieve not if your soul into Sheol has descended in grief,
And that in your life your body fared not according to your goodness,
But wait for the day of the judgment of sinners
And for the day of cursing and chastisement.
And yet when ye die the sinners speak over you:
"As we die, so die the righteous,
And what benefit do they reap for their deeds?
Behold, even as we, so do they die in grief and darkness,
And what have they more than we?
From henceforth we are equal.
And what will they receive and what will they see for ever?
Behold, they too have died,
And henceforth for ever shall they see no light."

I tell you, ye sinners, ye are content to eat and drink, and
rob and sin, and strip men naked, and acquire wealth and see the
good days. Have ye seen the righteous how their end falls out,
that no manner of violence is found in them till their death?
[The sinners answer:] "Nevertheless they perished and became
as though they had not been, and their spirits descended into
Sheol in tribulation."

Now, therefore, I swear to you, the righteous, by the
glory of the Great and Honored and Mighty One in dominion, and
by His greatness I swear to you.
I know a mystery
And have read the heavenly tablets,
And have seen the holy books,
And have found written therein and inscribed regarding them:
That all goodness and joy and glory are prepared for them,
And written down for the spirits of those who have died in righteousness,
And that manifold good shall be given to you in recompense for your labors,
And that your lot is abundantly beyond the lot of the living.
And the spirits of you who have died in righteousness shall live and rejoice,
And their spirits shall not perish, nor their memorial from before the face
    of the Great One
Unto all the generations of the world: wherefore no longer fear their
    contumely.

COMMENTARY

More Outside Books

As we noted in Part 1 of this unit, the books most frequently referred to as *apocryphal* are those in the Greek Septuagint which were included in the Christian, but not the Jewish, canon. In addition to these apocryphal works, many similar books were composed and circulated in Jewish and Christian groups between 200 B.C. and 200 A.D. Some of these works are still extant, although many have been lost. None are included in either the Jewish or the Christian canon.

The Book of Enoch

The selection you have read from Enoch is typical of the extra-biblical expressions of apocalyptic thought widely read by first-century Jews and Christians. The book itself was compiled from a variety of sources, apparently during the latter part of the second century and the early part of the first century B.C. in Jerusalem. In this example of apocalyptic writing, after the model of Daniel, we find references to the last judgment, to resurrection, to the messiah, to double destiny, and hence to the author's belief in ultimate moral retribution in a life after death.

This selection and the two in Part 1 of Unit Eleven contain some of the new ideas according to the authors' own beliefs and understandings. One can anticipate, if he has some acquaintance with later religious literature, how the apocalyptic viewpoint was to exercise a profound influence on Christian literature, with its gospel claims, while the wisdom orientation would inform more generally the literature that the rabbis developed as a continuing interpretation of torah in a changing world.

REFLECTION QUESTIONS

1. What elements in the Enoch passage clearly mark it as apocalyptic writing? What similarities and differences do you find between Enoch and Daniel?
2. What differences in general attitude can you discern between the Enoch passage and the two wisdom passages in this unit?
3. What would be the basic differences involved for you in making plans for tomorrow's apocalypse as compared with making plans for tomorrow's revolution?

THE JEWISH COMMUNITY DEVELOPS CODES AND COMMENTARIES FOR LIVING THE TORAH

Part 1:

"THE SAYINGS OF THE FATHERS" EXPRESSES THE AUTHORITY AND METHOD BEHIND THE MISHNAH

The Mishnah is a code of rules and maxims developed and interpreted by the rabbis, a code by which Jews since the first century have ordered their lives. Except for the Hebrew Bible itself, no other body of writing bears greater authority than the Mishnah as a basic written guide in Judaism. It was accumulated during the scholar generations of the Tannaim (transmitters of tradition). The process began after Hillel the Elder, about 10 B.C., and lasted until Judah ha-Nasi (Judah the Prince) shortly after 200 A.D.

The Sayings of the Fathers (Pirke Aboth) traces the succession of authoritative interpreters of torah from Moses down to Rabbi Gamaliel III, the son of Judah ha-Nasi. Along with that succession of teachers, it demonstrates the method by which the rabbis taught the interrelated meaning of the biblical and oral traditions of Israel.

SEARCH CUES

1. the hedge for the Torah
2. on talking much with women
3. the advice of Hillel
4. the advice of Shammai
5. the reward of the righteous

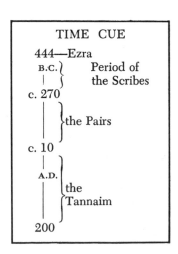

TIME CUE

444—Ezra

B.C. } Period of
the Scribes

c. 270

} the Pairs

c. 10

A.D.

} the
Tannaim

200

PIRKE ABOTH 1-2

Reprinted with permission from
Herford, R. Travers, trans. *Pirke Aboth*.
New York: The Jewish Institute of Religion
Press, 1930, Chapters I and II.

I

Moses received Torah from Sinai and delivered it to Joshua, and Joshua to the Elders, and the Elders to the Prophets, and the Prophets delivered it to the Men of the Great Synagogue. These said three things, "Be deliberate in judging, and raise up many disciples, and make a hedge for the Torah."

Simeon the Just was of the survivors of the Great Synagogue. He used to say, "Upon three things the world standeth; upon Torah, upon worship, and upon the showing of kindness."

Antigonos of Socho received from Simeon the Just. He used to say, "Be not like servants who serve the master on condition of receiving a gift, but be like servants who serve the master not on condition of receiving a gift. And let the fear of Heaven be upon you."

Jose ben Joezer, of Zeredah, and Jose ben Johanan, of Jerusalem, received from them. Jose ben Joezer, of Zeredah, said, "Let thy house be a place of meeting for the Wise, and dust thyself with the dust of their feet, and drink their words with thirst."

Jose ben Johanan, of Jerusalem, said, "Let thy house be opened wide, and let the poor be thy household, and talk not much with a woman." He said it: in the case of his own wife, much more in the case of his companion's wife. Hence the Wise have said, Everyone that talketh much with a woman causes evil to himself, and desists from words of Torah, and his end is he inherits Gehinnom.

Joshua ben Perahyah and Nittai the Arbelite received from them. Joshua ben Perahyah said, "Make thee a Master, and get thee a companion, and judge every man by the scale of merit."

Nittai the Arbelite said, "Keep far from the evil neighbor, and consort not with the wicked, and be not doubtful of retribution."

Judah ben Tabbai and Simeon ben Shetah received from them. Judah ben Tabbai said, "Make not thyself as they that prepare the judges; and when the suitors are before thee, let them be as wrongdoers in thy sight; and when they have departed from before thee, let them be in thy sight as innocent men, seeing they have accepted the sentence upon themselves."

Simeon ben Shetah said, "Examine thoroughly the witnesses, and be careful in thy words; perchance through them they may learn to lie."

Shemaiah and Abtalion received from them. Shemaiah said, "Love work and hate mastery, and make not thyself known to the government."

Abtalion said, "Ye Wise, take heed to your words, lest ye incur the guilt [that deserves] exile, and ye be exiled to a place of evil waters, and the disciples that come after you drink and die, and the name of Heaven be found profaned."

Hillel and Shammai received from them. Hillel said, "Be of the disciples of Aaron, one that loves peace, that loves mankind and brings them nigh to Torah."

He used to say, "Whoso makes great his name loses his name, and whoso adds not makes to cease, and he who does not learn deserves killing, and one who serves himself with the crown passes away."

He used to say, "If I am not for myself who is for me? and when I am for myself what am I? and if not now, when?"

Shammai said, "Make thy Torah a fixed duty. Say little and do much, and receive every man with a cheerful expression of face."

Rabban Gamaliel used to say, "Make thee a master and remove thyself from what is doubtful, and do not often tithe by conjecture."

Simeon his son said, "All my days I have grown up among the Wise, and I have not found anything better for one than silence; and not study is the chief thing, but action; and whoso multiplies words occasions sin."

Rabban Simeon ben Gamaliel said, "Upon three things the world stands: on truth, on judgment, and on peace. As it is said, 'Truth and judgment of peace judge ye in your gates.'"

II

Rabbi said, "Which is that right way which a man should choose for himself? Any that is an honor to him that does it and an honor to him in the sight of man. And be careful in the case of a light precept as in that of a weighty one, for thou knowest not how the rewards of the precepts are given. And count the loss by a precept against its reward, and the reward of a sin against its loss. Keep in view three things, and thou wilt not come into the power of sin; know what is above thee: a seeing eye, a hearing ear, and all thy deeds written in a book."

Rabban Gamaliel, son of Rabbi Judah the Prince said, "Study of Torah along with worldly occupations is seemly, for labor in the two of them makes sin forgotten. And all Torah without work ends in failure and occasions sin. And let all who labor with the congregation labor with them for the name of Heaven. For the merit of their fathers is their support, and their righteousness standeth forever. 'And ye—I confer upon you' [saith God] 'plenteous reward, as if ye had wrought.'"

Be cautious with the government, for they do not make advances to a man except for their own need. They seem like friends in the hour of their advantage, but they do not stand by a man in the hour of his adversity.

He used to say, "Make his will as thy will, so that he may make thy will as his will; make naught thy will before his will, so that he may make naught the will of others before thy will."

Hillel said, "Sever not thyself from the congregation, and be not sure of thyself till the day of thy death, and judge not thy associate until thou comest to his place; and say not of a word which is impossible to understand that it will be understood in the end; and say not, 'When I am at leisure I will study'—perchance thou wilt not be at leisure."

He used to say, "A rude man is not one that fears sin, nor is a man who knows not Torah a saint; nor does a shy person learn nor a passionate person teach, nor does one who engages much in business impart wisdom. And in a place where there are no men, strive to be a man."

Moreover, he saw a skull which floated on the face of the water, and he said, "Because thou drownedst, they drowned thee; and in the end they that drowned thee shall be drowned."

He used to say, "More flesh, more worms; more wealth, more care; more women, more witchcraft; more maidservants, more lewdness; more menservants, more thieving; more Torah, more life; more assiduity, more wisdom; more counsel, more understanding; more righteousness, more peace. He who has acquired a good name has acquired it for himself. He who has acquired words of Torah has acquired for himself the life of the world to come."

Rabban Johanan ben Zakkai received from Hillel and from Shammai. He used to say, "If thou hast learned much Torah, take not credit to thyself, for thereunto wast thou created."

Five disciples had Raban Johanan ben Zakkai, and these are they: Rabbi Eliezer ben Horkenos, Rabbi Joshua ben Hananyah, Rabbi Jose the priest, Rabbi Simeon ben Nathanel, and Rabbi Eleazar ben Arach.

He used to sum up their praise: "Eliezer ben Horkenos is a plastered cistern that loseth not a drop. Joshua ben Hananyah, happy is she that bore him. Jose the priest is a saint. Simeon ben Nathanel is one that feareth sin. Eleazar ben Arach is as a full-flowing spring."

He used to say, "If all the Wise of Israel were in one scale of the balance and Eliezer ben Horkenos in the second scale, he would weigh them all down." Abba Shaul said, in his name, "If all the Wise of Israel were in one scale of the balance, yea and Eliezer ben Horkenos with them, and Eleazar ben Arach in the second scale, he would weigh them all down."

He said to them, "Go and see which is that good way to which a man should cleave?" R. Eliezer said, "A good eye." R. Joshua said, "A good associate." R. Jose said, "A good neighbor." R. Simeon said, "One who sees the event." R. Eleazar said, "A good heart." He said to them, "I approve the words of Eleazar ben Arach more than your words, for in his words are included yours."

He said to them: "Go and see which is that evil way which a man should shun." R. Eliezer said, "An evil eye." R. Joshua said, "An evil associate." R. Jose said, "An evil neighbor." R. Simeon said, "He who borrows and does not pay. He that borrows from man is as he that borrows from the Omnipresent; as it is said: 'The wicked borroweth and payeth not, but the righteous showeth favor and giveth.'" R. Eleazar said, "An evil heart." He said to them, "I approve the words of Eleazar ben Arach more than your words, for in his words are included yours."

These said three things. R. Eliezer said, "Let the honor of thine associate be dear to thee as thine own; and be not quick to anger; and repent a day before thy death; and warm thyself at the fire of the Wise, and beware of their glowing coal lest thou be scorched. For their bite is the bite of a fox, and their sting the sting of a scorpion, and their hiss the hiss of a serpent, and all their words like coals of fire."

R. Joshua said, "The evil eye and the evil principle and hatred of mankind drive a man out of the world."

R. Jose said, "Let the property of thine associate be dear to thee as thine own. And dispose thyself to learn Torah, for it is not as inheritance. And let all thine actions be for the name of Heaven."

R. Simeon said, "Be careful in reading the Shema and in prayer. And when thou prayest, make not thy prayer a fixed form, but beseeching and entreaty before God; as it is said: 'For he is gracious and merciful, long-suffering and plenteous in mercy, and repenteth him of the evil.' And be not wicked in thine own sight."

R. Eleazar said, "Be alert to learn Torah and know what answer to give an *Epicuros*. And know before whom thou laborest and who is the master of thy work to give thee the wages of thy toil."

R. Tarphon said, "The day is short, and the work is great; and the laborers are sluggish, and the wages are high, and the householder is urgent."

He used to say, "The work is not upon thee to finish; nor art thou free to desist from it. If thou hast learned much Torah, they give thee much wages, and faithful is the master of thy work who will pay thee the wages of thy toil. And know that the giving of the reward to the righteous is in the time to come."

COMMENTARY

The Oral Tradition

After their return to Jerusalem from the exile, the Jews continued to develop the way of worship of the synagogue. The rebuilding of the temple at Jerusalem meant that the Jews now worshiped in two ways: by prayer and study in the synagogue and by prayer and sacrifice in the rites of the temple. The affairs of the temple came under the control of the Sadducees, while the Pharisees exerted the greater leadership in the synagogue. The institution of the synagogue, we have learned, probably had its beginnings during the exile, when the Israelites in Babylon were cut off from the temple worship in Jerusalem. In time the synagogue became another means by which they could keep the covenant and maintain their faithful relationship with God.

About 440 B.C., after the return from exile, Ezra the Scribe had established the Torah as the unchanging basis for Jewish life. In this sense, the Torah comprised the Pentateuch, that is, the first five books of the Hebrew Bible. The Torah was to remain the first and final authority in all matters of Jewish custom and law. It was the traditional understanding of the Jews that these five books were the very words Moses had written down after he was inspired by God on the heights of Sinai. Sinai was the event, and Torah was the means, by which God had identified himself and his will to his people, and by which the Israelites identified themselves as his people, in the manner of a wife, son, or servant.

From the early postexilic times, the synagogues and schools (*yeshibot*) had concerned themselves with the Torah and its interpretation. Along with their traditional understanding that the written Torah had been given directly to Moses by God, the Jews also held the conviction that an oral torah had begun with Moses at Sinai and had been passed down from generation to generation side by side with the written Torah. The purpose of this oral law, or oral tradition, was both to explain and interpret the written Torah and to adapt the teachings of the Torah to the changing times.

Thus the oral tradition always had been included directly or indirectly in the general meaning of torah. It was transmitted by word of mouth, and the Jews were instinctively hesitant to put it down into writing. This meant that people had to remember the oral tradition and pass it on. At the same time, people modified their memories in the light of their own experiences. A written record would have made memorization unnecessary and modification more difficult, for any written tradition was revered because it expressed teachings from distant generations closer to the original experience of the torah at Mount Sinai.

The Scribes and the Method of Midrash

From the time of Ezra on, the oral tradition was passed down by the scribes, or *Soferim*, who read and studied the written Torah in the schools and synagogues, from between about 440 B.C. to 270 B.C. An important part of the literature of Israel was specifically didactic, the authoritative teaching of certain rules by which the people were to regulate their lives according to God's will. When the Jews tried to live by teachings in such a large body of literature as the Pentateuch, they saw it necessary, to reinterpret the requirements in the literature to apply them to the changing conditions.

The process of studying the Pentateuch, reinterpreting it in the light of changing conditions, produced what we call *commentary*. This commentary, the oral tradition, was taught by the scribes through the use of a method called *midrash*. The scribes added a running commentary to the text of the written Torah. Since the Torah was read in sequence in the synagogues day by day, the text of the written Torah provided an aid to remembering the oral tradition that accompanied it. We will learn more of the *midrash* literature in Parts 5 and 6 of this unit.

The Pairs and the Method of Mishnah

The Soferim were succeeded after 270 B.C. by the five generations of teachers known as the *Pairs* (Zugot). They continued the transmission of the oral tradition until the end of the first century B.C. The major issues of discussion and debate in the synagogues were taken up by two opposing schools, each one led by a revered scholar (the Pairs). One school defended one side of the issue, while the other school defended the other side. By this means, both sides of an issue could be considered thoroughly, so that the people would not make hasty and ill-conceived judgments about their conduct in obedience to the will of God.

While the Soferim had used the method of *midrash* exclusively in teaching the oral tradition, the Zugot (Pairs) added another teaching method called *mishnah*. By this method, the scholars taught the oral tradition apart from the biblical texts which it accompanied. While ultimately the teachings of the oral tradition could be traced back to their biblical texts, this new method permitted a greater range of freedom in discussion. That is, the scholars could debate the major issues of the day as they arose, rather than following the day by day sequence of discussion accompanying the reading of the written Torah. In using this teaching method, the oral tradition was remembered not so much in relation to the written Torah as through repetition. Thus, the method was called *mishnah*, which means "repetition." From the time of the Zugot on, both methods, *midrash* and *mishnah*, existed side by side in the teaching of the oral tradition.

While the Pairs involved themselves in the *commentary* of the oral tradition, they also emphasized another process related to the reinterpretation of the Torah. They reduced the Torah to its essentials and then reapplied it to their current conditions. The process of reducing the Torah toward its essentials is the process of *codification*.

In the first two centuries, the Pharisees took an intense interest in the problems of coding and commenting. The Sadducees were content to understand their faith in terms of the Pentateuch, literally interpreted, and in terms of the fixed rituals and ceremonies of the temple.

The last of the Pairs opposed to each other two famous scholars named Hillel, a Pharisee, and Shammai, a Sadducee. Of these two, Hillel was the more generous and flexible in his interpretation of torah. Hillel was a Babylonian Jew who came to Jerusalem about 40 B.C. He was a contemporary of Herod the Great. More than any other pharisaic scholar, he influenced the development of other scholars, and, through them, the whole development of normative Judaism in the generations that followed him. He was responsible for providing the basic rules by which the rabbis would interpret torah. He even expressed the principle of codification and commentary when he said to an inquiring heathen who challenged him to say the whole torah while he stood on one foot, "What is hateful to you, do not do to your neighbor: that is the whole torah; the rest is commentary; go, study."

The Tannaim and the Mishnah

After the five generations of the Pairs, the accumulating mishnah teachings were passed down through a body of scholars known as the Tannaim ("repeaters," or transmitters of tradition). Under the Tannaim, the teachings in mishnah form were compiled and eventually put into writing. The codification process, as the teachings were drawn together and written down, produced the body of literature called the *Mishnah*. The Mishnah literature, compiled during the last generation of the Tannaim under Rabbi Judah ha-Nasi (the Prince), presented an authoritative codification of the rules and maxims governing Jewish thought and action from the time of the Soferim, through the period of the Tannaim, to the end of the second century A.D. This Mishnah codification of Rabbi Judah the Prince came to be accepted as the canon of oral tradition, and was studied and taught in the schools and synagogues after 200 A.D. Traditionally, while Hillel, the "father" of the Tannaim, is called simply Hillel, and not rabbi, Judah the Prince, on the other hand, is called simply "Rabbi." "Rabbi said," or "Rabbi used to say," always refers to Judah ha-Nasi.

The Mishnah in its codified form includes six main divisions, or orders. The orders relate to different aspects of Jewish life, such as agricultural laws, rules governing festivals, civil and criminal laws, and rules of purification, or ritual cleanliness. Each order contains from seven to twelve subdivisions, or tractates. There are sixty-three of these tractates all together. The tractates are divided further into chapters and paragraphs.

The Sayings of the Fathers

The Pirke Aboth, or Sayings of the Fathers, is the ninth tractate in the fourth order of the Mishnah. The maxims in the first two chapters of the Aboth trace tradition, beginning with Moses, through Joshua, the elders in Canaan, the prophets, the legendary Great Assembly of scholars in post-exilic Jerusalem, through the Pairs to Hillel and Shammai, from Hillel through the Tannaim to Gamaliel III, the son of Judah the Prince. The "line" then returns to Hillel and traces the succession of scholarship through Hillel's disciple Johanan (Yachanan) ben Zakkai and his five disciples.

The men described in these two chapters are considered the spiritual ancestors of normative Judaism. This is especially true of Hillel, whose style of phariseeism became the normal Jewish way in contrast to the militarism of the Zealots, the isolationism of the Essenes, the upper-class conservatism and biblical literalism of the Sadducees, and the apocalyptic claims by Christians that Jesus was the Messiah and that the final judgment and new age were already under way.

As an aid in understanding the first two chapters of the Aboth, we present the following comments, gleaned from scholars. The Aboth itself, as part of the Mishnah, is the subject of volumes of interpretive literature.

In paragraph 1 of the first chapter, the reference to "a hedge for the Torah" likens the Torah to a garden. Minor rules of conduct served to warn the faithful man that he was close to the precious commandments of the Torah itself. The phrase "he used to say," was a customary way of introducing the revered sayings of the Tannaim. Antigonos of Socho, referred to in paragraph 3, here opposes the Epicurean teachings, saying that one does not work merely for one's own well-being, nor does one act as if God has no interest in his affairs. Further on in the first chapter, "Gehinnom" refers literally to the valley of Hinnom where children had been sacrificed in ancient times in Canaanite rites to their god, Moloch. Generally it signified "hell" as opposed to "paradise." Paragraph 18 of the second chapter mentions the Shema, found in Deuteronomy 6:4-9, 11:13-21, and Numbers 15:37-41, parts of which you already have read. The Shema is considered to contain the principles of the Ten Commandments. The Amidah were the oldest congregational prayers said in the synagogue. They were repeated while the people remained standing.

REFLECTION QUESTIONS

1. Who is the first person mentioned in the Pirke Aboth, what does it say about him, and why do you think the Tannaim mentioned him first?
2. Which of his five disciples did Rabbi Johanan ben Zakkai consider to be the wisest, and why? Would you agree?
3. How would you describe the Pirke Aboth as a type of literature?
4. What do you think has made the rabbis so important in the Jewish tradition?
5. Compare the Torah and the Mishnah with the American Constitution and its Amendments. How are they similar? How are they different?

Part 2:

THE JEWISH FAMILIES REENACT WHO THEY ARE ON THE EVE OF PASSOVER

This reading, from the *Mishnah Pesahim,* describes the rules and the reasons for remembering on the eve of Passover what it means to be a Jew. The rules embrace not only words but actions, so that the act of remembering and the act remembered become united in one experience for the family of Israel. This is the Seder ceremony, a family service at which the father presides.

SEARCH CUES

1. the day and the wine
2. the four cups
3. the son's question
4. the disgrace and the glory
5. Rabbi Gamaliel's three essentials

NOW READ BELOW: FROM MISHNAH PESAHIM

FROM MISHNAH PESAHIM

Reprinted with permission from
Glatzer, N. N. *The Judaic Tradition.*
Boston: Beacon Press, 1969, pp. 188-190.

On the eve of Passover, when the late afternoon approaches, a man must eat naught until nightfall. Even the poorest in Israel must not eat unless he sits down to table, and they must not give them less than four cups of wine to drink even if it is from the [Paupers'] Dish.

After they have mixed him his first cup, the School of Shammai say: He says the benediction first over the [holy] day and then the benediction over the wine. And the School of Hillel say: He says the benediction first over the wine and then the benediction over the day.

When [food] is brought before him he eats it seasoned with lettuce, until he is come to the bread condiment [the bitter herbs]; they bring before him unleavened bread and lettuce, and the *haroseth,* although *haroseth* is not a religious obligation. Rabbi Eliezer ben Rabbi Zadok says: It is a religious obligation. And in the Holy City they used to bring before him the complete Passover-offering.

They then mix him the second cup. And here the son asks his father (and if the son has not enough understanding his father instructs him [how to ask]): "Why is this night different from other nights? For on other nights we eat seasoned food once, but this night twice; on other nights we eat leavened or unleavened bread, but this night all is unleavened; on other nights we eat flesh roast, stewed, or cooked, but this night all is roast." And according to the understanding of the son his father instructs him. He begins with the disgrace and ends with the glory; and he expounds from "A wandering Aramean was my father" (Deut. 26:5) until he finishes the whole section.

Rabban Gamaliel used to say: Whosoever has not said [the verses concerning] these three things at Passover has not fulfilled his obligation. And these are they: Passover, unleavened bread, and bitter herbs: "Passover"— because God passed over the houses of our fathers in Egypt; "unleavened bread"—because our fathers were redeemed from Egypt; "bitter herbs"— because the Egyptians embittered the lives of our fathers in Egypt.

In every generation a man must so regard himself as if he came forth himself out of Egypt, for it is written: "And thou shalt tell thy son in that day saying, It is because of that which the Lord did for me when I came forth out of Egypt" (Exod. 13:8). Therefore are we bound to give thanks, to praise, to glorify, to honor, to exalt, to extol, and to bless him who wrought all these wonders for our fathers and for us. He brought us out from bondage to freedom, from sorrow to gladness, and from mourning to a Festival day, and from darkness to great light, and from servitude to redemption; so let us say before him the Hallelujah.

How far do they recite [the Hallel]? The School of Shammai say: To "A joyful mother of children." and the School of Hillel say: To "a flintstone into a springing well." And this is concluded with the [benediction recounting] Redemption.

Rabbi Tarfon says: "He that redeemed us and redeemed our fathers from Egypt and brought us to this night to eat therein unleavened bread and bitter herbs." But there is no concluding benediction.

Rabbi Akiba adds: "Therefore, O Lord our God and the God of our fathers, bring us in peace to the other set feasts and festivals which are coming to meet us, while we rejoice in the building-up of Thy city and are joyful in Thy worship; and may we eat there of the sacrifices and of the Passover-offerings whose blood has reached with acceptance the wall of Thy altar, and let us praise Thee for our redemption and for the ransoming of our soul. Blessed art Thou, O Lord, who hast redeemed Israel!"

After they have mixed for him the third cup he says the benediction over his meal. [Over] a fourth [cup] he completes the "Hallel" and says after it the benediction over song. If he is minded to drink [more] between these cups he may drink; only between the third and the fourth cups he may not drink.

After the Passover meal they should not disperse to join in revelry.

COMMENTARY

Halakhah and Haggadah

In understanding the Mishnah, we also must understand the two principal ways by which the Jews had learned to obey the will of God by hearing his will in the words of the Torah. We see throughout the literature the presupposition that God teaches Israel sometimes by direct commandment through what the Torah prescribes and prohibits. He also teaches by implication, through the way the Torah describes life. In some instances, God says through the Torah, "Thou shalt" and "Thou shalt not." In other cases, God, through the Torah, describes the human situation in which Israel finds herself, and leaves it to Israel to infer what the nation or the individual should or should not do.

In both midrash and mishnah, the codes and commentaries which tell the Jew directly what to do and what not to do are called *halakhah*. The tradition that tells the story of Israel's human situation in parables, proverbs, and legends, is called *haggadah*.

Wisdom and Prophecy

In the language of Judaic tradition, the will of God for Israel comes both through revelation to the minds of inspired individuals and through the insights of the people which accumulate from their experience. God has revealed his will for Israel both through *prophecy*, given by divine inspiration, and through *wisdom*, emerging from human experience. The literature of the rabbis is a rich mixture of references both to prophecy and to wisdom.

God's teaching (torah), the rabbis assume, comes down through the generations, beginning with Sinai. Nevertheless, by the oral tradition, God's teaching comes also out of the contemporary experience of each generation. The task of the rabbis was to understand and interpret the Torah so that its codes and commentaries could be seen as one torah rather than many. In comparing the teaching of the rabbis with the record of torah, they could say with confidence, "Hear, O Israel, the Lord is our God, the Lord is One."

Mishnah Pesahim

The Seder ceremony that you have read comes from the tenth chapter of the third tractate of the second order of the Mishnah. "Mishnah Pesahim" indicates the study or recollection of the paschal lambs slain at the time of God's destruction of the Egyptian first-born in the Exodus. The blood of the lambs was sprinkled on the doorposts and lintels of the Israelites' dwellings.

After the destruction of the temple (587 B.C.) this home ceremony replaced the temple offering of the paschal lamb. This is primarily *halakhic* mishnah. It tells the Jewish family what to do. In this case, at the family table, the faithful Jew is to remember who he is in the presence of God as he reenacts symbolically God's delivery of Israel from Egypt.

What is accomplished by ceremony is *anamnesis*. By this symbolic ritual, that is, by this vivid recollection of the ancient deliverance, the faithful Jew participates in the original Passover event and shares the fullness of its meaning.

Some Details of the Seder

The posture of reclining, or sitting at table, is a sign of freedom and equality. The four cups of wine symbolizes the four words of redemption in Exodus 6:6-7: "I am the Lord, and *I will bring you out* from under the burdens of the Egyptians, and *I will deliver you* from their bondage, and *I will redeem you* with an outstretched arm and with great acts of judgment, and *I will take you* for my people. . ." To begin with the disgrace and to end with the glory is to teach first about Israel's bondage to Egypt and idolatry, and then about her deliverance. To appreciate the significance of the Seder ceremony on these points, read Deuteronomy 26:5-11.

The three essential things to be said at Passover are found in Exodus 12:27, Exodus 12:39, and Exodus 1:14. The Hallel is the six psalms of praise and thanksgiving (Psalms 113 through 118) which are said in whole or in part at Jewish worship on the festival days of New Moon, Passover, Weeks and Tabernacles, and Hanukah. The concluding benediction, or Redemption, begins, "All thy works shall praise thee, O Lord our God, and thy pious ones, the just who do thy will, together with all thy people, the house of Israel, shall with exaltation thank, bless, praise, glorify, exalt, reverence, sanctify and ascribe sovereignty unto thy Name, O our King. . . ." (From the Daily Prayer Book)

REFLECTION QUESTIONS

1. Why are this Mishnah Pesahim reading and the Seder ceremony it describes a codification of a previous writing and a previous event? What was the writing? What was the event?
2. Why do you suppose the Mishnah Pesahim specifically directs that the *son* shall ask the *father*, "Why is this night different from other nights?"
3. Scan the Hallel (Psalms 113-118). What appears to be the principal themes? Can you find where the School of Shammai said to stop reciting? Where the School of Hillel said to stop? Does the Hallel seem like an appropriate thing to recite at the Seder?

Part 3:

THE RABBIS COMMENT ON LOVE AND THE LAW

After the Tannaim developed the Mishnah code (c. 10 B.C. to 200 A.D.), those elder scholars, or "traditioners," were followed by rabbis called the Amoraim (singular, Amora). They interpreted the Mishnah for later times and circumstances by a vast commentary, involving many proverbs, parables, and problems of rules and wisdom. The name for this great body of Amoraic literature is the *Gemara*.

Thus the Tannaim codified the oral tradition in relation to the Hebrew Bible to produce the Mishnah code. The Amoraim later built an expanded commentary on the Mishnah called the Gemara. The Mishnah and the Gemara, taken together, is the *Talmud*.

The content of the *Sukkah*, from which these following two short selections are taken, spells out the meaning of the rules about the Feast of Tabernacles, one of Judaism's joyous festivals of praise and thanksgiving to God. In particular, this festival thanks him for the harvest and for his ancient care of the Israelites during their wilderness wandering. From the harvest, alms must be given. When alms must be given, the problem of love arises.

SEARCH CUES

1. almsgiving and love
2. torah and love

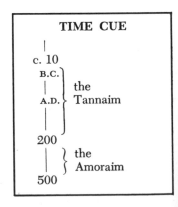

TIME CUE

c. 10 B.C.

A.D. } the Tannaim

200

} the Amoraim

500

FROM SUKKAH 49b

Reprinted with permission from
Montefiore, C. G., and Loewe, H.
A Rabbinic Anthology. New York:
Meridian Books, Inc., 1960, pp. 429
and 277.

R. Elazer said: Almsgiving is greater than all sacrifice, for it says, 'To give alms [lit. to do justice] is more acceptable to God than sacrifices' (Prov. XXI, 3). But loving deeds are greater than almsgiving, as it says, 'Sow in almsgiving [lit. righteousness], reap in love' (Hos. X, 12). Of his sowing, a man may eat or no; of his reaping, he will eat assuredly. And he said: Almsgiving becomes increasingly perfect according to the amount of love that is shown in it.

The torah [that is practised and studied] for its own sake is a law of love; the law [that is practised and studied] not for its own sake is a law without love. The torah which is studied in order to teach, is a law of love; the torah which is not studied in order to teach, is a law without love.

COMMENTARY

The Amoraim and the Gemara

The development of the rabbinic teachings did not stop after the codification of the Mishnah. The rabbinic scholars (Amoraim) who came after the Tannaim studied the Mishnah and added additional commentary, reinterpreting it to apply to their changing times. Some of the Amoraim (i.e., speakers, or completers) lived and worked in Palestine, but a greater number of them studied and debated the meaning of the Mishnah in Babylonia during the third to the fifth centuries A.D. Life dealt more kindly with the Jews in Babylonia than it did in the Roman and Christian Mediterranean world.

In contrast with the literary works of the Tannaim, which coded *halakhic* material for the most part, the works of the Amoraim, written in popular Aramaic as well as in Hebrew, consisted of a voluminous literature, the *Gemara*, which was mostly haggadic in nature. The Gemara ("completion") expanded the meaning of the Mishnah with extensive commentaries involving ethical, devotional, and other familiar lore.

The Talmud

Together, the Mishnah and the Gemara are called the *Talmud*. The Talmud contains both halakhah and haggadah, that is, codified legal material and expansive commentaries and folklore. Actually, the rabbis produced two Talmuds, one in Palestine and one in Babylonia, using the same Mishnah in each case, but adding a different Gemara. The Gemara of the Palestinian Talmud was codified at about the end of the fourth century A.D., whereas the Gemara of the Babylonian Talmud continued to be compiled and edited until the end of the fifth century A.D. Of the two, the Babylonian Talmud speaks with more authority in the Jewish tradition.

The Talmud is organized in orders and tractates, each of which has a name. These are the orders and tractates of the Mishnah. Selections from the Gemara of the Talmud become identified by references to the Mishnah tractate on which the Gemara selection is commenting. The selection is further identified by referring to a subdivision called a folio, or page, and then to a side of the folio, either the "a" side or the "b" side. Thus, our reading selections in this Part are from the "b" side of the 49th folio of the tractate called Sukkah in the Babylonian Talmud. The selections here are only a small fraction of Sukkah 49b.

When we read rabbinical literature correctly, we read *intensively* rather than *extensively*. We do not sweep through it to "get the plot," or to catch its emotional atmosphere. Instead, we dig into it, reading and rereading it, remembering who was writing it, and when, and for whom, searching it as much for what it seems to imply as for what it states more directly, inferring from it a variety of counsels and warnings addressed to our own experience and to our own times.

A Schematic Summary

In learning about the development of the rabbinic literature, it may be helpful to your understanding to view it schematically:

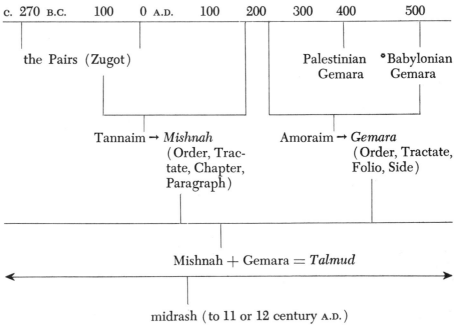

The Selections from Sukkah 49b

A *sukkah* is a booth, or tent, set up at the Feast of Tabernacles. The word *tabernacle* also means tent. The Festival of Tabernacles is based on Exodus 34:42, "And you shall observe the feast of weeks, the first fruits of wheat harvest, and the feast of ingathering at the year's end," and also on Leviticus 23:42, "You shall dwell in booths for seven days; all that are native in Israel shall dwell in booths, that your generations may know that I made the people of Israel dwell in booths when I brought them out of the land of Egypt: I am the Lord your God," and on verse 40 of the same chapter, "And you shall take on the first day of the fruit of goodly trees, branches of palm trees, and boughs of leafy trees, and willows of the brook; and you shall rejoice before the Lord your God seven days."

The content of the Tractate Sukkah, then, concerns itself with teasing out the meaning of the laws about the Feast of Tabernacles. As a commentary on the rules and rationale of the festival, the material we are reading is *haggadic*.

During the days of the Feast of Tabernacles, the people remembered gladly the survival of the Israelites in the wilderness, where they dwelt in temporary shelters and yet within the protecting tabernacle of God's care. At the time of this festival, they also enjoyed the fruits of the harvest from which alms were given. The problems of "What is righteousness?" "What is self-interest?" "What is law?" and "What is love?" occurred in connection with obeying the rules of almsgiving in those days of prosperity.

REFLECTION QUESTIONS

1. Do you find contradiction or agreement between R. Elazar's comment on almsgiving and love and the comment that follows on the torah and love?
2. Look up the biblical passages that Rabbi Elazar refers to in the first selection. How well do you think they support his argument?

Part 4:

A LEGEND
ABOUT RABBI ELIEZER BEN HYRCANUS

Baba Metzia (Middle Gate) is the second tractate of the fourth order of the Mishnah. It has been the object of a great deal of reference and commentary in the Gemara literature, since it contains a large number of the halakhic rules about right conduct in commerce and industry. The selection we are to read shows that the rabbis often moved beyond the subject matter of the tractate in pursuing their arguments and searching out the implications of the torah.

This selection from 59b recounts an incident that occurred within a much longer discussion. Just before these events, R. Eliezer had been arguing with his fellow sages over a matter of ritual cleanness and uncleanness in the preparation of food. Since cooking utensils were subject to the rules of cleanness and uncleanness, the one side held that the tiles forming an oven should be liable to uncleanness. The other side of the argument considered the tiles as separate objects, tile by tile, and therefore not liable to uncleanness. All the other sages took the first point of view, and declared the oven to be liable to uncleanness. Eliezer, a minority of one, took the latter point of view and declared the oven to be free of liability to uncleanness. The sequence of events in our selection begins at the point where these opposing opinions have been expressed.

SEARCH CUES

1. the leaning walls
2. after the majority must one incline
3. the comment of the Holy One

NOW READ BELOW: FROM BABA METZIA 59b

FROM BABA METZIA 59b

Reprinted with permission from
Glatzer, N. N. *The Judaic Tradition*.
Boston: Beacon Press, 1969, pp. 224-225.

... On that day Rabbi Eliezer [in dispute with other sages] brought all the proofs in the world [in support of his opinion], but the sages would not accept them.

He said to them: If the law is according to me, let this locust tree prove it.

The locust tree moved a hundred cubits. (And some say: four hundred cubits.)

The sages said to him: The locust tree cannot prove anything.

Then he said to them: If the law is according to me, let this stream of water prove it.

The stream of water turned and flowed backward.

They said to him: The stream cannot prove anything.

Then he said to them: If the law is according to me, let the walls of the House of Study prove it.

The walls of the House of Study began to topple.

Rabbi Joshua reprimanded the walls:

If scholars are disputing with one another about the law, what business is it of yours?

They did not fall down out of respect for Rabbi Joshua, and did not straighten up out of respect for Rabbi Eliezer, and they are still inclined.

Then Rabbi Eliezer said to them: If the law is according to me, let the heaven prove it.

A voice came forth from heaven and said:

Why do you dispute with Rabbi Eliezer? The law is according to him in every case.

Thereupon Rabbi Joshua rose to his feet and said:

"It is not in heaven" (Deut. 30:12):

the Torah has already been given once and for all from Mount Sinai;

we do not listen to voices from heaven.

For Thou hast already written in the Torah on Mount Sinai:

"After the majority must one incline" (Exod. 23:2).

[Later on] Rabbi Nathan came upon Elijah [the prophet].

He said to him: What was the Holy One, blessed be he, doing at that moment?

Elijah said to him:

He was smiling and saying: My children have defeated me, my children have defeated me!

COMMENTARY

Baba Metzia

This passage refers to a world in which an experience of miracle was common enough to make no overwhelming impression when used to bolster an argument. In the world of rabbinic literature, God could do what he wanted with the powers of nature. One man might invoke the miraculous

187

power of God, but so might another. Nor did the dramatic extent of a miracle seem to make much difference in the argument it was invoked to support. If God moved a locust tree a hundred cubits or four hundred cubits, the difference would have but slight effect on the argument.

In our selection, the reference to Elijah the prophet is based on the legend that Elijah, who had been taken "by a whirlwind into heaven" (Kings 2:11), still continued to appear now and again to the faithful to encourage them and to bring them news from the court of God.

The Talmudic Writing

We speak of "Folio 59b" of the tractate Baba Metzia according to the same system by which we speak of "Folio 49b" of the Tractate Sukkah. We keep it in mind also that when we use terms like "59b" we are referring to the Gemara related to the Mishnah tractate rather than to the tractate itself. Books in Hebrew are written first on the right hand page (recto) and then on the left (verso), which is the reverse of the way it is done in English. Thus, a reference to "59a" is a reference to the right hand page of an open folio, and a reference to "59b" as a reference to the left hand page.

One reason for this system of reference used for the Gemara is in the change in writing materials during the first few centuries A.D. The Torah had been read, and continued to be read, from a scroll, which was a rolled up document of leather or parchment. By the time of the Gemara, however, the most common form for documents was that of the *codex*, in which tablets of wood or pages of parchment were bound together at one edge, similar to our modern books.

We can now see the system by which the rabbi refers to passages in the Mishnah and Gemara. In referring to the Mishnah, he refers to the Mishnah order, the Mishnah tractate, then to the chapter, and finally to the paragraph. In referring to the Gemara, he refers, as in Mishnah references, to the Mishnah order, then to the Mishnah tractate. But then he refers to the Gemara folio (e.g., 59) and side, whether "a" (recto) or "b" (verso). Each Gemara folio contains the commentary of the Amoraim on a portion of a Mishnah chapter. Thus, we find a Gemara folio following a section of the Mishnah, and offering the comments and interpretations of the later rabbinic scholars which relate to the Tannaitic writings of the Mishnah.

REFLECTION QUESTIONS

1. Granted that the argument between R. Eliezer and his fellow rabbis began as an argument about ritual cleanness, what did it finally turn out to be?
2. Which line in the reading would you choose to represent the point against which R. Eliezer was really arguing?
3. What did the leaning walls of the House of Study suggest?
4. Do you think the comment by the Holy One decided the issue? What do you think the comment means?
5. Look up the biblical passages cited in this reading. How well do you think they support the arguments?

Part 5:

SOME SYNAGOGUE SERMONS
IN THE MIDRASH

The Midrash

When we speak of *midrash*, we refer to a literary product, and to the painstaking study of Scripture and experience which finds expression in the written product. Midrash is something far more profound than mere descriptive commentary by the rabbis. The midrash is Jewish thinking based on the supposition that the teaching that can be inferred from the Hebrew Bible is completely adequate to provide guidance from God for every situation. Such faith in the adequacy of the Scripture as God's teaching method required of the Jew, and especially of the rabbi, a continuing, diligent, and devoted searching of the canon to find that express will of God. That search went on in relation to the changing experience of the people, to discover how God's will applied to them and to their decisions.

Each portion of the midrash, whether directly or indirectly related to some passage of Scripture, is also called a midrash. Thus we have a midrash on Exodus, for example, or one on Numbers. In the plural, these portions are called midrashim. Unlike the Mishnah and the Gemara, which were formalized into codes by the end of the second and sixth centuries A.D. respectively, the midrash literature continued to grow and expand until the 11th or 12th century A.D. In an informal sense of the word, the process of midrash has never ceased, for people continue to develop commentary on the Scriptures. We should remember when reading selections from the midrash that the Bible bears more authority than the Mishnah, the Mishnah bears more authority than the Gemara, and all three bear more authority than the recorded midrash.

Mekhilta Bahodesh 5 is a midrash on the second verse of Exodus 20, "I am the Lord your God, who brought you out of the land of Egypt, out of the house of bondage." This is a rabbinic homily, a summary of interpretive sermons on the theme of Exodus 20:2. In this relatively short work, the rabbis refer to some 28 other texts from the Hebrew Bible in discussing the text that provides the theme.

This halakhic midrash begins with a *parable*, which is a short, imaginary story to illustrate a point in teaching or preaching.

SEARCH CUES

1. I am the Lord thy God
2. I have been called
3. why the Torah was not given in the land of Israel

NOW READ BELOW:
FROM MEKHILTA BAHODESH 5 ON EXODUS 20:2

FROM MEKHILTA BAHODESH 5 ON EXODUS 20:2

Reprinted with permission from
Lauterbach, Jacob Z., trans. *Mekhilta,*
Tractate Bahodesh, 5. Philadelphia:
The Jewish Publication Society of
America, 1933, on Exodus 20:2.

I am the Lord thy God. Why were the Ten Commandments not said at the beginning of the Torah? They give a parable. To what may this be compared? To the following: A king who entered a province said to the people, "May I be your king?" But the people said to him, "Have you done anything good for us that you should rule over us?" What did he do then? He built the city wall for them, he brought in the water supply for them, and he fought their battles. Then when he said to them, "May I be your king?" They said to him: "Yes, yes." Likewise, God. He brought the Israelites out of Egypt, divided the sea for them, sent down the manna for them, brought up the well for them, brought the quails for them. He fought for them the battle with Amalek. Then he said to them, "I am to be your king." And they said to him, "Yes, yes." Rabbi says: "This proclaims the excellence of Israel. For when they all stood before Mount Sinai to receive the Torah, they all made up their mind alike to accept the reign of God joyfully. Furthermore, they pledged themselves for one another. And it was not only concerning overt acts that God, revealing himself to them, wished to make his covenant with them but also concerning secret acts, as it is said, 'The secret things belong unto the Lord our God, but the things that are revealed,' etc. But they said to him, 'Concerning overt acts we are ready to make a covenant with thee, but we will not make a covenant with thee in regard to secret acts lest one of us commit a sin secretly and the entire community be held responsible for it.'"

I am the Lord thy God. Why is this said? For this reason: At the sea he appeared to them as a mighty hero doing battle, as it is said, "The Lord is a man of war." At Sinai he appeared to them as an old man full of mercy. It is said, "And they saw the God of Israel," etc. And of the time after they had been redeemed what does it say? "And the like of the very heaven for clearness." Again it says, "I beheld till thrones were placed." And it also says, "A fiery stream issued and came forth from before him," etc. Scripture, therefore, would not let the nations of the world have an excuse for saying that there are two Powers, but declares, "I am the Lord thy God." I am he who was in Egypt, and I am he who was at the sea. I am he who was at Sinai. I am he who was in the past, and I am he who will be in the future. I am he who is in this world, and I am he who will be in the world to come, as it is said, "See now that I, even I, am he," etc. And it says, "Even to old age I am the same." And it says, "Thus saith the Lord, the King of Israel, and his Redeemer the Lord of Hosts: I am the first, and I am the last." And it says, "Who hath wrought and done it? He that called the generations from the beginning. I, the Lord, who am the first," etc. Rabbi Nathan says, "From this one can cite a refutation of the heretics who say, 'There are two Powers.' For when the Holy One, blessed be he, stood up and exclaimed, 'I am the Lord thy God,' was there anyone who stood up to protest against him? If you should say that it was done in secret, but has it not been said, 'I have not spoken in secret,' etc.? 'I said not unto the seed of Jacob'—that is, to those only will I give it. 'They sought me in the desert.' Did I not give it in broad daylight? And thus it says, 'I the Lord speak righteousness, I declare things that are right.'"

Another interpretation: *I am the Lord thy God.* When the Holy One, blessed be he, stood up and said, "I am the Lord thy God," the mountains trembled and the hills wavered. Tabor was coming from Beth Elim and Carmel from Aspamea, as it is said, "As I live, saith the king whose name is the Lord of Hosts, surely as Tabor among the mountains and Carmel by the sea would come." This one was saying, "I have been called." And that one was saying, "I have been called." But when they heard from his mouth, "Who brought thee out of the land of Egypt," each one of them remained standing in its place, and they said, "He is dealing only with those whom he brought out from Egypt."

Another interpretation: *I am the Lord thy God.* When the Holy One, blessed be he, stood up and said, "I am the Lord thy God," the earth trembled; as it is said, "Lord, when thou didst go forth out of Seir, when thou didst march out of the field of Edom, the earth trembled." And it goes on to say, "The mountains quaked at the presence of the Lord." And it also says, "The voice of the Lord is powerful; the voice of the Lord is full of majesty," etc., up to "And in his palace everyone says, 'Glory!'" And their houses even were filled with the splendor of the Shekinah. At that time all the kings of the nations of the world assembled and came to Balaam, the son of Beor. They said to him; "Perhaps God is about to destroy his world by a flood." He said to them: "Fools that ye are! Long ago God swore to Noah that he would not bring a flood upon the world, as it is said, "For this is as the water of Noah unto me; for as I have sworn that the waters of Noah should no more go over the earth.'" They then said to him, "Perhaps he will not bring a flood of water, but he may bring a flood of fire." But he said to them, "He is not going to bring a flood of water or a flood of fire. It is simply that the Holy One, blessed be he, is going to give the Torah to his people. For it is said 'The Lord will give strength unto his people,' etc." As soon as they heard this from him, they all turned back and went each to his place.

And it was for the following reason that the nations of the world were asked to accept the Torah, in order that they should have no excuse for saying, "Had we been asked, we would have accepted it." For, behold, they were asked and they refused to accept it, for it is said, "And he said: 'The Lord came from Sinai,' " etc. He appeared to the children of Esau, the wicked, and said to them, "Will you accept the Torah?" They said to him, "What is written in it?" He said to them, " 'Thou shalt not murder.' " They then said to him, "The very heritage which our father left us was: 'And by thy sword shalt thou live.' " He then appeared to the children of Amon and Moab. He said to them, "Will you accept the Torah?" They said to him, "What is written in it?" He said to them, " 'Thou shalt not commit adultery.' " They, however, said to him that they were all of them children of adulterers, as it is said, "Thus were both the daughters of Lot with child by their father." Then he appeared to the children of Ishmael. He said to them, "Will you accept the Torah?" They said to him, "What is written in it?" He said to them, " 'Thou shalt not steal.' " They then said to him, "The very blessing that had been pronounced upon our father was: 'And he shall be as a wild ass of a man; his hand shall be upon everything,' And it is written, 'For indeed I was stolen away out of the land of the Hebrews.' " And when he came to the Israelites and "at his right hand was a fiery law unto them," they all opened their mouths and said, "All that the Lord hath spoken will we do and obey." And thus it says, "He stood and measured the earth; he beheld and drove asunder the nations." R. Simon b. Eleazar says, "If the sons of Noah could not endure the seven commandments enjoined upon them, how much less could they have endured all the commandments of the Torah! To give a parable. A king had appointed two administrators. One was appointed over the store of straw and the other was appointed over the treasure of silver and gold. The one appointed over the store of straw was held in suspicion. But he used to complain about the fact that they had not appointed him over the treasure of silver and gold. The people then said to him, 'Reka. If you were under suspicion in connection with the store of straw, how could they trust you with the treasure of silver and gold?' " Behold, it is a matter of reasoning by the method of *kal vahomer:* If the sons of Noah could not endure the seven commandments enjoined upon them, how much less could they have endured all the commandments of the Torah?

Why was the Torah not given in the land of Israel? In order that the nations of the world should not have the excuse for saying, "Because it was given in Israel's land, therefore we have not accepted it." Another reason: To avoid causing dissension among the tribes. Else one might have said, "In my territory the Torah was given." And the other might have said, "In my territory the Torah was given." Therefore, the Torah was given in the desert, publicly and openly, in a place belonging to no one. To three things the Torah is likened: to the desert, to fire, and to water. This is to tell you that, just as these three things are free to all who come into the world, so also are the words of the Torah free to all who come into the world.

Who brought thee out of the land of Egypt, out of the house of bondage.
They were slaves to kings. You interpret it to mean that they were servants
of kings. Perhaps it is not so, but means that they were slaves of servants.
When it says, "And redeemed you out of the house of bondage, from the
hand of Pharaoh King of Egypt" it indicates that they were servants of
kings and not servants of slaves. Another interpretation: *out of the house
of servants.* Out of the house of worshipers, for they worshiped idols.

COMMENTARY

Mekhilta Bahodesh 5

Some additional information about this second reading from the midrash
may aid your understanding of the passage. At one point, the sermon
becomes involved in the concept of *two powers.* Here the rabbi argues
against the Zoroastrian concept of eternal battle between a spirit of good
and a spirit of evil as he interprets the text. The word, *Shekinah,* further
on, speaks of the awe-inspiring experience of the presence of God.

The *seven commandments* given to Noah refer to the prohibition of (1)
the worship of other gods; (2) blaspheming the name of God; (3) cursing
judges; (4) murder; (5) incest and adultery; (6) robbery; (7) the eating
of flesh with the blood of life in it. According to tradition, the first six
of these were given to Adam, and the seventh was then given to Noah after
the flood. The idea behind this was that there are certain laws for all
mankind which had been revealed by God at the very beginning of man's
history. You may want to look back to the Noachide covenant and laws
here, about which you have read in Genesis 9.

Late in the sermon, the word *reka* can be translated "scoundrel." *Kal
vahomer* refers to one of the more important rules of scriptural interpretation employed by the rabbis. The first seven of these rules came into
use during the time of Hillel. *Kal vahomer* is the rule of "inference from
minor to major." The general principle of this rule is that if a person
acts in a certain way in circumstances which are relatively insignificant
to him, he is sure to act the same way in similar circumstances which are
much more significant. An example might be this: a person who can be
tempted to steal a penny can be even more tempted to steal a dollar. Or
this: if a human being can be trusted to love his own children, then God
can be trusted all the more to love his children.

REFLECTION QUESTIONS

1. What understanding of the relationship between God and Israel is
   illustrated by the parable at the beginning of this midrash?
2. What do you think is the point being taught by the story of the two
   mountains?
3. How does this midrash link the principle of moral retribution with the
   gift of the Torah?
4. Would you agree from reading this midrash that R. Simon ben Eleazar

was implying the following? All the sons of Jacob are also sons of Noah, but not all the sons of Noah are also the sons of Jacob.

5. Look up the word *ethnocentrism* in the dictionary. Do you think it applies to this selection? How widely do you think the ethnocentric attitude applies to religious literature being written today? To political literature being written today?

THE
CHRISTIAN
KERYGMA

Part 1:

PAUL THE APOSTLE SUMMARIZES THE CONTENT OF THE CHRISTIAN PROCLAMATION

In taking up the New Testament and the development of some of its important themes, we are entering a controversial area. The debate in the Christian church about the nature of the New Testament, and the whole Bible, has been a long and an important one, involving many issues. Central to the debate has been the question of inspiration. Most Christians, Roman Catholics and Protestants, believe that the Bible is an inspired book. But what form did the inspiration take?

Some believe that God dictated the Bible, word for word, to chosen scribes or authors. This is called the dictation theory, or verbal inspiration. Others believe that the Bible was inspired by God through faith—that it is a book written by faithful people, for faithful people. According to the first view, the Bible is a holy book because it was dictated by God. According to the second, it is holy because it is a witness of faith to faith: faithful people are describing the central events, interpretations, themes, and problems of faith to other faithful people. According to the first view, the Bible reflects the culture or the community from which it came only incidentally or accidentally. According to the second, the Bible is a book like most books: it reflects not only the faith, but the culture and background of the people who wrote it.

In keeping with our attempt to present an objective description of major characteristics and themes of the literature of Judaism, Christianity, and Islam, in this section we consider the New Testament as literature. In doing so, we represent the views of scholars who have studied the New Testament in relation to its development and its culture.

This is not to deny either the possibility or the validity of the various understandings of inspiration. It is to say, however, that the importance given to the New Testament and its themes, and the views of inspiration associated with it, are matters of choice for churches and individuals.

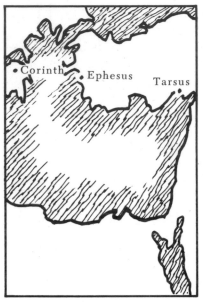

We cannot understand the significance of the Christian gospel, or "good news," apart from the fact that the Christian faith began as a movement within Judaism. That movement was rooted in the experience that certain Jews shared with each other concerning the significance of Jesus to the fulfillment of Israel's history and hope.

As literature, the New Testament is comprehensible only in relation to the Old Testament. The term *Old Testament,* for Christians, refers to all that Jews refer to as the *Bible,* plus, in some cases, certain of the apocryphal books that originally appeared in the Greek Septuagint. Christians generally apply the title *Bible* to all the books contained in the Old Testament, New Testament, and the biblical Apocrypha, although most Protestant Christians have not recognized the Apocrypha formally as canonical.

The New Testament records the experience of a community that believed in God's apocalyptic, or end-of-history, presence through Jesus to the Christian community, and through them to the rest of the world. They believed in it with all the certainty with which they and all Jews believed in God's guiding presence through the torah to historical Israel, and through Israel to the rest of the world. The literature of the New Testament argued the case for the Christian gospel by appealing for authority to the same Scriptures, and by referring to the same ideas that the great majority of Jews appealed to in practicing their faith.

The Christian claim that Jesus was the Messiah, and that the apocalypse was already happening, lay at the root of all that differentiated Christian literature from Jewish literature. The essential narrative content of the Christian claim has been called the *kerygma,* from a Greek word meaning to herald, or proclaim. One of the earliest examples of the kerygma is included in a letter written by Paul the Apostle to the Christian community he had started in Corinth. As *news,* the Christian proclamation described a dramatic act of God—an act occurring not at the beginning but at the *end* of Jesus' life as a man in history.

1. why Jesus died
2. the third day
3. the reference to the Scriptures
4. the church of God
5. the grace of God

NOW READ: 1 CORINTHIANS 15:1-11

COMMENTARY

The First-Century Jews

In viewing the conditions under which the Jews existed during the two first centuries, we looked at four different ways they chose to deal with their situation. In response to the question, "Who is Israel?" their lifeways provided four different answers. We saw in the Sadducees men who chose to accommodate themselves to the prevailing establishment of power and prestige, whether Jewish or foreign. Here was Israel conforming to the world.

We looked at the Pharisees and saw in them the mind and heart of those people who spent their lives in studious devotion to the law of their religion, in hopeful anticipation that their loyalty would be vindicated at the day of judgment and resurrection. Here was Israel persevering in the world.

We found in the Essenes an example of sectarian withdrawal from the mainstream of daily life. They strove to live the pure torah in private communities where the faithful could wait for that coming day of God untempted by the competitions of public business and national politics. Here was Israel withdrawn from the world.

We saw in the Zealots the militant urge of political patriotism in men willing to plot and fight relentlessly toward the overthrow of the Roman power in Palestine and toward the reestablishment of the Jewish state. Here was Israel at war with the world.

Jews and Christianity

The primitive Christian community, inasmuch as it was born a Jewish movement, shared in many ways the general views of the Pharisees and the Essenes. It either rejected or spiritualized the central ideas of the Sadducees and Zealots. In their literature the Christians shared with the Pharisees and the Essenes belief in a messiah, in the resurrection of the dead, in a final judgment, and in double destiny to either heaven or hell. The difference between the views of the Christians and those of the normative Judaism of the Pharisees and their rabbis centered in issues of when

199

and how these beliefs might become accomplished reality. To the primitive Christian claim, "Already," the Pharisees answered, "Not yet."

The Pharisees believed that the resurrection experience was yet to come, while the Christians believed it had already begun with Jesus. The Pharisees asserted that in the future God would render a final judgment on the present world, while the Christians proclaimed that he already had rendered the judgment. The Pharisees believed that one day the Messiah would come to announce the day of judgment and preside over the new creation, while the Christians believed that the Messiah already had come and that the great apocalyptic event already was taking place. Where the Pharisees understood that the faithful would one day live a life of triumph under God's kingship in a new age, the Christians claimed that the disciples of the risen Messiah already were living that life, awaiting the final consummation at the end, which would soon arrive.

Where the Pharisees believed that the faithful sons of Israel should persevere in faithful obedience to the torah, awaiting God's great day to come, the Christians believed that both Jew and non-Jew should accept the new age as already arrived. They proclaimed that the torah already was fulfilled through the death and resurrection of Jesus. In the death and resurrection of Jesus, God had inaugurated the new humanity through a radically new *identifying event.* Those who put their trust in the significance of the resurrection of Jesus would constitute a new humanity dwelling in a new creation.

Christian literature began as a record of this proclamation. The old covenant of the torah, according to the Christian gospel, was fulfilled and superseded by the new covenant centered in Jesus as the Christ (Messiah). To the Christians, the risen Christ, as Lord of the great new creation and host of their intimate communal table, reconciled Jew with Jew, and Jew with non-Jew in the open and inclusive community of the new Israel. From the Christians, yet another answer came to the question, "Who is Israel?"

Christianity thus began as a movement within Judaism. This movement met only limited success among the Jewish people, even among the Pharisees, to whose ways it seemed most akin. The Pharisaic reaction was generally one of revulsion against the radical claims of the Christians concerning Jesus as the Messiah, and against what seemed to be an attack on the torah that comprised the heart of their faith. However, among Gentiles, or non-Jewish people, and especially among Gentiles with personal sympathies toward Judaism, the Christian movement grew rapidly.

The Figure of Paul

The giant figure in Christian history who stands as the great example of the Christian appeal to the Gentiles is Paul the Apostle. Not long after the first persecutions of the Christians in Jerusalem, marked by the stoning of Stephen, Paul became a Christian. Paul, whose original name was Saul, was a Jew of the tribe of Benjamin, a resident of the city of Tarsus, and a Roman citizen. He was well-educated in rabbinic doctrine, a devout Pharisee, and militantly anti-Christian up to the moment of his conversion.

This occurred in a dramatic experience of the presence of Christ while Paul was carrying letters of arrest against Christians from Jerusalem to Damascus.

Paul and his missionary journeys throughout the eastern and northern Mediterranean world have become the prime example of the way Christianity became diffused throughout the Mediterranean world during the first century A.D. His *epistles,* which were teaching and preaching letters, or essays in letter form, are the earliest examples of Christian literature we possess. As a person trained in Pharisaic scholarship who spent his youth in a center of Hellenistic culture (Tarsus), he filled his epistles with the thought forms both of Israel and of Greco-Roman culture, as did many contemporary scholars among the rabbis.

Paul's Letter to Corinth

One of Paul's most effective efforts at forming a Christian community took place at Corinth in southern Greece. Later, probably when he was in Ephesus, Paul sent to these Corinthian Christians a letter, written between 52 and 55 A.D., in which he urged them toward sobriety of conduct and the building up of doctrinal integrity in their community. At one place in the letter he summarized the heart of the message he had brought to them, the passages you have read in 1 Corinthians 15.

We find in this passage a reflection of the Christian reliance on the Old Testament, recollecting that the Christians did not view their gospel as destroying the torah, but rather as exalting and fulfilling it. His reference to Cephas is to the apostle Peter, "the Rock." In writing of "the twelve," he is referring to the disciples of Jesus. Paul's reference to the grace of God embraces the idea of God's powerful and empowering good will bestowed on an undeserving recipient, in this case Paul. With Paul, as with all the Christians, the kerygma, the story and meaning of the death and resurrection of Jesus, was the good news he had to tell.

REFLECTION QUESTIONS

1. What words and phrases in this passage suggest that Paul was referring in part to ideas and events that were not described in the Old Testament?

2. Look up the word *testament* in the dictionary. How is it related to the words *witness, will,* and *covenant?*

3. What experience apparently had to happen to a person to mark him as a member of the earliest Christian community, according to Paul in the passage you have read?

4. In terms applicable to rabbinic literature, would you call this passage more similar to halakhah or to haggadah?

Part 2:

A LATER EVANGELIST DETAILS THE NARRATIVE OF THE CHRISTIAN COMMUNITY'S ORIGINAL IDENTIFYING EVENT

Many Christians believe that the Gospel of John was written by one of Jesus' apostles. Others believe that the fourth Gospel was probably written sometime between 90 and 110 A.D. by an unknown author. Paul wrote his New Testament letters, according to this theory, almost a half century earlier, between 50 and 60 A.D. Thus the chapter we are reading from the Gospel of John presents a later written account of the resurrection of Jesus. It is also more complete than the abbreviated record we read in Paul's letter to the Corinthians. Nevertheless, each writer was vitally intent on testifying to his readers that the resurrection of Jesus was central to the faith.

SEARCH CUES

1. the empty tomb
2. the orders to the disciples
3. the element of doubt
4. he breathed on them

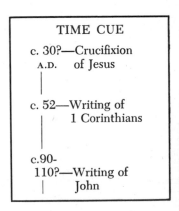

TIME CUE

c. 30?—Crucifixion
A.D.   of Jesus

c. 52—Writing of
        1 Corinthians

c.90-
110?—Writing of
        John

NOW READ: JOHN 20:1-31

COMMENTARY

The Christian Oral Tradition

When we read Christian literature, we need to keep in mind that behind and around that literature, as in the case of the Jewish literature, there existed a great body of oral tradition. Most scholars believe that people told the Christian gospel before they wrote it down. In fact, the very earliest Christians saw little need for writing down the gospel, since they believed the risen Christ would return at any hour to complete the act of judgment on the old creation and to reign over the new. However, as time went by, and the great apocalyptic event that had begun with the resurrection of the Messiah failed to complete itself, the oral tradition concerning Jesus took on codified forms for memorization as stories and sayings that could be transmitted from generation to generation and from place to place.

As Christians moved throughout the Mediterranean world to carry abroad the message of their new faith, they modified and expanded the original account of their gospel to teach and defend it in dialog and debate with the dispersed world of Judaism and with the world of Greco-Roman religion and philosophy.

Codification and Commentary

Many scholars see in the Christian tradition a parallel to that in the Jewish tradition, a similar process of contraction and expansion of the accounts. While Judaism was sifting the Mishnah code from the oral tradition of the torah, the Christians were sifting out basic corresponding elements, called the kerygma, from the many oral accounts of the gospel. Similarly, while the commentaries of the oral tradition were developing among the Jews, Christians were also developing commentaries that would become the larger part of the New Testament.

However, where the Mishnah reflected the Jewish faith that life began with one's obedience to the law given by God, the kerygma reflected the Christian faith that life began with one's belief that Jesus had fulfilled the law by his obedient life, that he gave his life in death for all men, and that the gift of new life comes through the resurrection of Jesus as the Messiah. Where the halakhic Mishnah told men that God requires men to do and not do certain things, the haggadic Mishnah and midrash spelled out the meaning of this required conduct. Where the kerygma told men about the events that formed the essential gospel message (i.e., the ministry, crucifixion, death, and resurrection of Jesus, his ascension, and the gift of the Spirit), most of the New Testament spelled out the meaning of that message to the faithful.

New Testament Literature: Epistles and Gospels

A most important literary form in New Testament literature is the letters Christian leaders wrote to the new Christian communities and to individuals as a means of admonition, teaching, and encouragement. The letters Paul wrote to the Romans, to the Galatians, and to the Corinthians between 50 and 60 A.D. are the earliest examples not only of Christian letters but of Christian literature generally.

Chronologically, according to many Christian scholars, the book of Mark was written about 70 A.D., and the books of Matthew and Luke sometime between 85 and 100 A.D. The epistles of Paul were written significantly earlier than the latter three works, called the Synoptic Gospels. The fourth Gospel, that of John, was probably written even later, possibly between 90 and 110 A.D.

A comparative reading of the Pauline epistles and the four Gospels can show the ways in which the gospel message was expressed during the latter half of the first century A.D., according to the experience and circumstances of the men who compiled and wrote the several books. Yet the purpose of each author remained clear. Each was concerned with what the people to whom he was writing believed about Jesus as the crucified, dead, and risen Messiah, and with the effects of that belief on Christian conduct.

John 20

In the passage you have read, Mary Magdalene, or Mary of Magdala, was a disciple of Jesus from the region of Galilee. Scholars debate as to whether or not the "other disciple" referred to here can be identified as the apostle John. References to Jesus as "the Lord" sometimes carry the meaning merely of "teacher," or "master," and sometimes, especially in the post-resurrection episodes, imply his identity with God.

The empty tomb, and the arrangement of the burial cloths, are presented as indications that Jesus had arisen. The author portrays the "other disciple" as recognizing at once the significance of the grave cloths as evidence of Jesus' resurrection.

The references to the shut doors set the stage for the appearance of the risen Jesus in the midst of the disciples, discernible as a spiritual presence, yet not bound by such things as the opening and closing of doors.

REFLECTION QUESTIONS

1. What common claims are made in this account and in the kerygma you read in Paul's letter to the Corinthians?
2. What possible explanations might the author have had in mind for the fact that Mary and the disciples failed to recognize Jesus when he first appeared to them?
3. What significance do you see in the phrase, "he breathed on them"?
4. What did the words about the forgiveness and retention of sins appear to predict about the subsequent activity of the disciples?
5. What particular purpose might the author of the Gospel of John have had for telling in about 100 A.D. the story of Doubting Thomas?

FURTHER PORTRAYALS
AND TEACHINGS OF JESUS

Part 1:

THE EARLIEST OF THE NEW TESTAMENT GOSPELS PROVIDES A VISTA VIEW OF THE CHRISTIAN EXPERIENCE

Our purpose in reading the whole book of Mark is to appreciate by extensive reading the particular emphases the Christians generally put into their New Testament writing. Mark was written about 70 A.D. by an unknown author, probably a gentile member of the Christian community in Rome. The author's purpose was to portray as convincingly as possible the figure of the resurrected Jesus as the Messiah who was anticipated by the Pharisees and Essenes. The burden of the book is an expansion of the kerygma to include, in its emphasis on both the power and the humiliation of Jesus, the whole scope of his activity.

SEARCH CUES

1. Jesus as the Messiah
2. the need for suffering
3. the Kingdom of God
4. the use of parables
5. origins of Christian rites

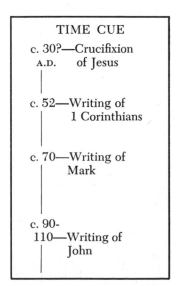

TIME CUE

c. 30?—Crucifixion
A.D.   of Jesus

c. 52—Writing of
          1 Corinthians

c. 70—Writing of
          Mark

c. 90-
110—Writing of
          John

COMMENTARY

The Book of Mark

As with the other Gospels, scholars disagree as to who the author of Mark might have been. Some believe that it was written by one of Peter's disciples. Others think that it is impossible to determine who wrote it. This earliest of the Gospels contains a selection and compilation of materials current in the oral tradition of the Christian community at Rome right after the persecution of the Christians by the emperor Nero. During this persecution, according to tradition, the apostles Peter and Paul had both suffered martyrdom. The author-compiler doubtless was a gentile Christian of the Roman Christian group.

In offering encouragement to his Christian readers, the author's account emphasized the necessity of Jesus' suffering and crucifixion, accenting the paradox of the Christian claim that the bad news of the crucifixion meant at the same time the good news of God's love. The message of the author of Mark was presented neither as a biography nor as a history. Instead, it began as a claim that although the historical Jesus was dead, nevertheless, by a singular act of God, he was reborn as the risen Messiah.

Through both their oral and written testimony, the Christians meant to present the risen Christ to the world as the covenant of God's relationship with men in a new and final form. The new covenant was new because it occurred in the form of a human person who had triumphed in behalf of everyone over the related tragedies of human death and human disobedience to God. The Christians both wrote and taught that in this new life the former torah, God-given and necessary though it had been as a preparation, now itself was transformed.

The Christian Message

We recall that the Hebrew Bible began with a story of creation. The literature of Christianity begins as an announcement of a new creation as radically new as the first. The Christian kerygma described the central, discernible events of that new creation, some of which were discernible to the eyes of ordinary sense experience, others discernible only to the eyes of those who embraced the faith.

While anyone seeing him could discern the historical Jesus, only the Christians discerned in him the Messiah. Anyone could see the activity of the Christian community, but only the members of that community perceived that activity as guided by the spirit of the ascended Messiah. Within the Jewish community, devout Pharisees looked forward to the coming of the Messiah. Christians on the other hand claimed to remember his coming, to enjoy his presence as the ruling spirit of their enterprise, and to anticipate his coming again to complete his universal mission.

The Kingdom of God

Time passed and the ascended Christ did not return to history as a presence discernible to either sight or faith. The first Christian proclamation said that the Messiah had come already. The Pharisees responded by denying the claim, insisting that the Messiah was yet to come. According to some scholars, as time went by, the Christian community soon adopted a third point of view in its literature, which said in effect, "Already, but not yet; not yet, but already." In other words, they spelled out the belief that the Messiah had come already for the first time, but not yet for the second. The kingdom of God as the new creation, cosmic in scope, had not come yet, but already it had come as the new humanity manifest in the Christian community as it was ruled and guided by the Spirit.

The writers of the Gospels reflected this paradoxical belief that the kingdom of God was at the same time a present reality and a coming event. Many scholars think that the author of Mark believes Jesus had announced the messianic kingdom as a present reality, but in such a way that the meaning of the event was hidden. This emphasis is particularly notable in the parables in Mark 4.

Parable of the Kingdom in Mark

Chapter 4 contains three parables with a "seed" motif. The first pointed out various possible reactions to the announcement by Jesus that the kingdom of God had arrived. The second pointed to the mysterious quality of the kingdom's growth. The third dramatized the vast comparison to be made between the kingdom's initial impact and its full manifestation, between the first secret signs of its presence as a reality, and the full meaning of those signs of the kingdom as a coming event.

Mark is consistent in representing the gospel in the form of parables which only those "in the know" can understand. Some scholars contend that this was Mark's way of explaining why the Jews generally refused to accept what to the Christians was an obvious truth.

The short sayings in Mark 4:21-25 seem to imply that the secret Jesus shared with the disciples was meant to bear fruit later in what they told to others, and that they could expect others to learn from them to the extent that they themselves were willing to learn from Jesus. Nevertheless, the growth and progress of the messianic kingdom would remain God's secret and not theirs.

The Tension Between Christians and Jews

In Mark we frequently find evidence of the tension between the Jewish and Christian communities. Just as the Jewish reader of the Bible was forced to seek answers to basic questions in his efforts to live the torah, so the Christian reader of the Bible was troubled by similar questions in his efforts to trust the Christ. The answers others have found nourish the reader of great religious literature as he attempts to adopt or produce his own answers to universal questions.

In Jerusalem, the paschal lambs were killed and offered in the temple during the afternoon prior to the evening Passover meal, when they were eaten between sundown and morning. The seven-day Feast of Unleavened Bread began at that same sundown. We can better understand Mark's association of the Last Supper with the Feast of the Passover in chapter 14 by reviewing our reading from *Mishnah Pesahim*. According to scholars the little story of the anointing at Bethany portrays Mark's view that Jesus lived with a premonition of his death that was not shared by his disciples. *Nard* was an expensive brand of those ointments sometimes used to refresh guests after a journey, and sometimes to anoint the corpses of the dead before burial. The woman used it in the former sense. Jesus took the opportunity to interpret it in the latter sense.

In verse 13 of chapter 14, a man, rather than a woman, carrying a water jar would be an unusual sight, employable as a signal. The titles *Teacher* and *Rabbi*, both used by Mark in reference Jesus, mean the same thing. The householder, or "goodman of the house," would be the head of the household. Custom in Jerusalem required that local residents offer hospitality to visitors to enable them to keep the Feast of the Passover.

Mark 14:20 refers to the dish of *charoseth*, the mixture of vinegar, raisins, and dates in which the bread and bitter herbs were dipped during the Passover meal. The verbs *took, blessed,* and *gave* reflect the basic action of the Christian communion meal. The reference to the "blood of the covenant" may refer not only to the original Passover, but also to the blood of the covenant described in Exodus 24:3-8. Note that the blood thrown against the altar, plus the blood thrown on the people, serves symbolically to unite God and the people in one blood (life). The hymn referred to in Mark 14:26 may be one or more of the Hallel psalms mentioned in *Mishnah Pesahim*. The quotation in verse 27 is from Zechariah 13:7. Here, as elsewhere in Christian literature, we find the assumption that significant events in the Christian tradition are prefigured in the Hebrew Bible.

The procedures portrayed in Mark 14:53-65 do not follow the rules of the Mishnah with regard to trials, especially that requiring the agreement of testimony given by separated witnesses. (For interest, read *Susanna and the Elders*, one of the books of the Apocrypha. It is a classic story concerning agreement of testimony in a judgment.) The mood of this account again reflects the hostility between Christians and Jews.

In chapter 15 Barabbas may have been a popular leader with Zealot tendencies. The crowd may have been there not primarily to watch the trial of Jesus before the procurator, Pontius Pilate, but to plead with Pilate for the release of Barabbas. At the time of Jesus, and until the time of Emperor Constantine I (c. 300 A.D.), crucifixion was a Roman form of execution ordinarily used for slaves or political insurgents, regarded as beneath the dignities of ordinary citizenship.

Mark quotes, "My God, my God, why hast thou forsaken me?" as the last words of Jesus on the cross. These compare with those quoted by Luke, "Father, into thy hands I commit my spirit!" and with those quoted by John, "It is finished." Matthew uses the same words as does Mark. These words are the opening verse and title of Psalm 22. Some scholars regard these words in isolation, and see in them an expression of despair. Others see them as a reference to the whole psalm, and therefore regard them as a shout of confidence and triumph.

The inner curtain of the temple stood between the people and the Holy of Holies, that is, the forbidden place of the overpowering presence of the living God. Mark may have implied that the crucifixion-resurrection of Jesus dramatically destroyed the separation between man and God, and that, indeed, the body of the Messiah himself turned out to be the place of the divine presence. Others see in the rending of the curtain a prediction of the fall of the Temple in 70 A.D.

REFLECTION QUESTIONS

1. The Gospel of Mark at times "quotes Scripture." Find two such instances and read both the New Testament and Old Testament forms of the quotations. Are they similar? Are they different? What point is being made in the Old Testament version? What point is being made in the New Testament version?

2. What evidence can you find in Mark that the author was writing to encourage a Christian group living in fear of persecution?

3. What does the phrase "Kingdom of God" refer to in Mark? How did he imply that it was present, but hidden?

4. Find two parables in Mark that are also allegories.

5. In the book of Mark, find passages that you believe fit our definitions of the following: prophecy, wisdom, apocalyptics, didactics.

6. See if you can observe how a concern for the identity of one's own community occurs both in Mekhilta Bahodesh 5 and in the attitude portrayed in the parables of the Kingdom in Mark 4.

7. Where would you turn in a modern newspaper to find writing similar to prophecy? To wisdom?

8. In what kinds of organizations and gatherings today would you expect to find attitudes like those of the writers of apocalyptic literature? Of didactic literature?

Part 2:

AN EVANGELIST RECOUNTS THREE PARABLES OF JESUS SHOWING GOD'S ATTITUDE TOWARD SINNERS

In the 15th chapter of the book of Luke we find three parables reflecting the theme of "the lost." They demonstrate a somewhat different attitude and purpose from the three "seed" parables we have read in the fourth chapter of Mark. Although many scholars believe that the writer remains anonymous, tradition ascribes authorship of the book to a physician named Luke, who was a Gentile and a fellow worker with Paul. Opinions vary as to where Luke might have been written. The best possibilities appear to be Greece, Rome, or Antioch. According to many scholars, the book was written between 85 and 100 A.D. and was directed toward a Gentile community.

SEARCH CUES

1. the repenting sinner
2. the celebration upon recovery
3. God's attitude toward the righteous

NOW READ: LUKE 15:1-32

COMMENTARY

Luke-Acts

The books of Luke and Acts are in reality two volumes of the same work. The author concerns himself in the two volumes with the beginnings of the Christian community. He does this first through telling the story of the life and death of Jesus, and then by relating the early development and expansion of the Christian movement up to the end of Paul's work.

One of the primary reasons the author wrote Luke-Acts may have been to show that the Christian movement was religious rather than political. The Roman Empire was suspicious of newly developing sects, fearing political uprisings. Christians already had suffered persecution from Rome. The writer, in telling the story of the movement's development, may have sought to allay the fears of Rome that the Christans were a subversive group. Rather, he portrayed Christianity as a world religion, possessing the spirit of the New Israel, whose membership was comprised of Jews and Gentiles alike.

Luke's Parables

The three parables in Luke 15 illustrate the claims of Jesus concerning God's love and initiative toward those who, having broken his covenant, now looked toward God for reconciliation. God's loving initiative is understood here as uniquely apparent in the Christian gospel. These three parables are in fact parables and not allegories. The point they make is simple and clear, not veiled and subtle as in the parables you read in Mark 4.

REFLECTION QUESTIONS

1. How would you compare the emotional attitude expressed in these Lukan "lost" parables with that expressed in the three "seed" parables of Mark?
2. In comparing these three parables with the three parables in Mark 4, which, the Markan or the Lukan, do you think are told more dramatically? Why?
3. What special evidence do you find in the lost son story to indicate not only the hunger but also the humiliation of the son?
4. How would the Christians have explained the causes of the prodigal son's humiliation as compared with the causes of the humiliation of Jesus?
5. Briefly outline a *Christian* sermon you might write based on the prodigal son parable, then briefly outline a *Jewish* sermon you might write on the same parable if it appeared in the Talmud instead of the New Testament.

Part 3:

THE GOSPEL ACCORDING TO MATTHEW PROVIDES A NARRATIVE OF THE BIRTH OF JESUS

Only the books of Matthew and Luke contain stories describing the birth of Jesus and its circumstances. The birth narratives present the Christian community's account of how the messiah of their faith had been born as a Jewish child into ordinary human circumstances.

SEARCH CUES

1. the meaning of Mary's pregnancy
2. Herod's plot
3. the flight into Egypt and the return

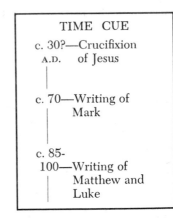

TIME CUE
c. 30?—Crucifixion A.D. of Jesus
c. 70—Writing of Mark
c. 85-100—Writing of Matthew and Luke

NOW READ: MATTHEW 1:18-2:23

COMMENTARY

Matthew's Orientation

Matthew more than any other writer of the Gospels was concerned with relating the beliefs of the Christian community to the principles of Judaism. One of his ways was to demonstrate, through his selection of stories, that the life of Jesus was the fulfillment of the Old Testament

214

prophecies. This is evident in the passage you have read in Matthew 1 and 2.

The Birth Narrative

In Matthew 1:18, "before they came together" is based on the Jewish custom that the betrothed couple enjoyed a very close relationship, but were not considered married until they began living together in one residence. The wise men referred to in the second chapter of Matthew were the magi, Zoroastrian priests and seers from the regions of Persia. They often regarded stars as heavenly angels identified with important human persons, as "guiding stars" or "guardian angels." The gifts from the magi are gifts appropriate to royalty. Later Christian interpretation gave each particular gift a special significance. The reference to "two years old or under" in Matthew 2:16 would seem to indicate that the visit of the magi took place months after Jesus' birth.

REFLECTION QUESTIONS

1. What appears to be the writer's understanding of the phrase, "child of the Holy Spirit"?
2. Look up the following Old Testament verses quoted in this birth narrative: Isaiah 7:14, Micah 5:2, Hosea 11:1, and Jeremiah 31:15. What seems to be the general purpose of references such as these, that occur with great frequency both in the New Testament and in the Talmud?
3. What events in this birth narrative might remind you of the story of Moses and the Exodus? What events might remind you of the story of the exile?

Part 4:

THE SERMON ON THE MOUNT GATHERS TOGETHER THE TEACHINGS OF JESUS

INTRODUCTION

The Sermon on the Mount in the book of Matthew presents the teachings of Jesus as proclamations and arguments regarding the kingdom of God and his listeners' relation to it. The style is rabbinic throughout, replete with didactics, parables, legal arguments, and wisdom sayings. Its sermonic structure incorporates an introduction, body, and conclusion.

SEARCH CUES

1. descriptions of the blessed (Beatitudes)
2. the importance of the torah
3. a choice of masters
4. one who had authority

NOW READ: MATTHEW 4:23-7:29

COMMENTARY

Jesus' Teachings in Matthew

In his efforts to show the relationship of Christianity to Judaism, the author of Matthew not only portrayed the ways in which Jesus had fulfilled the Scriptures, but also included more of the ethical teachings of Jesus related to the torah than did the other Gospel writers. He presented Jesus as the rabbi Christians would know as the Messiah, the Lord of the new age. As we have seen, that new age would be a reign of God acknowledged by the whole world. It would fulfill the long dramatic history of God's covenant with Israel.

The Coming of the Kingdom

The account of Jesus' teaching you have read in this part expressed a Christian understanding of the way Jesus himself interpreted the coming of the kingdom of God. The way Jesus reasoned and argued was basically the rabbinical method of teaching characteristic of his day. Nevertheless, the claims he made about the coming of the messianic kingdom of God differed radically from the doctrine of the rabbis among whom the development of the Mishnah was well under way.

The Sermon on the Mount

Some scholars think that the Sermon on the Mount is a collection and arrangement of sayings and parables by Jesus as they existed in the growing oral and written tradition of the Christians during the last two decades of the first century A.D.

To locate such a sermon "on the mountain" is to present it as a message of great significance. The Beatitudes at the beginning describe the kinds of people whom God has destined to enjoy the unmatched happiness of the kingdom. The sermon describes the style of life required of those who would live in the kingdom. One can no more summarize the teaching of Jesus in the so-called "Golden Rule" (Matthew 7:12) than can one summarize the teaching of Hillel the Elder in the same saying, written down some two generations earlier.

The Sermon on the Mount does not substitute some simple "law of love" for the torah, but it requires of those who would live the life of the messianic kingdom of God a perfection, or fulfillment, of the torah's purposes. To the need for a right behavior Jesus adds the necessity of a right attitude. To live the life of the kingdom, one certainly must act out the righteous ways of the torah fully and completely, as hopeful acts of obedience to God by one who longs to reach the kingdom.

REFLECTION QUESTIONS

1. If the Sermon on the Mount does have an introduction, body, and conclusion, at what verse would you say the body begins, and at what verse would you say the conclusion begins? What are the first and last verses of the sermon?
2. If the word "blessed" means about the same as "happy," what do you think that Jesus meant by applying the word "blessed" to "the poor in spirit," "the meek," "those who hunger and thirst for righteousness," "those who are persecuted"?
3. How might Matthew 5:17-20 be interpreted to agree with the general claim of the Christian gospel? To disagree with it?
4. What interpretation did Jesus give to the principle of moral retribution? How did the saying, "An eye for an eye and a tooth for a tooth" constitute a call for justice in life as over against surrender to unbridled vengeance?
5. From whom might Jesus have heard the Golden Rule?

Part 5:

THE BOOK OF JOHN BEGINS BY PORTRAYING AN ETERNAL CHRIST

The prolog to the book of John makes the Christian experience of the meaning of Jesus a universal message. Its style reminds us more of the creation story, or of the poetic wisdom literature, than of the more concrete birth narratives in the books of Matthew and Luke.

SEARCH CUES

1. the word
2. the agent of God's creation
3. the motifs of light and truth
4. the function of grace

NOW READ: JOHN 1:1-18

COMMENTARY

The Eternal Christ in the Prolog to John

Christians understood Jesus not only as the messianic agent of God in history, but also as the agent of God acting at the very beginning of God's creation and at the final end of God's fulfillment of that creation. Christians identified Jesus with the person of God. For the Christians, to speak of the presence of Jesus, or of the presence of Christ, or of the presence of the Spirit, was the same as to speak of the presence of God.

With this concept of the eternal Christ went the concept of incarnation. To be incarnate meant to be "in the flesh," or more specifically, to be a spirit taking the form of a mortal human being, experiencing the birth, death, and experiences that characterize all human existence. In the prolog to the book of John we find a portrayal of the eternal Christ, who becomes incarnate as the first and decisive step in God's final act to reconcile men with himself.

John, borrowing a term from his Stoic neighbors, describes the preexistent Christ as the Word (Logos) of God. The idea is that just as a man's word is inseparable from himself, so also is the Christ inseparable from the Creator.

Taking up the ongoing argument with Judaism, the author of John says that this new creation has not come through the torah. Rather, it has come as the eternal Christ incarnate, that is, as the person of God who has made himself present to the world as the human personality whom men have called Jesus.

The Book of John

The content of the book of John is quite different from that of the Synoptic Gospels. Some scholars think the author of the fourth Gospel was a Jewish Christian who had been influenced by hellenistic philosophy and religious thought. While his book describes events in the life of Jesus, he appears to have been much less concerned with recording the parables and sayings of Jesus than with reinterpreting the meaning of Jesus' life and ministry as a whole, in the light of his belief in Jesus as the eternal Christ who had become incarnate.

Scholars think that the author of John drew much of his material from a different stream of tradition in the early church than the one used in the Synoptic Gospels. They also believe John was written later than the other Gospels, probably between 90 and 110 A.D. Whether or not the author was familiar with the earlier works, he does not appear to have incorporated much of their content in his writings.

REFLECTION QUESTIONS

1. How does the first paragraph of the prolog to John's Gospel appear to modify the first paragraph of the book of Genesis with respect to God and creation?
2. How does this passage express the humiliation theme found in the Christian gospel?
3. What influence from Greek philosophy seems to appear in John's prolog? What parallel influence can you find in the Jewish apocryphal writings you have read?
4. John's prolog uses the term *light* in a different sense, apparently, than does the first chapter of Genesis. What is that difference?

Part 6:

A CHRISTIAN AUTHOR DESCRIBES HIS VISION OF THE CITY OF GOD'S NEW CREATION

The vision of the New Jerusalem in the passage we are reading from the Revelation to John is a dramatic example of apocalyptic literature written from a Christian perspective. It was written, according to tradition, by an author named John during the last decade of the first century A.D. He wrote for the benefit of Christians under persecution by the Roman Empire in Asia Minor.

SEARCH CUES
1. the descent of the new Jerusalem
2. the fate of the wicked
3. the wife of the Lamb
4. the four-square city
5. the tree of life
6. they shall see his face

NOW READ: REVELATION 21:1-22:5

COMMENTARY

The Revelation to John

In true apocalyptic fashion, the author of Revelation looks forward to the Last Day, and does so as a means of encouraging his fellow believers in his own day who suffer under persecution. The book contains such themes as the endurance of the faithful under oppressive circumstances;

the vision of the eternal Christ; the presence of God in this evil world; the Roman Empire (referred to as Babylon) as the prime manifestation of evil; the coming millennium, or thousand years of messianic rule; and, finally, the ultimate judgment and fulfillment of all things in the New Jerusalem.

The passage you have read portrays the New Jerusalem as the endless circumstance in which all things are fulfilled in joy and bliss for the faithful. This new creation is God's reward to the saints (martyrs) for the humiliation and pain they have suffered from the evil powers that have oppressed them before the day of judgment.

REFLECTION QUESTIONS

1. According to Revelation, do the faithful go to their reward, or does their reward come to them?
2. The most holy part of the temple in Jerusalem was cubical in shape. What connection do you see between this and the shape of the New Jerusalem in the vision?
3. Compare the symbolic relationship between this author's reference to the tree of life and the references to it in Genesis 2, verses 8-9 and 22-23.
4. What significant similarities and differences do you see between this passage and the passage you read in the book of Daniel?
5. Which do you think are more credible, the visions of the apocalyptic writers or the modern visions you read describing urban renewal and the cities of the future? Why?

THE GROWTH
OF THE CHRISTIAN
COMMUNITY

TONGUES LIKE FIRE AND A SOUND LIKE RUSHING WIND SIGNIFY THE COMING OF THE SPIRIT

Through the fourth quarter of the first century A.D. the Christian community continued as a movement, gaining converts in great numbers throughout the Mediterranean world. But it also was adjusting to the prospect that its initial expectation of an early return of the risen Christ was not to be fulfilled, at least in the manner Christians had first anticipated. The movement that began with a universal proclamation increasingly was becoming stabilized as an institution with its own particular tradition.

Part of that tradition was the story in the Acts of the Apostles that described how the Holy Spirit, by this time identified both with the God of torah and with the Christ, had entered into the community of the first disciples, or apostles. From this story the Christians learned that from their earliest days they had been inspired as a movement, established as an institution, and provided with an authoritative leadership.

SEARCH CUES

1. wind and fire
2. speaking in tongues
3. repentance and baptism

NOW READ: ACTS OF THE APOSTLES 2:1-47

COMMENTARY

The Situation of the Early Church

Christian literature during the latter two-thirds of the first century A.D. increasingly reflected an understanding that the Christian church was living an extended "in the meantime," between the Messiah's first coming as Jesus of Nazareth and his second coming to complete the final judgment of mankind. The second coming would mark the establishment of the kingdom of God in its final form.

The Christians understood their role in this historical "in the meantime" to be that of an agency, or missionary movement, proclaiming the gospel to all humanity. All men should have an opportunity to join the New Israel, which was enjoying the life of the Kingdom even now, "in the meantime." Thus the Christians understood themselves to be a kind of beachhead of the future kingdom of God, living already in the midst of the old creation, and working there diligently to persuade as many people as they could to believe the good news and to join the beachhead community that took its guidance and derived its vitality from the spiritual presence of its risen Lord. The second chapter of the book of Acts gives us an account of the dramatic experience by which the earliest Christians realized themselves to be inspired by the Spirit to take up their mission as the Christian church.

The Book of Acts

As we have noted earlier, the whole book of Acts is a continuation of the Gospel of Luke. We know more about the history of the early Christian church from Acts than from any other source. Nevertheless, the book of Acts, like the Gospels, intentionally presents an account of the faith-experience of the primitive church rather than an account of its history. As we see vividly in the second chapter, the book of Acts emphasizes the Christian understanding of the spirit of God as the Holy Spirit of the church. It also dramatizes the growing Christian understanding that their gospel was meant not only for those Jews who would accept it, but also and equally for the Gentile world beyond the compass of the torah. In this, the book of Acts parallels the general position of the apostle Paul. In fact, Paul and his missionary journeys are the subject of the second half of the book.

Some Details of Acts 2

Pentecost (fiftieth day) was a designation given by Greek-speaking Jews to the Feast of Weeks that took place at the end of the seven-week harvest season. Later Christian tradition reassigned the term to refer to the fiftieth day after Easter. In verse 27, Hades indicated in Greek the underworld place that was the melancholy abode of the dead. The reference to David in this passage implies the priority of the kingship of Jesus as the Messiah over the Davidic kingship which it superseded and fulfilled, according to the Christian gospel.

REFLECTION QUESTIONS

1. What do you think the passage that told about "speaking in other tongues" meant to the Christian who read it?
2. Compare this account of how the risen Jesus inspired the Christian church with the account in John 20. Since in both instances the account

was written to convince the reader, which of the two would you say was the more credible? Why?

3. Would *The Acts of the Holy Spirit* be a better title for this book than *The Acts of the Apostles,* if this chapter is typical? Why?

4. What significance do you suppose the Christian reader inferred from the account of shared possessions?

5. Do you see any similarities between the general attitudes and conduct of the converts described in Acts 2, and the general attitudes and conduct of youth groups today? Any differences?

Part 2:

PAUL THE APOSTLE DEVELOPS A BASIC CHRISTIAN INTERPRETATION OF GOD'S COVENANT

Paul, in writing to the Roman Christians, was speaking to Gentiles rather than to Jews. He was proclaiming and defending what he understood to be an act of God that applied equally and universally to Jews and non-Jews. Central to his argument was the assertion that to be trusted and cared for by God was a reality not to be received as if it were earned, but to be accepted as given. His argument was complicated and paradoxical. Neither those who accepted it nor those who rejected it found it easy to explain. Nevertheless, it remained at the heart of Christian teaching.

SEARCH CUES
1. the knowledge the torah gives
2. the gift of grace
3. the meaning of baptism
4. sin and death vs. faith and life
5. two kinds of slavery

NOW READ: ROMANS 3:1-6:23

COMMENTARY

Paul's Letter to the Romans

Paul wrote his letter to the Christians at Rome sometime between 53 and 58 A.D. He probably wrote the letter from Corinth. Paul had not yet visited the Roman Christian community at that time, so the letter served to introduce both himself and his gospel message. The letter contains Paul's most extensive account of the central aspects of his thought.

Some Features of the Letter

In the selection you have read, Paul makes a number of major points. He notes that all people have sinned, Jews and Gentiles alike. That is, they have not taken part in an obedient relationship to God. Paul expresses the belief that all men share the responsibility and guilt for Adam's sin before God at the very beginning of time. However, God has redeemed men from sin, has removed their guilt, and has justified them in spite of their sins—all by God's freely given action which he performed in Jesus. Therefore, since God has acted to restore the right relationship between himself and man, man in response will do the will of God. He will do it not out of obligation to the law, but rather because he could live no other way, since God has removed the barrier of sin and guilt through his justifying act performed in Jesus.

In the passage, Paul offers an explanation of his view that God looks with favor on men not primarily because of their behavior in obedience to the torah but rather by virtue of their faith in God. This faith may be the faith of a Hebrew prior to the giving of the torah, or it may be the faith of one who keeps the torah, or it may be the faith lodged by a Gentile in Jesus, the Messiah. Paul uses the example of Abraham. If we read Genesis 17:1-14, we can better understand the gist of Paul's argument. The statement, "For the law brings wrath . . ." makes a subtle but important point in Paul's reasoning, accenting the central issue of gospel vs. torah in Paul's argument with his fellow Jews. In thinking about this reading, you will want to consider thoroughly the meaning Paul gives to these terms: sin, grace, faith, redemption, expiation, justification, salvation, righteousness.

REFLECTION QUESTIONS

1. If you were to say to Paul, "A man gets from God what he deserves," what do you think his response would be?

2. Look up the word *paradox* in the dictionary. What ideas in this passage might be considered paradoxical?

3. Paul seemed to understand faith as an attitude on the part of a human being, and grace as an attitude on the part of God. Also he said both that a man is justified by grace and that he is justified by faith. Which— the faith or the grace—do you think Paul would say actually makes *real* the justification?

4. If you were to ask Paul, "What is freedom?" what do you think his answer might be? How might his answer differ from an answer Judah ha-Nasi might give?

Part 3:

A LATER CHRISTIAN TEACHER PROVIDES A CONTRAST TO PAUL'S VIEWS ON FAITH

The initial expectation of the Christian community shortly after its experience of the resurrection was that the risen Christ would return very soon—any day or hour—to reign over the new creation. The old history of sin and death, already superseded in principle, no longer would pertain to the faithful. For those already justified by faith, righteous conduct would be their freely chosen way of life. But the risen Christ did not return as expected. Sin and history did not end. The faithful continued, apparently, to be involved in both.

In these circumstances, the author of James raised again for Christians the apocalyptic threat of judgment. He called on them to behave in a manner consistent with love as a summary of God's law. They should do this not only to demonstrate their faith that their Lord would come, but also in recognition that they still remained liable to judgment under the torah.

SEARCH CUES

1. partiality to the rich
2. the royal law (Leviticus 19:15-18; Matthew 5:39)
3. faith apart from works

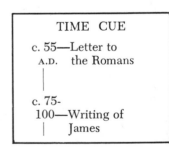

TIME CUE

c. 55—Letter to
A.D.   the Romans

c. 75-
100—Writing of
James

NOW READ: JAMES 2:1-26

COMMENTARY

The Letter of James

The content of James reflects the outlook more of a Jewish Christian than of a Gentile Christian. Support for the author's arguments is drawn not from the teachings of Jesus but from the Old Testament, and even Jesus himself is seldom mentioned in the epistle.

The author, besides having an intimate knowledge of Judaism, had an excellent command of Hellenistic literary style. For example, in the passage you have read, the author employs a Hellenistic literary form called the *diatribe*. This means that he wrote as if he were debating orally with an opponent. He expressed the opponent's point of view and then responded with this own argument. If you check back to the selection from the letter to the Romans, you can see that Paul also used this literary device in his writings.

James and Paul

On first reading the second chapter of James, you might think that the author was directly refuting the assertions that Paul made in the passage you read from his letter to the Romans. However, if you look more closely at the letter of James, you can see that, first, the author of James gave a different meaning to the word *faith* from the meaning Paul gave the word. Second, you will find that in reality, both Paul and the author of James were arguing against the same position, rather than against each other. As you read, think about the similarities and differences in these two arguments.

REFLECTION QUESTIONS

1. Read James 2:1-9 and then Leviticus 19:15. When the author discusses "partiality" in James 2, is his attitude consistent with the law as he himself describes the law? Explain the reason.
2. Does the law of neighbor love appear to be easier to obey than other directives of torah, or more difficult? Why?
3. Comparing the author of Romans 3:1-6:23 with the author of James 2:1-26, which of the two seems more preoccupied with mental attitude and which with social behavior as the key to being in the right relationship with God?

Part 4:

PAUL DESCRIBES THE CHURCH AS A COMMUNITY INSPIRED BY THE SPIRIT AND PRAISES THE REALITIES OF FAITH, HOPE, AND LOVE

Just prior to the passage we are about to read Paul had briefly described the Christian reenactment of the Lord's Supper. This common meal was the central act of worship by which the church continued in its identification with the risen Christ, who was understood as presiding at this humble but heavenly banquet. Simultaneously, the Christian communion meal also celebrated the sense of unity among the members, whatever their social backgrounds might be.

It was largely out of concern for maintaining and enhancing the solidarity of the Christian church as a community that Paul, in chapters 12 and 13, interpreted the variety of talents that might mark the membership. With that same interest in group solidarity, he dramatized the qualities of faith, hope, and love.

SEARCH CUES

1. gifts from the Spirit
2. the effect of baptism
3. the interdependence of the parts

NOW READ: 1 CORINTHIANS 12:1-13:13

COMMENTARY

Paul's Description of the Christian Community

The Christian community was a voluntary community. Nobody had to be a Christian if he didn't want to. One could not be born a Christian, except in a spiritual sense, and then only as he was moved by the Spirit to become one. The fact that the Christian movement was open to individuals from all families or nations meant that the early Christian had no sense of nationality at the center of his faith. Being the beachhead of the new creation, and itself a creature only of the Spirit, the Christian church could lay no claim to being an historical nation. On the contrary, the very newness of the new Israel consisted in the understanding that it was not a nation like the old Israel, or like Persia, or Greece. Therefore, the social solidarity of the Christians had to be recognized not in a sense of nation, but in a sense of community. In modern terms, the Christian church as a social institution was a voluntary organization.

In this second reading from 1 Corinthians, Paul likened the various members of the Christian church to the members of a human body. Paul's ideas here were similar to those of the Stoics, who understood nature and society to be a single organic whole, knit together by a common indwelling spirit. His ideas were also like those of Plato, who argued in the *Republic* that the ideal body politic behaves corporately as though it were a single individual. Paul saw, then, the Christian church as a new society in which all the members were mutually responsible and mutually interdependent. The one spirit of the risen Christ related equally to them all. Each of them lived in this new creation, sharing with all his fellows a common dependence on the love and guidance of their one ruling Lord.

You should observe that what Paul was teaching the Corinthians differed from both the Stoic and the Platonic philosophies in that Paul saw the Christian church as a body of people reunited and reconciled as a new creation serving in the old creation as the body of Christ. Paul considered apostles, prophets, and teachers as leaders of the church. Nevertheless, these and any other gifts of the Spirit became as nothing if they did not participate in love, which to him was the supreme principle of integrity in the new creation. The 13th chapter of 1 Corinthians spells out his description of that love.

REFLECTION QUESTIONS

1. Does it appear that the Christians shared any group characteristic holding them together which was directly comparable to the tribal kinship of the Jews or the state citizenship of the Romans?

2. Faced with the problem of maintaining community organization and discipline, what advantages and disadvantages did the Christians have in comparision with the Jews or Romans?

3. How were the Roman, Jewish, and Christian communities organized about 100 A.D.? Consider in each case: (a) its supreme reason for existing, (b) its normal requirements for membership, (c) its organization of leadership, (d) its authorized methods of dealing with disobedient members, and (e) its usual methods of dealing with its enemies.

4. How would you compare the communities in question three, using the same considerations, with the following communities today: (a) Israel,

(b) Spain, (c) the United States, (d) the Christians in the United States, and (e) the Jews in the United States?

5. Almost everybody today would share Paul's good opinion of love, and would agree that you should love your parents, brothers and sisters, sweethearts, teachers, and the poor. You also should love beauty, truth, goodness, nature, your country, God, and maybe even your enemy and yourself. Is such an apparently universal reality as love easy to identify in yourself? In other people? Why?

Part 5:

A WRITER COMBINES THE THEMES OF PRIESTHOOD, FAITH, AND THE HEAVENLY CITY TO COME

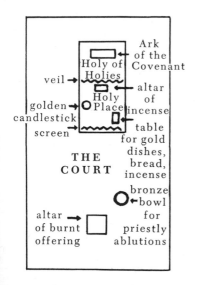

By the latter part of the first century A.D., the new blend of ideas we have identified with the religious literature of the two first centuries was taking sophisticated form in the writings of such Jews as Philo, a contemporary of Jesus, and such Christians as the author of the Letter to the Hebrews. To understand the author's mind and purpose in writing the Letter to the Hebrews, the following "directions" may help.

(1) Examine carefully this drawing of the tabernacle sanctuary. (2) Review again the basic dualistic concept of Plato's idealism, that our present world is only a shadow of the real one. (3) Recall the basic Old and New Testament notion that faith is active trust in the purposive activity of God. (4) Recollect the apocalyptic expectation, stressed among the Christians, of a final judgment on history and the creation of a new existence. (5) Picture again the ancient figure of Moses, acting as a priest, realizing the covenant between God and Israel. He did this by sprinkling the blood of the sacrificial victim first on the altar of God and then on the people, thus symbolizing their life of obedient unity with their Lord.

235

SEARCH CUES

1. the Holy Place and the Holy of Holies
2. the blood of the new covenant
3. once for all at the end of the age
4. a single offering
5. what faith is

NOW READ: HEBREWS 9:1-12:2

COMMENTARY

Date and Authorship

Scholars think that the letter to the Hebrews was written between 90 and 95 A.D. The vague title, "to the Hebrews," gives us little help in discovering to whom it was addressed. From the content of the epistle it seems likely that it was written to a Roman Christian community. Early Christian tradition ascribed authorship of the letter to Paul. However, most interpreters today think the style and thought are not Pauline, and the author remains unknown.

The Sacrificial Priesthood

The author presupposes several factors as he develops his thought. First, he assumes that direct access to God can come only through worship. Specifically, this access comes through the sacrificial aspect of worship performed by the high priest. With this assumption, the author carefully constructs a comparison between the sacrificial priesthood performed under the old covenant, using the temple worship as a model, and the sacrificial priesthood of Jesus.

Second, the author presupposes a two-dimensional world, somewhat akin to Plato's idealistic philosophy. That is, he sees the present world as only a shadow or an imperfect copy of the perfect heavenly real world. Even as the shadow world differs from the real world, so the world of the present differs from the world of the time to come. The author thus looks at the two worlds *eschatologically*.

With these assumptions in mind, we can see how the author has developed his thesis. He views Jesus both as the perfect and necessary priest and as the perfect and necessary sacrifice, who provides the faithful with direct access to God and forgiveness of sins.

REFLECTION QUESTIONS

1. Without pressing for detailed comparisons, what did the author of Hebrews say that Christ acting as high priest had done that no other high priest could do?

2. Explain how the high priest passage asserts the superiority of actual self-sacrifice as a priestly way to bring one's people into the presence of God. Do you think the author was opposed to priesthood generally?

3. Would you agree or not that the author of Hebrews expressed a forward-looking and optimistic point of view? Why?

4. The first verse of chapter 11 of Hebrews is the only outright definition of faith in the New Testament, that is, "the assurance of things hoped for, the conviction of things not seen." With this definition in mind, answer these questions:

   (a) How does a young man know for sure that his girl loves him?

   (b) How do you know for sure that you are forgiven when someone says, "I forgive you"?

   (c) How would the definition apply to martyrs facing the lions in the Colosseum?

   (d) In what sense is faith always an investment of trust in the unknown?

5. What seems to have been the situation of the people for whom the author wrote the Epistle to the Hebrews, and what do you think the author hoped to accomplish for them by writing it?

6. List several human communities that you know about. Would you say in each case that some commonly held faith in a reality that transcends the group is largely what holds the group together? Why?

THE QUR'AN

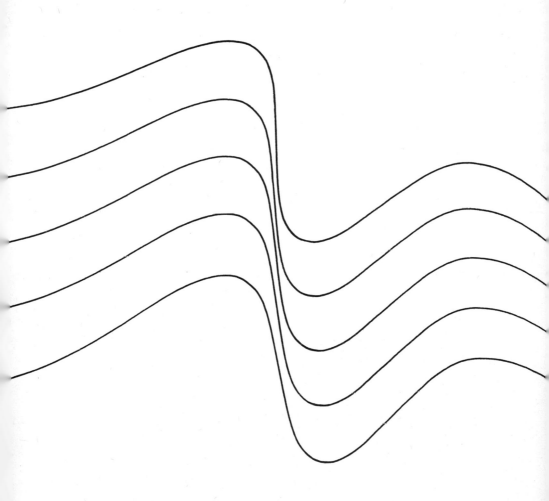

A BRIEF INTRODUCTION TO MUHAMMAD AND HIS WORLD

THE INTERVENING CENTURIES

In 570 A.D., in the Arabian city of Mecca, a child was born whose name was to be Muhammad. Just five hundred years had passed since the Romans had destroyed Jerusalem and the Temple. During that time, Jews and Christians, as refugees or missionaries, had moved out from Palestine along the travelways that stretched to the west, to the east, and southward into Arabia. The Christian movement had gone on to become an international religion, distinct from Judaism. It was zealously aggressive; by the year 325 A.D., it had been endorsed and adopted by the Roman Empire itself in the person of the Emperor Constantine. He saw in it a means of cohesion for the great Pax Romana, which by then was very strained, held together almost entirely by military strength. Both Jews and Christians had found their way during those intervening centuries into Arabia, and to the trading town in the Hijaz where Muhammad was born, far south of the Empire's control.

MUHAMMAD GROWS UP IN ARABIA

Muhammad's father, Abdullah, died a short time before the child's birth. Therefore, the child came under the protection of Abdul Muttalib, his paternal grandfather. According to custom, the boy spent his first three or four years living with nomad foster parents in the desert. Wellborn children of Meccan society grew from infancy to childhood nursed and weaned by desert women like Haleema, Muhammad's foster mother.

Both Muhammad's mother and his sponsoring grandfather died shortly after he was returned to Mecca. Thereupon his uncle, Abu Talib, became responsible for his care. Apparently Muhammad enjoyed affectionate treatment from all the elders with whom he lived as a child. According to tradition, he grew to young manhood with a reputation for generosity, industry, honesty, and confidence. When he was in his mid-twenties, he married the twice widowed Khadeeja, by whom he had previously been employed to conduct her business in the caravan trade. She was fifteen years his senior. The marriage continued with a high degree of mutual love and understanding.

ARABIA IN THE SIXTH CENTURY A.D.

In those days Mecca was not only a leading town on the overland trade route between Palestine and the Yemen, but also the chief religious shrine of the pagan Arabs. The Christian Byzantine Empire held sway over the eastern Mediterranean, while Persia, its opposing oriental counterpart, exercised dominion to the east across the Fertile Crescent. These two great powers were locked in a lingering war of attrition. South from the Fertile Crescent lay Arabia, a vast sandy region supporting a sparse population. To neither of the two great powers did Arabia represent booty worth a major effort. Nevertheless, both Byzantium and Persia had developed spheres of influence in the eastern and western areas of northern Arabia. The Arabs considered their country, Arabia, to be a great peninsula, encompassed by the headwaters of the Tigris and Euphrates on the north, the Red Sea on the west, the Indian Ocean on the south, and the Persian Gulf and Persian mountains on the east.

ARABIAN JEWS AND CHRISTIANS

Within Arabia one could find in those days settlements of both Jewish and Christian tribes. They had wandered there long centuries ago. Some of the Jewish tribes may have been there before the Babylonian exile. Both the Jews and the Christians in Arabia lived far from the Palestinian headwaters of their respective faiths and from the ongoing mainstreams of their history in the cities to the north and westward around the Mediterranean.

The religious ideas of the Christians in Arabia varied considerably from those of the Byzantine Church with its hellenized culture, centered in Constantinople on the Bosporus, where Europe and Asia meet. Quarreling with each other, the Arabian Christians nevertheless shared with one another and with the Arabian Jews a common fear and hostility toward the Byzantine giant to the north, which had from time to time rejected and oppressed these peoples. Within Arabia, the Jewish communities and tribes apparently were more solidly united religiously and more prosperous economically than were the Arabian Christians.

TRIBAL LIFE

The majority of Arabs before the days of Islam were Semitic nomads related to the ancient Hebrews. Apparently their religion took a variety of forms, but in general it was animistic. It identified gods and spirits under the forms of natural phenomena, from the sun, moon, and stars to more mundane objects like trees and rocks. These Arabs lived outside the settled towns and oases and measured their wealth in their camels and herds of sheep and goats. Theirs was an austere desert life, where necessity bred hard men, warlike and proud, tribally organized and highly individualistic. Poverty and relative overpopulation often forced them to raid the settled places on the rim of the desert. Sometimes they died on those raids, sometimes they returned with loot to the desert, and sometimes they stayed and settled down as emigrants. The pagan Arabs were basically a pastoral nomad people who habitually found themselves forced by necessity and enticed by opportunity to undertake ventures in trading, raiding, and emigration.

It was in this culture that Muhammad lived. His own tribesmen, the Quraysh, constituted the leading pagan tribe of Mecca. He knew the Jewish and Christian tribes and Jewish and Christian individuals who lived in Mecca and elsewhere in the Hijaz region along the Red Sea, where Mecca was located. Into this Arabian culture of hard men and hardship he would bring what he believed to be a new revelation from God, whom he called by the Arabian name Allah. Out from this desert sub-continent his followers would invade most of the territories of the great powers with a new religion and a new empire, called by the Arabic name, Islam.

244

MUHAMMAD RECITES THE QUR'AN

According to Islamic tradition Muhammad received his first command from Allah to recite from the Qur'an, the heavenly book of God's righteous will, in the year 610 A.D. Throughout the following twenty-two years, until his death in 632 A.D., he continued to receive from time to time revelations of additional portions of the Qur'an until finally the revelation was complete. His first four converts to Islam were his wife, Khadeeja; an eleven-year-old cousin named Ali; Abu Bakr, his close friend; and his freed slave, Zaid.

His early efforts at preaching the way of Islam, the religion of the Qur'an met with scant success and massive opposition in Mecca. The Jews and Christians generally rejected his proclamation. The pagan Meccans continually harassed and persecuted his small following. Muhammad's loyal wife and kindly uncle, Abu Talib, both died during the hardships of those earlier Meccan years.

In the meantime, the number of Muhammad's revelation experiences grew into a greater and greater volume of Qur'anic recitations, which his listeners either memorized or wrote down on whatever was at hand at the time. According to tradition Muhammad himself was illiterate.

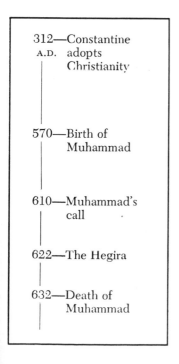

312—Constantine
A.D. adopts Christianity

570—Birth of Muhammad

610—Muhammad's call

622—The Hegira

632—Death of Muhammad

THE GROWTH OF ISLAM

Eventually Muhammad converted to Islam a group of men from Medina, an agricultural center in the Hijaz to the north of Mecca. They returned to Medina and started a Muslim movement there, where Islam was much more hospitably received. This experience with the Medinians led to an emigration by all the Muslims in Mecca to Medina, including Muhammad himself. The year was 622 A.D. This was a dramatic event in the development of Islam. Indeed, all subsequent Islamic dating of time begins with that year, *the Year of the Hegira,* as the emigration is called.

Muhammad quickly came to assume religious and political control of Medina. He established a kind of confederacy, in which the various Arab and Jewish tribes, generally hostile to each other even though living within the city, administered their own domestic affairs and joined together when necessary for the common defense of the city against external aggression. Subsequently, after a series of truces and offensives between the Muslims of Medina and the Meccans, the forces of Islam, led by the Prophet Muhammad, permanently defeated the Meccans and brought Mecca under Islam's control.

Muhammad proceeded to destroy the signs of idol worship, or polytheism, at the Ka'ba, the Meccan shrine to which he had made a pilgrimage as a Muslim the year before. Ka'ba means *cube,* and tradition tells that it first was constructed by Ibrahim (Abraham) and Ismail (Ishmael). To the Muslims it represented the heavenly abode of God and contained a Holy of Holies, a cubical room like that in the Temple of Jerusalem. When Muhammad cleared the Ka'ba of the idolatry associated with it, he was clearing away the pagan corruptions of its original purpose as a shrine of the one God, Allah. These corruptions had been introduced during the intervening centuries by the Arabian polytheists, the worshipers of many gods.

Meanwhile Muhammad had converted or subdued the neighboring bedouin tribes of Arabia through his religiously inspired missionary, diplomatic, and military activity. After a brief excursion against the Byzantines, Muhammad fell ill of fever in 632 A.D. while planning a campaign against Syria. A few days later he died.

GOD, THE BOOK, AND THE PROPHETS

Part 1:

MUHAMMAD THE PROPHET RECITES GOOD NEWS AND WARNINGS

In the tradition of Islam, as well as in the prophetic traditions of Judaism and Christianity, the prophet was known as a prophet solely by virtue of his message and never because of his character. The prophet himself, in the case of Muhammad, was highly revered as a man. But no question existed in the orthodox Muslim mind regarding the priority of things. The prophet's message did not originate with the prophet himself. He only recited what had been spoken in heaven beforehand and conveyed verbatim to him by one of God's angels. Thus to the Muslim the Qur'an had been sent as the spoken word of God, borne into human experience through the lips of Muhammad, the inspired messenger.

SEARCH CUES

1. inspiration
2. God's pronouns of self-reference
3. the succession of prophecy
4. good news and warnings
5. the supremacy of God

NOW READ BELOW:
SURAHS 21:25; 4:163-166; 33:40-48; 5:16-21

Note: The selections from the Qur'an have been translated from the Arabic for this course by Dr. A. H. Abdel Kader and Dr. A. Muhsin El-Biali, Director and Assistant Director of the Islamic Center, Washington, D.C. They have been put into idiomatic English by Dr. John R. Whitney, Assistant Professor of Religious Studies, The Pennsylvania State University.

We never sent a messenger prior to sending you without also sending to him our inspiration, namely, that no god exists but me. Therefore serve and worship me alone.

21:25, The Prophets.

We have sent you inspiration, Muhammad, just as we sent it to Noah and to the messengers after him. Thus we sent inspiration to Abraham, Ismail, Isaac, Jacob and the tribes, and to Jesus, Job, Jonah, Aaron, and Solomon. Also we gave the Psalms to David.

We already have told you the story of some of the messengers, but of others we have not—(although God spoke directly to Moses)—messengers bearing good news coupled with warnings, that mankind, the messengers having come, should have no excuse before God, for God is exalted in might, wise.

But God bears witness that the word he has sent to you he has sent from his own knowledge. The angels also bear witness: though God is witness enough.

4:163-166, The Women.

Muhammad does not act the father to any of your men, but as the messenger of God, the last of the prophets. God alone has full knowledge of all things.

O you who believe! Celebrate praises to God, and do so often. Glorify him morning and evening. He is the one who sends blessings upon you, as do his angels, that he may bring you out from the depths of darkness and into the light. And he is full of mercy for the believers. Their greeting on the day they meet him will be "Peace!" He has prepared for them a generous reward.

O Prophet! Truly we have sent you as witness, a bearer of glad tidings, and also to warn—as one called into God's grace at God's behest to act as a lamp spreading light.

Then give the glad tidings to the believers, that they may receive from God a truly great reward. Do not submit to the unbelievers and hypocrites, and do not heed their annoyances, but put your trust in God. For God is sufficient as a judge of affairs.

33:40-48, The Clans.

O people of the book! Our messenger has come to you revealing to you much in the book that you used to hide, at the same time omitting much that now is not needed.

There has come to you from God a new light of the illuminating book, whereby God guides to ways of peace and safety all who seek his good pleasure, bringing them by his will out of darkness to light, leading them to a path that is straight.

In blasphemy indeed are those that say that God is Christ, son of Mary. But you say, "Who would have the least power against God, were it his will to destroy all—Christ, son of Mary, his mother herself, and each and all on earth? For to God belongs the dominion of the heavens and the earth, and all that is between. God creates what he pleases, for he has power over all things."

Both the Jews and the Christians say: "We are children of God, and his beloved." But you say, "Why then does he punish you for your sins? No, you are but men among men that he has created. He forgives whom he pleases, and he punishes whom he pleases. To God belongs the dominion of the heavens and the earth, and all that is between, and to him is the final return."

O people of the book, now our messenger has come to you, making things clear to you, after the break in the sequence of our messengers, lest you should say, "There came to us no herald of glad tidings and no one to warn us." But now a messenger of glad tidings and of warning has come to you. God has power over all things.

5:16-21, *The Table.*

COMMENTARY

God and the Prophet

The Muslim saw himself as a member of Islam. This meant that he was one of those who had made his peace with the active will of God. The Muslim was a person who had submitted to God's command. He accepted the divine charge that he make manifest in his own life the faith and law he received from God in the holy book.

That full and final revelation from God came in the ecstatic moments of Muhammad's prophetic recitations. Veneration for the Prophet by the Muslims was the veneration men gave to one through whom the words of God's command had come to them. He, like any Muslim, contributed to the Qur'an nothing except his own belief, obedience, and interpretation after its utterance. All else that made him famous as the Prophet came as an influence of the Qur'an.

The Ways of Muhammad

Muslims understood that Muhammad, inasmuch as he was called to be the Prophet, was profoundly influenced by the experience of being God's messenger. In addition to his extraordinarily fine character, the prophetic influence made him an excellent example of Muslim submission to God. In many ways, then, where the Qur'an would express a general rule of righteousness, the habits of the Prophet might provide suggestions as to how the law might be applied in practice. Thus a Muslim might ask, first, when facing an ethical decision, "What does the Qur'an say concerning this?" And then, if he could not understand fully what to do after reference to the Qur'an, he might further ask, "What would the Prophet do in such circumstances?" The answer to this latter question would come when he referred to the record of the Prophet's own ways and judgments, preserved in a body of revered tradition called the *Hadith*. The Prophet's "trodden path," or way of doing things, is referred to as the *Sunnah*.

Thus the Muslim learned from the Qur'an that he must pray. But he learned from the Hadith the particular form of prayer appropriate for a Muslim as commended by the practice of Muhammad. From the Qur'an the Muslim learned that he must give alms. But he learned particular procedures for giving alms from the Hadith as it cited the custom and advice of the Prophet in this respect. In each case the Muslim traced the Hadith tradition back to prescriptions and prohibitions laid down by the Prophet, and to the practices he followed from former times or initiated himself to be the way of Islam.

The Islamic Oral Tradition

According to Hadith tradition itself, the companions (close disciples) of Muhammad did not write down the Hadith during his lifetime because of his apprehension that his own human sayings might be confused with those of the Qur'an. Thus an oral tradition (Hadith) developed in Islam that later was written down. It was based on the doings and sayings of the Prophet as an exemplar of Muslim conduct. Like the Jewish midrash and the gospel elaborations of the New Testament kerygma, the Hadith detailed the implications of Qur'anic verses. For example, one finds in the Hadith the story of how once Muhammad was taken by a mysterious animal at night to Jerusalem. From there he was translated (i.e., he ascended without dying) into heaven and returned again. While involved in this experience, he met Jesus, Moses, and, in the highest of the seven levels of heaven, Abraham. The angel Gabriel, the heavenly messenger by whom God delivered the words of the Qur'an to Muhammad, acted as his guide for this ascension, as the Hadith tells it.

REFLECTION QUESTIONS

1. How might the use of personal pronouns in these passages make it difficult for you to keep in mind the Muslim assumption that God and God alone was the author of the Qur'an?
2. Consider whether the following is true or false: All prophets are messengers, but not all messengers are prophets.
3. Which of the new ideas that developed in the two first centuries appear to be present in these passages? Do you think the reading, besides reflecting the tradition of the Hebrews, reflects more the influence of Greece or of Persia? Explain.

Part 2:

GOD SPEAKS OF THE BOOKS BY WHICH HE HAS REVEALED HIS WILL TO MEN

In the preceding passage we read the greeting, "O people of the book." For the Muslims, the great revelations from God to man had come always in God's words as inscribed in a book somehow pre-existing in heaven. Such a book had been given to Abraham, though it long since had disappeared. The Torah and Gospel had been similar books, later in large part forgotten or corrupted, though fragments of the originals remained.

It is sufficient for us now to observe that Muslims could see a family relationship between the Torah, the Gospel, and the Qur'an. The Muslims understood that God sent each originally in its true form as a book from God: the Torah to Moses, the Gospel to Jesus, and finally the Qur'an to Muhammad.

SEARCH CUES

1. the book
2. the people of the book
3. the succession of the prophets
4. the seal of the scripture
5. concerning the Jews and Christians
6. the judgment of God

NOW READ BELOW:
SURAHS 17:2; 2:87; 5:47-69

THE TORAH

We gave Moses the book, and made it a guide to the children of Israel, commanding, "Take none other than me as judge of your affairs."

17:2, The Children of Israel

We gave Moses the book and followed him with a succession of messengers. We gave Jesus the son of Mary clear signs and strengthened him with the Holy Spirit. Is this it, that whenever there comes to you a messenger with news that you yourselves do not desire, you puff up with arrogance? Some of these you have called imposters, and others you slay!

2:87, *The Cow*.

THE QUR'AN

We are the One Who revealed the law to Moses. In it was guidance and light. Through the standards of Torah, Jews have been judged by the prophets who bowed in submission to God's will. The rabbis and doctors of law similarly have judged, for likewise the Torah was entrusted to them and they were witnesses to it. Therefore, do not fear men, but fear me, and do not sell my tidings for a cheapening price. The ones who fail to judge by the light of what God has revealed, they are the unbelievers.

In it we ordained for them "Life for life, an eye for an eye, nose for nose, an ear for an ear, tooth for tooth, and wounds equal for equal." However if one does forego to retaliate for reason of charity, it becomes thereby an act of atonement for himself. If there are any who fail to judge by what God has revealed, they do wrong.

We sent Jesus the son of Mary, following in their footsteps, confirming what was revealed before him. We also gave him the Gospel, wherein is guidance and light, confirming that which was given before it in Torah— a guide and an admonition to those who fear God. Let the folk of the Gospel judge by that which God has revealed within it. And whatever ones do not judge by what God has revealed, they are transgressors.

To you we sent the scripture in truth, sealing the scripture that came before it, guarding it safely. So judge between them by what God has revealed, and do not follow their vain desires that diverge from the truth that has come to you. To each among you we prescribed a law, and an open way. If God had so willed, he would have made you one people, but his plan is to test you in what he has given you, so therefore strive in all virtues as though in a race. The goal of you all is God. It is he that will show you the truth concerning the matters in which you dispute.

So judge between them by what God has revealed, and do not follow their low desires. Be cautious of them, lest they should seduce you from part of what God has revealed to you. Then, if they turn away, know that God intends to chastise them for some of their sins. Surely many of the people are transgressors.

Is it not judgment from out of the time of ignorance they are seeking? Who then, for a people whose faith is assured, can give better judgment than God?

O you who believe, do not take Jews and Christians for friends. They are friends to each other. He among you who takes them for friends is one of them. Truly, God does not guide the wrongdoing people.

But you see those in whose hearts is disease hastening toward them and saying: "We fear lest calamity strike us." Perhaps God will bring a commandment or victory to you from himself, so they will regret what they hid in their souls.

And those who believe will say, "Are these the men who swore their strongest oaths by God that they were with you?" All that they do will be in vain, and they will fall into ruin.

O you who believe, and he among you who may become a renegade from his religion, know that God will provide a people he loves and who love him. They will be humble regarding believers, stern toward unbelievers, striving in the way of God, not fearing the reproach of those who find fault. Such is the grace of God, which he gives to whomever he will. God is all-embracing, all-knowing.

Only God, his messenger, and those who believe are your friends—those who establish regular prayers and regular alms, and bow down in worship. And those who take God, his messenger and those who believe as friends—the party of God, certainly they shall triumph.

O you who believe, do not take for friends those who make sport or mockery of your religion. Neither take them from those who received the Scripture before you, or from those who turn away faith. Instead, if indeed you have faith, fear God.

When you issue the call to prayer, they take it as mockery and sport. That is because they are people without understanding.

Say, "O people of the book, do you find fault with us for no other reason than that we believe in God and in that which has been revealed to us, as well as in that which was revealed before, while most of you are transgressors?"

Say, "Shall I point out to you something much worse than this, to judge by the treatment it had from God? Those who incurred the curse of God and His wrath, that is, those who worshiped evil, are far more astray from the straight path and are many times worse off. Some he transformed into apes and swine."

When they come to you, they say, "We believe," but, truly, they enter with unbelief and they leave the same way. But God knows best what they hide.

And many of them you see strive with each other in sin and transgression, consuming their illicit gain. Truly, they do what is evil. Why do not rabbis and doctors of law forbid them their sinful utterances, and from devouring forbidden gain? Certainly, the works that they do are evil.

The Jews say, "God's hand is tied. May *their* hands be tied, and may they be accursed for the blasphemy they utter. On the contrary, both his hands are widely outstretched. He gives and spends of his bounty just as he pleases. But the revelation that comes from God to you increases in most of them their stubborn rebellion and blasphemy.

We have placed among them hatred and enmity until the day of judgment. Whenever they kindle the fire of war, God extinguishes it. But they keep striving to do mischief on earth. And those who do mischief God does not love.

If only the people of the book had believed and had done their duty! We certainly would have removed their evils from them, and would have made them enter gardens of bliss. If only they had observed the Torah and Gospel and what was revealed to them from their Lord! They surely would have been nourished from above them and from under their feet. Among them are people who are moderate, but many of them do evil.

5:47-69, *The Table*.

COMMENTARY

The People of the Book

Great prophets had come and gone before Muhammad, but, according to Muslims, he was born to be the seal of all the prophets. When, through the experience of Muhammad, God opened the Qur'an to the minds of men, all former books of prophecy could then be closed. They were all here, corrected and completed, in this book that God gave to be the heart of Islam. The Qur'an would suffice as a revelation by which to judge all revelation, and as a law by which to judge all the issues of righteousness that the future might produce. The prophetic greatness of Abraham, Moses, and Jesus would be vindicated in the Islamic discipline and teaching. What had been corrupted or forgotten of the original books of the Torah and the Gospel in the biblical record that Jews and Christians had preserved, the Qur'an restored and set right again. What no longer was necessary in those former records, the Qur'an omitted. What originally had been lacking in those partial revelations to the former prophets, the Qur'an now added for the benefit of human progress.

The Muslim believed that the Torah of the Jews first had been a book revealed to Moses. Likewise, the Gospel of the Christians first had been a book revealed to Jesus. Jews and Christians had forgotten or corrupted their partial versions of the heavenly book, but they, together with the Muslims, were people of the book, none the less. However, the term *Muslim* could apply only to Jews and Christians who could see the final truth in Islam. Before their prophecies had been forgotten or corrupted by their later followers, men like Abraham, Moses, and Jesus had in truth been great prophets and fellow Muslims, foreshadowing the advent of the Qur'an.

According to Islam, all the words in the Qur'an are the words of God. Sometimes he speaks as "I," sometimes as "we." Sometimes he speaks to the Prophet, sometimes to the Muslims, sometimes to all the people of the book. The book, said the Muslims, is a revelation of God's Command.

The Language of the Qur'an

Scholars agree that the Qur'an is the most beautiful of all Arabic literature, and perhaps the first literary work in that language. It speaks a language rich in concepts and filled with emotion. It speaks of Islam, the way of the Muslim, the surrender of act and mind to God, and the surrender, too, of one's emotions. The rhythmic flow of thought and feeling in the Qur'an implies to the Arabic listener a wealth of subtle implications which become lost in translation. This is not to say, however, that the message of the Qur'an is lost altogether in translation. The meanings within it, in terms of acts and concepts, become quite clear in English, according to the testimony of those well versed in both languages.

The Literary Structure of the Qur'an

The Qur'an as it now exists is a *recension*, or collection of the Prophet's recitations, which the faithful followers of the Prophet memorized or wrote down in the twenty years during which he was voicing them. This recension was approved as the authorized version of the Qur'an during the regime of Uthman, the third of the first four caliphs of Islam. The first of these four orthodox caliphs had been Abu Bakr. He was the close friend and father-in-law of Muhammad through the Prophet's marriage to Ayesha, Abu Bakr's daughter, two years after the Hegira. The second caliph had been Umar. Uthman, the third caliph (644-656 A.D.), preceded Ali, the last of the four. Each of these men was closely associated with Muhammad through marriage. The caliphs carried on Muhammad's rule of Islam as his succeeding representatives, both in the political and in the religious sense. In no sense, however, did they succeed him in anything resembling the prophetic nature of Muhammad's authority in Islam.

Muhammad recited the Qur'an in the Hijaz dialect. However it may vary technically between being prose and poetry, in quality it remains poetic throughout to the Arabic ear. To the faithful, its words are the words of God, sent to the Prophet, who in turn recited them to the world of men, faithfully and fully. The book remains subject to interpretation while at the same time its utterances to the Muslim are infallible, being the pure words of God himself. Because it is the product of an experience of direct inspiration from God in words, the book falls under the classification of literature known as prophecy.

A certain progression of concern marks the book, in that some portions show the effects of having been recited in Mecca, while others reflect their having been recited in Medina. The Qur'an argues strongly against the Jewish interpretation of the Torah and the Christian expression of the Gospel in the terms of incarnation. For the most part, the book is didactic, a commanding communication from God. Through the lips of the Prophet, God directs the faithful to act out his righteous command. Islam, or submission to God, fulfilled the life of the person, and glorified that greater brotherhood of the faith to which each Muslim belonged.

The Qur'an's chapters are of varying length, each called a *surah*, and named arbitrarily by some word significant in the surah, usually appearing near the beginning. Each surah in turn comprises a number of verses (*ayat*). Thus to cite "surah and ayat" in the Qur'an is parallel to citing "chapter and verse" in the Bible. But the Qur'an, unlike the Bible, consists of one book rather than many. The longest surahs appear first in the Qur'an, the shorter ones later. This arrangement in the authorized recension is a conventional, or arbitrary, way of putting the surahs in a logical order.

257

Christians and Jews

The audience to which the Prophet recited the Qur'an consisted not only of pagan Arabs but also of people to whom both the Jewish and Christian traditions were familiar. The biblical references could have prompted scant interest among pagan listeners unrelated to the life of either the Jewish or the Christian tribes.

In this connection we notice the high frequency of passages that warn Muslims against intimate friendship with Christians and Jews. Fraternization would imply equality of truth between those corrupted or incomplete traditions and the truth of the Qur'an. Because this was the full and final book from God and the complete expression within history of his heavenly command, for the Muslim no other book and no other tradition could equal it.

REFLECTION QUESTIONS

1. In what sense does it appear that the "people of the book" also were the people of the books? Who were "the people of the book" referred to at the beginning of the passage from *The Table* (5:16-21)?
2. How would a Muslim answer these questions? Which existed first, (a) Moses or the Torah? (b) Jesus or the Gospel? (c) Muhammad or the Qur'an?
3. Would an orthodox Muslim have any theoretical problems regarding the authorship of the Qur'an? Why?
4. What signs of ethnocentricity do you find in the Qur'an thus far? How would a Muslim explain them?

Part 3

THE QUR'AN RECOLLECTS GOD'S CALL AND TESTING OF ABRAHAM

We have read previously in this course several biblical stories and interpretations concerning Abraham. They have given an account of his faithful obedience to God. We recall the family affairs involving Abraham, Sarah, Hagar, Isaac, and Ishmael, as the biblical tradition interpreted them. Now, out of Arabia and a later time, we encounter in the words of the Qur'an the Muslim's view of Abraham, his faith, and his family, and what they meant.

SEARCH CUES

1. God's revelation to Abraham
2. giving partners to God
3. the building of the house
4. peace, surrender, and Islam
5. Abraham's nearest of kin

NOW READ BELOW:
SURAHS 6:74-90; 2:124-132; 3:65-68

ABRAHAM

Behold! Abraham said to his father Azar, "Do you take idols for gods? For I see you and your people in manifest error."

Now this is how we show Abraham the kingdom of the heavens and the earth, that he might be one of those possessing certainty.

When the night overshadowed him, he saw a star, and he said, "This is my Lord." But when it set, he said, "I do not love things that set."

And when he saw the moon rising, he cried, "This is my Lord!" But when it set, he said, "Unless my Lord guides me, I surely shall become one of the people who are going astray."

When he saw the sun rising in splendor, he said, "This is my Lord; this is the greatest of all." But when the sun set, he said, "O my people! I am indeed free from your guilt in giving partners to God. Behold! I have turned my face toward him who created the heavens and the earth, as one by nature upright, therefore I am not of the idolaters."

His people argued with him. He said, "Do you dispute with me concerning God when he has guided me? I do not fear in any way those that you set up beside him, unless my Lord agrees. My Lord comprehends all things in his knowledge. Security is for those who believe, and do not mix their faith with iniquity, but go aright."

And this was our argument we gave Abraham against his people. We exalt in degrees whom we please. Surely the Lord is wise, knowing.

And we bestowed upon him Isaac and Jacob. We guided each of them, and Noah beforehand, and among his progeny David, Solomon, Job, Joseph, Moses, and Aaron. Thus do we reward the good. And Zacharias and John and Jesus and Elias; each of these was one of the righteous, as well as Ismail and Elisha, Jonas and Lot; and to all we gave favor above the nations. And we chose and guided to the right way some of their fathers, their descendants and their brethren.

This is the guidance of God: he gives that guidance to whomever he pleases of his worshipers. Yet if they were to join other gods with him, all that they did would be vain for them.

Those were the ones to whom we gave the Scripture, and command, and prophethood. But if these do not believe in them, then indeed we shall entrust it to a people who will not be disbelievers.

They were the ones whom God guided, so follow their guidance. Say, "I do not ask you for any reward for it. It is only a reminder to the nations."

6:74-90, *The Livestock.*

And remember that Abraham was tried by his Lord with certain commands, which he fulfilled. God said, "I will make you a leader to the nations." Then Abraham pleaded, "And also from my offspring?" God answered, "But my promise is not within reach of doers of evil."

Remember we made the house a resort for mankind and a sanctuary. Take as your place of worship the place where Abraham stood. And we enjoined Abraham and Ismail. Purify my house for those who go around it, and for those who meditate within, and those who bow down and prostrate themselves.

And remember, Abraham said, "My Lord, make this a city of peace, providing with fruit those of its people who believe in God and the last day." He said: "And whoever disbelieves, I shall grant him enjoyment for a short while, then I shall drive him to the fire of chastisement, an evil destination."

And remember that Abraham and Ismail raised the foundations of the house, "Our Lord! Accept this from us. Behold! You, only you, are the hearer, the knower. Our Lord, make us both submissive to you, and from our offspring a nation submitting to you, and show us our ways of devotion and turn to us; for surely you are the oft-Returning, the merciful. Our Lord! Raise up in their midst a messenger from among them, who will recite them your revelations and instruct them in scripture and wisdom, making them grow. Behold! You, only you, are the mighty, the wise."

And who are they who turn away from the religion of Abraham but those who debase their souls with folly? We chose him and rendered him pure in this world; and in the hereafter he will be in the ranks of the righteous.

When his Lord said to him, "Surrender!" he said, "I surrender to the Lord of the worlds."

And this was the legacy that Abraham left to his sons, and so also Jacob, "O my sons! God has chosen the faith for you; so do not die except in the faith of Islam."

2:124-132, *The Cow.*

You people of the book! Why do you dispute about Abraham, when the Law and the Gospel were not revealed until after him? Have you no understanding?

Behold! You have disputed over matters concerning which you had knowledge. God knows even as you do not.

Abraham was not a Jew, nor yet a Christian; but he was an upright man who had surrendered to God, and he was not one of the idolaters.

Without doubt, among men, the nearest of kin to Abraham are those who follow him. So also are this messenger and those who believe. And God is the protector of those who have faith.

3:65-68, *The Family of Emran.*

COMMENTARY

The Judeo-Christian Division

We have seen how the biblical story of Israel is for the most part the history of a people that was unified. True, the tribes had quarreled with each other, the northern kingdom had contested with the southern, and partisan debates and prejudices had continued in the Jewish community throughout the latter centuries B.C. But not until the advent of the Christian church did there occur a division of such scope and duration that it has endured to the present day.

Parallel to the development of Judeo-Christian estrangement had been the development of a religious literature expressing and continuing that division in controversy over the relative truth or falsehood of one revelation in opposition to another. Thus the tradition, religious and literary, reflected a deep and continuing difference of conviction existing between the Christians and the Jews. At the same time, both traditions encountered tension in their relationships with political states.

Another Division Comes with Islam

Five centuries after the beginning of the Jewish-Christian division, a third experience of revelation, once again both in history and in literature, set the new against the old. As the Christians had claimed their revelation to be the fulfillment and successor of the revelation to Israel, now the Muslims proclaimed their revelation to be the fulfillment and successor to the revelations of both the Jews and the Christians.

Thus Islamic literature, beginning with the Qur'an, is oriented both to the literature of the Jews and to that of the Christians. Where the Christian literature, according to its view, pointed to the inadequacy of the torah as the means by which men might be reconciled to God, the Muslim literature, according to the faith of Islam, pointed both to the inadequacy of the Jewish interpretation of the torah and to the inadequacy of the Christian interpretation of Jesus as the Christ. Neither of these interpretations according to the convictions of the Muslims, was anything more than a partial or corrupted representation of the true revelation of God. The Muslims pointed to the teaching of the Qur'an as God's chosen means by which to correct the errors, to omit what was unnecessary, and to provide what was lacking in the Jewish and Christian records of those former revelations.

Sorrow as Well as Anger

The alienation among men displayed in the division between the three peoples who each worshiped the God of Abraham frequently expressed itself in literature not only as anger but also as sorrow. The sorrow of the Jews might be seen as the sorrow of a parent over the profound and continuing mistakes of his children. The sorrow of the Christians would be like the sorrow of an elder son with a precious gift to give which neither his parent nor his brother would accept. The sorrow of the Muslims would then be like the sorrow of a youngest son bearing the last best hope for peace in the family, only to find the family elders adamant in refusing it.

The Qur'an Speaks of Abraham

Each of the three religions you have studied traces its tradition back to Abraham. According to Jews, Christians, and Muslims, Abraham was the patriarchal archetype of the man of faith. In the Qur'anic story of Abraham which you have read, *Azar* refers to Terah, the father of Abraham, as we read of him in Genesis 11:24-32.

The *house* refers to the Ka'ba, in Mecca. Islam's understanding was that Abraham and Ismail came with Hagar into Arabia. Tradition associates Abraham and Ismail together in the story of Abraham's temptation, and furthermore identifies Mecca as the place of Hagar's visitation by the angel of God. Abraham and Ismail thus were the first Muslims. Cf. Genesis 16.

REFLECTION QUESTIONS

1. Animism, as a form of primitive religion, involves worshiping the spirits associated with any of a wide variety of natural objects. The Arabs

of the seventh century A.D. were largely animistic in their religious belief. What effect might the story of the revelation to Abraham have on such belief?

2. How might the Qur'an's account of how Abraham and Ismail built the House (Ka'ba) be described as an etiological story?

3. How would you explain your agreement or disagreement with the following assertion? "It is impossible to show the common beliefs included in the literatures of Judaism, Christianity, and Islam without also making evident the controversies involved."

4. Compare the faith of animists in the powers associated with such natural objects as stones and storms with the faith of modern consumers in the powers associated with such manufactured objects as vitamins and cleansers. What are the differences and similarities?

Part 4:

THE QUR'AN TELLS ITS VERSION OF THE STORY OF MOSES AND THE EXODUS

According to the Qur'an, all true faith in God was a response to his command delivered from the lips of inspired prophets reciting the book. Muslims accepted, as a fundamental part of their belief, the reality of Abraham, Moses, and Jesus as prophets preceding Muhammad. Now we read an account in the Qur'an of the role of Moses as the prophet chosen not only to overcome Pharaoh, but also to lead the Israelites out of Egypt, and to give them the Torah, written down on tablets.

SEARCH CUES

1. the power of Moses vs. the power of the sorcerers
2. the conversion of the sorcerers
3. the arrogance of Pharaoh's people
4. by no means can you see me directly
5. seeing but not believing
6. the calf

NOW READ BELOW: SURAH 7:103-157

MOSES

Then, after them, we sent Moses with our signs to Pharaoh and his chiefs, but they wrongfully rejected them. So see what the fate was of those who made mischief.

Moses said, "Pharaoh, I am a messenger from the Lord of the worlds. I am one for whom nothing is right but to say the truth about God. Now

I have come to you from your Lord with a clear sign. So let the children of Israel leave with me."

Pharaoh said, "If indeed you have come with a sign, and tell me the truth, demonstrate it."

Then Moses threw down his rod, and behold, it was a serpent, plain for all to see! And he drew out his hand, and behold, it was white to all who beheld!

The chiefs of the people of Pharaoh said, "This is indeed a skillful sorcerer. His plan is to get you out of your land. What, then, is your counsel?"

"Keep him and his brother in suspense," they said, "and send men to the cities to round up and bring to you all the well-versed sorcerers."

So the sorcerers came up to Pharaoh. They said, "Of course we shall have a reward if we win!"

He said, "Yes, because in that case you all shall be raised to positions nearest my person."

They said, "O Moses, will you throw first, or shall we have them throw first?"

Moses said, "Throw first." So when they threw, they bewitched the eyes of the people, and struck terror into them, for they demonstrated powerful magic.

We put it into Moses' mind by inspiration. "Throw your rod," and behold, it swallowed up straightway all the falsehoods they pretended!

Thus the truth was confirmed, and all that they did became ineffective. So the great ones were vanquished then and there, and were made to look small. Therefore the sorcerers fell down prostrate in adoration, saying, "We believe in the Lord of worlds, the Lord of Moses and Aaron."

Pharaoh said, "Do you believe in him prior to my giving you permission? Surely this is a trick you have planned in the city to drive out its people. But soon you shall know the consequences. Be sure that I will cut off your hands and your feet on opposite sides, and I will cause you to die on the cross."

They said, "For us, we are but sent back to our Lord. But you wreak your vengeance on us simply because we believed in the signs of our Lord when they reached us! Our Lord, pour out on us patience and constancy, and take our souls to you as Muslims who bow to your will!"

The chiefs of Pharaoh's people said, "Will you leave Moses and his people to spread mischief in the land, and to abandon you and your gods?" He said, "We will slay their male children; only their females will we save alive. We have irresistible power over them."

Moses said to his people, "Pray for help from God, in patience and constancy, for the earth is God's to give as a heritage to such of his servants as he pleases. And the end is best for the righteous."

They said, "We have had trouble, both before and after you came to us." He said, "It may be that your Lord, destroying your enemy, will make you inheritors of the earth. Thus he may test you by your deeds."

We punished the people of Pharaoh with years of drought and shortness of crops, that they might receive warning.

But when good came, they said, "This is all due to us." When gripped by calamity, they ascribed it to evil omens connected with Moses and those with him! But behold, in God's sight the omens of evil in truth pertain to them, though most of them fail to understand!"

They said, "No matter what signs there may be by which you bring sorcery upon us, we shall never believe in you."

So we sent on them wholesale death, locusts and lice, frogs and blood, signs obviously self-explaining. But they were steeped in arrogance, a people given to sin.

Every time the penalty fell on them, they said, "O Moses, on our behalf call on the Lord by virtue of his promise to you. If you will remove the penalty from us, we shall truly believe in you, and we shall send away the children of Israel with you."

But every time we removed the penalty from them, under fixed terms they had to fulfill, behold, they broke their word! So we exacted retribution from them. We drowned them in the sea, because they rejected our signs and failed to take warning from them.

And we made a people considered weak inheritors of lands in both east and west, lands where we sent down our blessings. The fair promise of the Lord was fulfilled for the children of Israel because they had patience and constancy, and we levelled to the ground the great works and fine buildings which Pharaoh and his people erected.

We took the children of Israel across the sea. They encountered a people entirely devoted to some idols they had. They said, "O Moses, fashion for us a god like the gods they possess." He said, "Surely you are a people without knowledge. As for this folk, the cult they belong to is a fragment of ruin, and the worship they practice is vain."

He said, "Shall I seek a god for you other than the true God, when it is God who has endowed you with gifts above the nations?"

And remember, we rescued you from Pharaoh's people, who afflicted you with the worst of penalties, who, while saving alive your females, slew your male children. In that was a tremendous test from your Lord.

We appointed for Moses thirty nights, and finished the period with ten more, thus was completed the term of communion with his Lord, forty nights. And Moses had charged his brother Aaron, "Act for me among my people. Do right, and do not follow the way of those who do mischief."

When Moses came to the place appointed by us, and his Lord addressed him, he said, "O my Lord, show yourself to me, that I may look upon you." God said, "By no means can you see me directly, but look at the mountain. If it abides in its place, then you shall see me." When his Lord showed his glory on the mountain he made it like dust, and Moses fell down in a swoon. When he recovered his senses, he said, "Glory be to you! I turn to you in repentance, and I am the first to believe."

God said, "Moses! I have chosen you above other men by the mission I have given you and the words I have spoken to you. Take, then, the revelation which I give you, and be one of those who give thanks."

And we ordained laws for him in the tablets concerning all matters, both commanding and explaining all things, saying, "Take and hold these with firmness, and enjoin your people to hold fast by the best in the precepts. Soon I shall show you the homes of the wicked."

Those who act arrogantly on the earth in defiance of right, I will turn away from my signs. Even if they see all my signs they will not believe in them. And if they see the way of right conduct, they will not adopt it as the way; but yet if they see the way of error, that is the way they will choose. For they have rejected our signs, and have failed to take warning from them.

Vain are the deeds of those who reject our signs and the confrontation in the hereafter. Can they expect to be rewarded except as they have wrought?

The people of Moses made in his absence the image of a calf from their ornaments. It seemed to low. Did they not see that it neither could speak to them nor show them the way? They took it for worship and did wrong.

When they repented, and saw that they had erred, they said, "If our Lord does not have mercy upon us and forgive us, we shall indeed be among those who perish."

When Moses came back to his people, angry and grieved, he said, "Evil is what you have done in my place in my absence. Did you make haste to bring on the judgment of your Lord?" He put down the tablets, seized his brother by the hair of the head, and dragged him to him. Aaron said, "Son of my mother! The people indeed reckoned me as nothing, and came near to slaying me. Do not make the enemies rejoice over my misfortune, nor count me among the people of sin."

Moses prayed, "O my Lord, forgive me and my brother! Admit us to your mercy. For you are the most merciful of those who show mercy!"

Those who took the calf will indeed be overwhelmed with wrath from their Lord, and with shame in this life. Thus do we recompense those who invent falsehoods.

However, to those who do wrong but afterward repent and believe, truly the Lord thereafter is oft-forgiving, most merciful.

When the anger of Moses was appeased, he took up the tablets. In the writing on them there was guidance and mercy for such as fear their Lord.

And Moses chose seventy of his people for our place of meeting. When they were seized with violent quaking, he prayed, "O my Lord! If it had been your will you long ago could have destroyed both them and me. Would you destroy us for the deeds of the foolish ones among us? This is no more than your testing. By it you cause whom you will to stray, and you lead whom you will into the right path. You are our protector, so forgive us and give us mercy, for you are the best of those who forgive. And ordain for us that which is good, in this life and in the hereafter, for we have turned to you." He said, "With my punishment I visit whom I will, but my mercy extends to all things. That I shall ordain for those who do right, who practice regular charity, and believe in our signs, those who follow the messenger, the unlettered prophet, whom they find mentioned in their own scriptures, in the Law and the Gospel. For he commands for them what is just and forbids to them what is evil. He allows to them as lawful what is good and prohibits to them what is bad. He releases them from their heavy burdens and from the yokes that are upon them. Therefore, they are the ones who believe in him, honor him, help him, and follow the light which is sent down with him—it is they who will prosper."

7:103-157, The Heights.

COMMENTARY

Prophecy in Islam

According to Islam, God's way of revealing his command always had been the way of prophecy. Prophecy might occur in three degrees of significance. God might inspire the prophet to an abrupt expression of insight in the midst of other activity; this was the least degree of significance. Secondly, God might inspire the prophet through the medium of dreams or visions, which the prophet then would recount. But the highest degree of significance in prophecy was that in which the angel of God would speak directly to the prophet in words, which the prophet then would recite to those around him. These recited words constituted the words of the heavenly book, the archetype of all the revealed books of prophecy.

The Former Prophets

Thus the Muslims believed that Abraham had recited from the book, but that the record of his recital had been lost by his followers. They believed that the torah was a recitation by Moses of the book, the record of which had been partly corrupted, partly forgotten. They believed that the gospel was in fact a similar prophecy given to Jesus and recited by him. This, too, had been corrupted in the record written by his followers.

All the same, these former prophecies were significant. Originally they all had been prophecies in the words of the book. The prophets who recited them were important as God's human messengers. But the Qur'an, as received and recited by Muhammad, served as a completion of that Book of God's revelation that the former prophets had partially recited. Likewise, it served to correct the record of those prophecies which had been corrupted by the followers of Abraham, Moses, and Jesus.

REFLECTION QUESTIONS

1. What event, central to the story of the Exodus in the Bible, is not mentioned in this story in the Qur'an?

2. How would you explain why the Qur'an's account of Moses' encounter with the sorcerers shows an effect on the sorcerers not described in the biblical account, that is, their conversion?

3. In its attack on idolatry, to whom do you think the Qur'an was primarily addressed, to the Jews, the Christians, or the pagan Arabs?

4. In its attack on "giving partners to God," do you think the Qur'an intended to speak primarily to the Jews, the Christians, or the pagan Arabs?

5. Does the figure of Moses seem to you to be more true to life in the book of Exodus or in the Qur'an? Can you give your reasons as a literary critic supporting your decision?

6. Do you think this passage points out a basic difference between prophecy and magic? If so, what does the difference seem to be?

Part 5:

THE QUR'AN DESCRIBES THE BIRTH AND SIGNIFICANCE OF JESUS

The Qur'an regarded Jesus as especially important in the long succession of the prophets, from Adam, through Abraham and Moses, to Muhammad. Jesus was of cardinal significance, too, in the Muslim understanding of Islam's relationship to Christianity and Judaism. He, like Abraham and Moses, was a Muslim, according to the Qur'an. The similarities and differences between the Muslim and New Testament accounts of the birth, life, and death of Jesus dramatize the distinctive points of difference between Islam and Christianity.

SEARCH CUES

1. Mary and Zechariah (Zakariya)
2. the birth of John the Baptist (Yahya)
3. the angels' announcement to Mary
4. the legend of the clay bird
5. Jesus to be vindicated
6. the similitude of Jesus

NOW READ BELOW: SURAH 3:35-63

JESUS

Behold! The wife of Emran said, "My Lord, I have dedicated unreservedly what is in my womb to your service. So accept this of me, since you hear and know all things."

When she gave birth to her, she said, "My Lord, I have given birth to a baby girl!" (And God knew best what she had given birth to.) "And indeed the male is not quite like the female. I have named her Mary, and I commend her and her offspring to your protection from Satan, the rejected one."

With grace her Lord accepted her, and with grace he made her grow up, and she was assigned to the custodianship of Zakariya. Each time he entered her chamber to see her, he found her supplied with nourishment. He said, "O Mary! Where does it come from?" She said, "From God, for God provides sustenance to whom he pleases, without measure."

At this point, Zakariya prayed to his Lord, saying, "My Lord! Grant me a blessed progeny from you, for you are he that hears prayer!"

While he was standing in prayer in the chamber, the angels called to him, "God gives you glad tidings of Yahya, who shall bear witness to the truth of a word from God. He will be noble, chaste, and a prophet, of the good company of the righteous."

He said: "My Lord! How shall I have a son when I am very old, and my wife is barren?" "Thus," was the answer, "does God accomplish what he wills."

He said: "My Lord! Give me a sign!" "Your sign," was the answer, "shall be that you shall speak to no man for three days except by signals. Then remember and praise your Lord again and again, and glorify him in the evening and in the morning."

Behold! the angels said, "O Mary! God has chosen you and purified you— you above the women of all nations. Mary, worship your Lord devoutly. Prostrate yourself, and bow down in prayer with those who bow down before him." This which we reveal to you is part of the tidings of things unseen, O Muhammad! For you were not with them when they cast lots with arrows, as to which of them should be charged with the care of Mary, nor were you with them when they disputed the point.

When the angels said, "Mary, God gives you glad tidings of a word from him! His name will be Christ Jesus, son of Mary, held in honor in this world and the hereafter, and of the company of those nearest God. He shall speak to the people in childhood and in maturity, and he shall be of the company of the righteous." "O my Lord!" she said, "How shall I have a son when no man has touched me?" God said, "Even so, God creates what he wills. When he has decreed a plan, he but says to it, 'Be,' and it is!"

"And God will teach him the book and wisdom, the Law and the Gospel, and send him as a messenger to the children of Israel, with this message: 'I have come to you with a sign from your Lord, in that I make for you out of clay, as it were, the image of a bird. I breathe into it, and it becomes a bird by God's command. Furthermore I declare to you what you shall eat, and what you shall store in your houses. Surely all this becomes a sign for you if you are believers. I have come to you to witness to the law which came before me, and to make lawful for you part of what was forbidden to you. I have come to you with a sign from your Lord, so fear God, and obey me. It is God who is my Lord and your Lord; therefore worship him. This is the straight way.'"

When Jesus discerned unbelief on their part he said, "What will be my helpers to bear the message of God?" The disciples said, "We want to be

God's helpers. We believe in God. Bear witness that we are Muslims. Our Lord! We believe in what you have revealed, and we follow the messenger. Therefore write us down among those who bear witness."

And the unbelievers plotted and planned, and God planned too, but the best of planners is God.

Then God said, "O Jesus! I will cause you to die and raise you to myself and clear you of the falsehoods of those who blaspheme. I will make those who follow you superior to those who reject faith, until the day of resurrection. Then shall you all return to me, and I will judge between you touching the matters which you often disputed."

"As to those who reject faith, I will punish them with terrible agony in this world and in the hereafter, nor will they have anyone to help. As to those who believe and do righteous deeds, God will pay them their reward in full. But God does not love those who do wrong. This is what we rehearse to you of the verses and the book of wisdom."

The similitude of Jesus before God is to Adam; he created him from dust, then said to him, "Be," and he was.

The truth comes from your God alone; so do not be among those who doubt. If anyone now disputes in this matter with you after full knowledge has come to you, say, "Come! Let us gather together, our sons and your sons, our women and your women, ourselves and yourselves. Then let us earnestly pray, and invoke the curse of God on those who lie!"

This is the true account. There is no god except God; and God is indeed the exalted in power, the wise. But if they turn back, God has full knowledge of those who do mischief.

3:35-63, *The Family of Emran.*

COMMENTARY

The Qur'an Story of Jesus

The Muslims believed in the Christian doctrine of the virgin birth, but not in the crucifixion of Jesus as an historical event. Nor did they believe in the doctrine of Jesus' resurrection. Furthermore, they did not believe in the doctrine of Jesus as the Son of God. For them, these doctrines evidenced the sin of *shirk*. To the Muslim, God utterly transcended any possible human attempt to comprehend him or depict him except as he gave men ways of reverence toward him in the Qur'an. No man had the mind or the right to equate any person or any thing in history with him. God was without partner and without similitude. To think otherwise was to commit the ultimate sin of *shirk*, that is, of associating a human understanding, or a human person or natural thing with God.

As the Qur'an provided them, men might adopt a whole host of personal attributes by which to refer to God (i.e., the 99 names), such as *most high, lord of the worlds, subtle, wise*. But these all failed to comprehend him, even though they became the Muslim's way by which to pay him reverence. The Muslim understood that these words were merely a way of *referring* to God; they did not *describe* him.

In the selection you have read, Emran refers to Amram, the father of Moses, Aaron, and Miriam, as described in the Bible. Cf. 1 Chronicles 6:1-3. Zakariya refers to Zechariah, and Yahya refers to John the Baptist.

As the rabbis taught a doctrine of the torah as preexistent with God before creation, and as the Christians taught a similar doctrine with respect to Jesus as the *logos,* or Word of God, so the Muslims taught a doctrine of the preexistent "Mother of the Book," being with God as the mystical source of all the revelations of the book to men.

REFLECTION QUESTIONS

1. How does this passage dramatize Mary as a dedicated and protected person? Dedicated by whom? Protected by whom?
2. In what principal respects does the Qur'an account of the birth of Jesus agree with the birth account in Matthew 1:18-25?
3. What points of Muslim teaching about Jesus become apparent in the story of the clay bird?
4. Do you agree or disagree that the tone of the Qur'an is both more defensive of monotheism and more severe in moral judgment than that of the Hebrew Bible? The New Testament? Why?

UNIT EIGHTEEN:

THE BELIEFS
AND LAWS
OF ISLAM

Part 1:

THE QUR'AN CITES THE
ONENESS OF GOD

God, the heavenly creator and ruler, is one God, according to Islam. He is one, and not two, three, or many. He creates and sustains everything in the spiritual and natural world, whether men, stones, the spirits (jinn) who live in the natural world, or the heavenly angels, God's messengers, who go from his heavenly court to do his bidding. All are his creatures. Everything in his creation. Everything happens because of his permission or in obedience to his command.

SEARCH CUES

1. the absolute God
2. what the blasphemers say
3. God provides and cares for all
4. the angels praise him and do his bidding
5. the creator of man

NOW READ BELOW:
SURAHS 2:255; 5:75-76; 6:95-103; 29:46;
39:75; 66:6; 7:189; 23:12-14

GOD: HIS ONENESS AND ATTRIBUTES

God! There is no god except him—the living, self-subsisting, eternal. No slumber can seize him nor sleep. To him belong all things in the heavens and on earth. Who can intercede in his presence unless he permits? He knows what pertains to his creatures as happening after, before, or behind them. Nor shall they achieve any of his knowledge except as he wills. His throne extends over the heavens and the earth. He feels no fatigue in preserving and guarding them, for he is most high, supreme in glory.

2:255, The Cow.

They blaspheme who say, "God is Christ, son of Mary." For Christ said, "O children of Israel! Worship God, my Lord and your Lord." Whoever joins other gods with God, God will forbid him the garden, and hell will be his abode. There will be no one to help the wrongdoers.

They blaspheme who say God is one of three in a trinity, for there is no god but the one God. If they do not desist from their words, truly a grievous penalty will befall the blasphemers among them.

5:75-76, The Table.

It is God who causes the seed-grain and the date-stone to split and to sprout. He causes the living to come from the dead, and he is the one who causes the dead to come from the living. That is God. Then how are you deluded away from the truth?

He cleaves open the dawn. He has made the night for rest and tranquility and the sun and the moon for reckoning. Such is the measure of the mighty, the knowing. It is he who makes the stars to be beacons for you, so that with their help you may guide yourselves throughout the dark spaces of land and sea. We detail our signs for people who know.

It is he who has produced you from a single being and has given you a habitation and a resting place. We have detailed our revelations for a people who have understanding.

It is he who sends down rain from the skies. With it we produce vegetation of all kinds; from some we produce grain, heaped up at harvest. Out of the datepalm and its sheaths come clusters of dates hanging low and near. Then, too, there are gardens of grapes, olives, and pomegranates, each similar in kind yet distinct in variety. When they begin to bear fruit, feast your eyes on the fruit and the ripeness of it. Behold! In these things there are signs for people who believe.

Yet they take the jinn as partners with God, though God created them, and without knowledge they falsely ascribe to him sons and daughters. Glory be to him! How highly exalted he is above what they ascribe to him!

To him is due the primal origin of the heavens and the earth. How can he have a son when he has no consort? He created all things, and of all things he has full knowledge.

Such is God, your Lord. There is no god except him, the creator of all. So worship him! He takes care of all things. No vision can grasp him, but his grasp includes every vision. He transcends all comprehension, yet he is acquainted with all things.

6:95-103, The Livestock.

Do not dispute with the people of the book, except with means better than mere disputation, save with those who inflict wrong and injury. But say, "We believe in the revelation which has come down to us and in that which has come down to you. Our God and your God is one, and to him we surrender."

29:46, The Spider.

ANGELS

You will see angels surrounding the throne on all sides, singing glory and praise to their Lord. In justice will be the decision between them, and the cry on all sides will be, "Praise be to God, the Lord of the worlds!"

39:75, The Throngs.

O you who believe! Save yourselves and your families from a fire whose fuel is men and stones, over which are appointed angels stern and severe, who do not flinch from enacting the orders they receive from God, precisely as they are commanded.

66:6, The Banning.

CREATION OF MAN

It is he who created you from a single person whose mate he made of like nature, in order that he might dwell with her in love. When they are united, she bears a light burden which she carries about unnoticed. When she grows heavy, they both pray to God their Lord: "If you give us a goodly child, we vow to be grateful forever."

7:189, The Heights.

From a quintessence of clay we created man; then we made him a small sperm in a firm resting-place; then into a clot of congealed blood we transformed the sperm; then out of that clot we made a lump; then out of that lump we made bones and clothed the bones with flesh. Then from it we developed another creature—so blessed be God, the best of creators!

23:12-14, The Believers.

COMMENTARY

The Oneness of God

Nothing in the Qur'an commands the attention of the reader more than its focus on the oneness and the attributes of God. Central to all Islamic thought is the reverence expressed in the first surah, the creed of Islam, the very essence of the book. This first surah, called the *Fatiha*, or opening chapter, contains seven verses. Each verse, or ayat, in each surah of the Qur'an becomes to the Muslim mind a sign from God, and each surah is a degree. Thus God leads the faithful by ayat and surah (i.e., by signs and degrees) to the fullness of revelation as comprehended in the full Qur'an. This first surah, then, the Fatiha, became wedded to the Muslim mind as did the Shema to the Jewish mind, and the Lord's Prayer to the Christian. It can be translated as follows:

"In the name of God, most gracious, most merciful.
Praise be to God, the cherisher and sustainer of
    the worlds, most gracious, most merciful,
    master of the day of judgment.
We worship you, and we seek your aid.
Show us the straight way, the way of those on whom
    you have bestowed your grace,
Those whose portion is not wrath, and who do not
    go astray."

Intergroup Relations

To appreciate the experience of the Muslim in his relationship with God, we turn our attention to the relationship which he, the Jew, and the Christian, each understood to exist between his own people and those who were not members of his people's faith or nation.

In comparing our selections from the Hebrew Bible and the apocryphal and rabbinic literature with those from the Christian New Testament, we have seen a difference of emphasis concerning inter-group relations. Christians taught that all the non-Christian world would be blessed, or at least have that opportunity, through the Christian revelation. The Jews taught that all the non-Jewish world would be similarly blessed through the Jewish revelation. The Hebrew Bible and the apocryphal and rabbinic literature informed Jews that the blessings from God which they were to share with all the nations of the world did not necessarily involve a sharing of their own nationality. One need not be a Jew to enjoy the blessings from God which Israel was called to mediate to the nations. In contrast, the Christian New Testament required quite specifically that the way to enjoy the blessings of Christianity consisted necessarily, at least as a first step, in becoming a member of the Christian church.

Even though at all times gentiles might be accepted as converts to Israel, and even though sometimes a strong missionary movement existed among the Jews, nevertheless as a rule the Jews abided in the extended familial kinship of Israel as a national community with a common tribal origin and ancestry. From their point of view, the gentile nations were destined to be blessed as neighbors to Israel rather than as members of it. Conversely, the blessing which the non-Christian would inherit through the church required that the individual become a member of that church regardless of his nationality. This implied an ultimate loyalty on the part of the Christian to the church community which transcended his loyalty to his nation.

We can see in these contrasts something of the conflicting social attitudes that were manifested in the controversy of so much Jewish and Christian literature whenever one dealt with the claims and conduct of the other.

When Muhammad introduced the Qur'an into history, a second wave of missionary fervor swept the Western world, like the earlier and still-persisting missionary enterprise of the Christians. Unlike the Christians, however, and more like the Jews, this religion carried with it a sense of national identity among its adherents. Like the Christians, and unlike the Jews, the

Muslims reached out in a universal quest for members. Islam would be both religious and political. It would build its society as a community of converts and as an empire of political order. All men could join themselves as members to Islam. Meanwhile, Islam was called to impose its political rule wherever Jewish, Christian, or pagan tribes or nations appeared to plot against those who lived as Muslims. Thus God, through the Qur'an, would create among men not only a growing community of God's grace and mercy, but at the same time, an expanding political nation. The missionary community and the aggressive nation would be one undivided society of men acting in history under the command of the one and undivided God.

Islam, therefore, from the first recitation of the Qur'an, proclaimed God as the one and only God, whose name was Allah, who had inspired all tribes and nations in some degree through the sudden insights, the visions, and the prophecies he had given to their leading men. Yet for any religious community or political nation to claim in direct opposition to Islam a full and final revelation and authority from God was blasphemy and the worship of a man-made idol.

God's Creation

The Muslim's faith included many ideas shared with, or akin to, the ideas of the Christians and Jews. According to the Muslim, one above all ascribed mercy and graciousness to God, mercy to help men when the need arises, and grace to guide them in the way of righteousness and peace before any need arises.

God creates and sustains all that is in the spiritual and natural world, even the jinn, the invisible and hidden spiritual forces in the world. They are led, according to tradition, by Satan (Iblis), spoken of in the Qur'an both as a fallen angel and as one of the jinn. If the latter, then like the other jinn Satan is made of fire, as men are made of clay.

God's court, like the heavenly court depicted in the Bible, is populated with angels who are the messengers of God. These messengers keep God in touch with the world of men.

REFLECTION QUESTIONS

1. What resemblances do you see, if any, between surahs 2:255, 6:95-103, and the biblical Psalms?
2. How does the Qur'an avoid irreverence toward Jesus while at the same time attacking certain Christian teachings about Jesus?
3. In surah 6:95-103, would you say that the references to things of nature were especially appropriate for Muhammad's listeners? Why?
4. What are some similarities and differences between this Qur'an account of the creation of man (23:12-14) and those in the first two chapters of Genesis?
5. How might a person explain the sources of natural and human existence without reference to a god?

Part 2:

THE QUR'AN TELLS HOW MEN REACH THE PLEASURES OF PARADISE AND THE HORRORS OF HELL

According to the Qur'an a man would end up either in the gardens of paradise or in the flames of hell, depending on his moral behavior while living in this world. The recitations of Muhammad portrayed the dramatic distinction between paradise and hell, and contrasted the meaning of belief and disbelief, obedience and disobedience, in the experiences of men.

SEARCH CUES

1. the rivers beneath
2. men on the high places
3. chains, pitch, and fire
4. wives of the prophets
5. obedience to God and his messenger

NOW READ BELOW:
SURAHS 7:42-53; 14:48-50; 33:28-36; 4:36-38

PARADISE

Now those who believe and work righteousness (for we put no burden on any soul, but one which it can bear), will be companions in paradise, to dwell there forever.

And we shall remove whatever ill-feeling may be in their hearts, and rivers shall flow beneath them. And they will say, "All praise be to God, who led us to this! Nor would we have found the way if God had not guided us. Truly the heralds of our Lord brought the truth." And it will be proclaimed to them, "This is paradise which you are made to inherit for what you did."

And the dwellers in paradise cry to the dwellers in hell, "We have found to be true that which our Lord promised us. Have you found to be true that which your Lord promised you?" They say, "Yes, truly." And a crier between them cries: "The curse of God is on doers of evil, those who would try to keep men from the path of God and would seek in it something crooked. They are the ones who denied the hereafter."

And between them is a veil. On high up places are men who know all by their marks. And they call to the owners of paradise: "Peace be with you!" Not yet have they entered it, although they hope.

And when they turn their eyes toward the dwellers of hell, they say: "Our Lord! Do not put us with the wrongdoing people."

The men on the heights will hail certain men they will know from their marks, saying, "Of what profit to you were your hoards and your arrogant ways? Are these the ones about whom you swore that God would not show mercy? Enter paradise. No fear shall come upon you, nor is it you who will grieve."

The companions of hell then call out to the owners of paradise, "Pour on us some water or some of that which God has provided you." They reply, "Surely God has forbidden them both to the disbelievers, to those who took their religion to be mere amusement and play, and to those deceived by the life of the world." That day shall we forget them as they forgot the meeting of this day, and as they used to reject our signs. For truly, we have brought them a scripture which we expound with knowledge, a way of guidance and mercy for a people who believe.

Do they just wait for the final fulfillment of the event? On the day the event is finally fulfilled, those who ignored it before will say: "The messengers of our Lord indeed brought true tidings. Have we no intercessors now to intercede on our behalf? Could we be sent back? Then would our conduct be different from our behavior in the past." They in fact will have lost their souls, and the things they invented will leave them in the lurch.

7:42-53, *The Heights.*

HELL

One day the earth will be changed to a different earth, and so will the heavens, and men will be marshalled before God, the one, the irresistible. And you will see the guilty on that day linked together in chains—their garments, liquid pitch, and their faces covered with fire.

14:48-50, *Abraham.*

ETHICS

O Prophet, say to your consorts, "If it be you desire the life of this world and its glitter—then come! I will provide for your pleasure setting you free quite handsomely. But if you seek God and his messenger, as well as the abode hereafter, then surely God has prepared for the doers of good among you a mighty reward."

O wives of the prophet! Whoever shows manifest lewdness, the punishment for her will be doubled, and that is easy for God. As for any of you who works righteousness, remaining devout in the service of God and his messenger, to her shall we doubly grant her reward. We have prepared her a generous sustenance.

O wives of the Prophet! You are not like any other women. If you keep your duty to God, then do not be soft of speech, lest he in whose heart is disease may aspire. Instead, speak the customary way. And stay in your houses and do not display your beauty like the display of women in the era of ignorance. Keep up prayer, pay the poorrate, and obey God and his messenger. God only desires to take uncleanness away from you, O people of the household, and to purify you thoroughly. Bear in mind what is recited in your houses about wisdom and God's revelations. Behold! God is subtle, aware.

For Muslim men and women—for believing men and women, for devout men and women, for true men and women, for men and women who are patient and constant, for men and women who humble themselves, for men and women who give in charity, for men and women who fast, for men and women who guard their chastity, for men and women who spend much time engaged in the praise of God—God has prepared forgiveness for them, and a great reward.

It is not fitting for a believer, whether a man or a woman, when a matter has been decided by God and his messenger, to have any option about their decision. If anyone disobeys God and his messenger, he is indeed on a clearly wrong path.

33:28-36, *The Clans.*

Serve God, and do not join any partners with him. And do good—to parents, kinsfolk, orphans, those in need, neighbors who are near, neighbors who are strangers, the companion by your side, the wayfarer, and those whom your right hands possess. For God does not love the arrogant, the vainglorious, those who are niggardly and bid people to be niggardly, hiding that which God has given them out of his grace. And we have prepared for the disbelievers an abasing punishment—and those who spend their wealth in order to be seen of men, and who do not believe in God or the last day. Whoever takes Satan for a companion, what a dreadful companion he is!

4:36-38, *The Women.*

COMMENTARY

Man's Behavior Leads to Paradise or Hell

According to Islam, God maintains a constant interest in the faith and ethics of mankind. He points out in the Qur'an the proper relationship between a man and his wife, or wives, and between persons in trade and politics. God teaches even the proper behavior toward those whom "their right hands might possess," that is, toward captives, slaves, or any creature existing under the Muslim's power to sustain or destroy.

The Muslim, like the Christian, looked forward to a resurrection and a day of judgment. The hereafter is real in the teaching of the Qur'an. The spirit of a man lives on eternally according to the will of God, suffering the punishments or purgings earned for him by his sins—and this is hell—or enjoying the heavenly Gardens of God, where fruit hangs low from the trees, where waters flow beneath one's feet, and where companions live to bring one gladness—and this is paradise.

REFLECTION QUESTIONS

1. How do the destinies of the faithful and the unfaithful in the Qur'an seem to compare with those of the faithful and the unfaithful in the New Testament?
2. What kind of behavior seems to have been the mark of a good Muslim wife? According to the Qur'an, would the conduct of the typical modern American woman be satisfactory to Muslim ethics? Why?
3. Comparing the writings of the Hebrew Bible, the New Testament, and the Qur'an, how would you rank them with regard to emphasis on *individual* as over against *corporate* human destiny?

Part 3:

THE PROPHET RECITES SOME OF
THE RULES OF ISLAM'S CULTIC LIFE

The religious community in the Abrahamic tradition, whether Jewish, Christian, or Muslim, lived within the discipline of its own peculiar cult, or religious rule of life. For Islam, this included rules of prayer, of ceremonial cleanness, of diet, charity, and devotion to Islam's holy place of origin, where the full meaning of the Muslim life first was revealed through Muhammad the Prophet.

SEARCH CUES

1. the covenant
2. a mind befuddled
3. ceremonial impurity
4. the qiblah
5. unconditional almsgiving
6. pilgrimage
7. carrion, blood, and swine

NOW READ BELOW:
SURAHS 2:40-46; 4:43; 2:142-146; 2:177;
2:261-266; 3:96-97; 16:114-115

PRAYER: GENERAL PRESCRIPTION

O children of Israel! Call to mind the favor I bestowed upon you, and fulfill your covenant with me as I fulfill my covenant with you, and fear none but me.

And believe in that which I have revealed, verifying that which is with you, and do not be the first to deny it; neither charge a cheap price for my messages. Keep your duty to me, and to me alone. Do not conceal truth with falsehood, nor knowingly hide the truth. Be steadfast in prayer; practice regular charity; and bow down your heads with those who bow down in worship.

Do you urge men to be good yet neglect your own souls while you read the Book? Have you no sense? Seek help in patience and prayer. Truly this is difficult except for the humble-minded, who bear in mind the certainty that they will meet their Lord, and that they will return to him.

2:40-46, *The Cow.*

ABLUTION AND GENERAL CLEANLINESS AS A CONDITION FOR PRAYER

O you who believe! So that you may understand all that you say, do not approach prayers with a mind befuddled with alcohol, nor in a state of ceremonial impurity, (except when traveling on the road), until after washing your whole body. If you are ill, or on a journey, or one of you comes from offices of nature, or if you have been in contact with women, and you find no water, then take for yourselves clean sand or earth, and rub your faces and hands with it. For God blots out sins and forgives again and again.

4:43, *The Women.*

THE QIBLAH, OR THE DIRECTION TOWARD MECCA

The fools among the people will say: "What has turned them from the Qiblah to which they were accustomed?" Say, Both east and west belong to God. He guides whom he will to a way that is straight.

Thus we have made you an exalted nation, that you may be bearers of witness to the people that the messenger may be a bearer of witness to you. And we appointed the qiblah which formerly you were used to, only that we might know him who follows the messenger from him who turns on his heels. In truth, it was a hard test except for those whom God guided. But it was not God's purpose that your faith should be in vain, for God is full of pity, and merciful toward mankind.

Surely, we see your face turning to heaven, so indeed we shall make you master of the qiblah which you like. Then turn your face towards the sacred mosque. Wherever you are, turn your faces toward it. And those who have been given the Book certainly know that it is the truth from their Lord. And God is not heedless of what they do.

Even if you were to bring to the people of the Book all the signs, they would not follow your qiblah. Nor are you going to follow their qiblah; nor indeed will they follow each other's qiblah. If, after the knowledge has reached you, you were to follow their desires—then indeed you would be in the wrong.

Those whom we have given the Book recognize him as they recognize their sons. But a part of them surely conceal the truth which they know.

2:142-146, *The Cow.*

CHARITY

It is not righteousness that you turn your faces toward east or west; rather it is righteousness to believe in God and the last day, and the angels, and the Book, and the messengers; to spend of your substance out of love for him, for your kin, for orphans, for the needy, for the wayfarer, for those who ask, and for the ransom of slaves; to be steadfast in prayer, and to practice regular charity; to fulfill the contracts which you have made; to be firm and patient, in pain and adversity, and throughout all periods of panic. Such are the people of truth, the God-fearing.

2:177, *The Cow.*

The parable of those who spend their substance in the way of God is that of a grain of corn. It grows seven ears, and each ear has a hundred grains. God gives manifold increase to whom he pleases, and God cares for all, and he knows all things.

Those who expend their wealth in the way of God, and do not follow up what they have spent with reproach or injury, their reward is with their Lord, and they shall have no fear nor shall they grieve.

A kind word with forgiveness is better than almsgiving followed by injury. God is self-sufficient, forbearing.

O you who believe! Do not cancel your charity by reminders of your generosity or by injury, like those who spend their substance to be seen of men, but believe neither in God nor the last day. In parable, they are like a hard, barren rock, on which is a little soil. On it falls heavy rain, leaving it just a bare stone. They will be able to do nothing with anything they have earned. And God does not guide those who reject faith.

And the parable of those who spend their wealth to seek God's pleasure and for the strengthening of their souls is the parable of a garden on raised ground, upon which heavy rain falls, so that it brings forth its fruit twofold. But if heavy rain does not fall on it, light rain suffices. And God observes of what you do.

Does any of you wish that he had a garden with date-palms and vines, and streams flowing underneath, and all kinds of fruit, which, when he is stricken with old age, and his children are not strong, should be caught in a whirlwind of fire and burnt up? Thus does God make clear to you his signs, that you may consider.

2:261-266, *The Cow.*

PILGRIMAGE

The first house appointed for men was at Bakka, full of blessing and of guidance for all kinds of beings. In it are manifest signs, the station of Abraham. Whoever enters it finds security. Pilgrimage to it is a duty that men owe to God—those who can afford the journey. But if any deny faith, God does not stand in need of any of his creatures.

3:96-97, *The Family of Emran.*

DIETARY LAWS

So eat of the good and lawful sustenance which God has provided for you. And be grateful for the favors of God, if it is he whom you serve.

He has only forbidden you dead meat, and blood, and the flesh of swine, and anything over which the name of other than God is invoked. But if one becomes forced by necessity, without willful disobedience, or transgressing due limits, then God is oft-forgiving, most merciful.

16:114-115, *The Bee.*

COMMENTARY

The Creed

The Qur'an, believed to be a revelation from God became the written authority and guide to which every Muslim turned his heart and mind. From the content of the Qur'an, the Muslim derived five great dimensions for his life as a member of Islam. Those five dimensions centered themselves in five activities of Islamic faith often called the Five Pillars of Islam.

At least once in his life, each Muslim had to repeat the creed of Islam with complete commitment and understanding. This formal creed, spoken to every child at birth and to every person at the moment of his dying, constituted the first and last affirmation of his life. It said, "There is no god but God: Muhammad is the Prophet of God." To say this creed in good faith was to become a Muslim, and to keep on saying it, together with acting in the patterns of devotion it implied, was to remain one.

Prayer

The heart of Muslim devotion was prayer. Daily, when the *muezzin* (crier) voiced at the five appointed hours his call to the faithful to enter the mosque, the place of prayer and learning, the Muslim responded, entering the mosque and following the *Imam* (leader) in the sequence of prayers and obeisances. If unable to join his brother Muslims at the mosque, he observed the Islamic requirements for prayer wherever he happened to be, insofar as it was possible. Always, with all the faithful, he faced in the direction of the Ka'ba (Mecca) when he prayed. This, his direction of facing when he prayed, was the *qiblah* of Islam. While the Prophet remained in Mecca (Bakka), before the Hejira, the qiblah of the Muslims was Jerusalem, after the pattern of the Jews and Christians. But after the Hejira the qiblah of Islam became and remained Mecca.

Almsgiving

Each Muslim expressed Islam by following the rule of charity (*zakat*) through almsgiving. Almsgiving in part was required and in part was a matter of voluntary decision. In almsgiving the Muslim expressed his devotion to man as in his offering of prayer he expressed his devotion to God.

Pilgrimage

Not all Muslims possessed either the financial resources or the physical strength to make a pilgrimage *(hajj)* to Mecca. Each one who did have the means was required to make the pilgrimage at least once during his lifetime. The focus of the hajj was on the Ka'ba. Each pilgrim walked around it at prescribed times during his pilgrimage. Each pilgrim also ran between two mounds called the Safa and the Marwah. He did this to commemorate how Hagar, the mother of Ismail, ran seeking water for her infant son when Abraham brought them into the desert. Later the boy would help to build the Ka'ba as the sacred house of prayer where Muslims would praise and glorify God in Mecca, the city of peace *(salam)*.

Fasting

During the month of Ramadan, the month in which Muhammad first received a revelation of the Qur'an from the angel Gabriel, each Muslim had to fast *(saum)* throughout each day in order to commemorate that great event. This meant abstaining from food, drink, and sexual intercourse from sunrise to sunset.

These, then, were the Five Pillars of Islam: the creed, the prayers, the alms, the pilgrimage, and the fast. In the Qur'an selections for this part, you have read several of the many passages which pertain to these and other practical devotions by which the Muslim expressed his peaceful submission to the command of God.

REFLECTION QUESTIONS

1. In addressing Israel in surah 2:40-46, what is implied by the phrase, "Fulfill your covenant with me as I fulfill my covenant with you"?

2. How would you interpret the fact that the Qur'an's prohibition against consuming alcohol has lasted much longer than the similar prohibition that appeared in the American Constitution?

3. How does praying toward a certain point in space become also a prayer toward a certain point in time? What made, for Islam, that certain point in time and space significant?

4. Compare the attitudes toward charity and almsgiving that you have found in the religious literature studied in this course.

5. What similarities and differences in the cultic practices of Judaism, Christianity, and Islam have you discovered in the literature or observed elsewhere?

Part 4:

THE QUR'AN TEACHES THE WAYS
OF ISLAM WITHIN THE FAMILY

The Qur'an touched with commanding guidance on practically every significant aspect of human life, including the affairs of the domestic household. The rules of Muslim life describe the right relationships between parents and their children, husbands and their wives, masters and their servants. Those rules in part were the same and in part quite different from the family household laws of Judaism.

SEARCH CUES
1. the wing of humility
2. two, or three, or four
3. first, next, and last
4. family arbitration

NOW READ BELOW:
SURAHS 17:23-24; 4:2-3; 4:34-35

FAMILY RELATIONSHIP
Your Lord has decreed that you worship none but him, and that you be kind to parents. Whether one or both of them attain old age in your lifetime, say not a word of contempt to them, nor repel them, but address them in terms of honor. And, out of kindness, lower to them the wing of humility, and say: "My Lord! Bestow on them your mercy, as they cherished me in childhood."

17:23-24, *The Children of Israel.*

POLYGAMY
Restore to the orphans their property, not substituting worthless things for good ones; and do not devour their substance by mixing it up with your own, for this is indeed a sin.

291

And if you fear that you cannot do justice to the orphans, marry such women as seem good to you, two, or three, or four. But if you fear that you will not do justice, then marry only one, or that which your right hands possess. That will be more proper, to prevent you from doing injustice.

4:2-3, *The Women.*

DIVORCE, REMARRIAGE AND ALIMONY

Men are the protectors and maintainers of women, because God has given the one more strength than the other, and because they support them from their means. Therefore, the righteous women are devoutly obedient, and guard in absence what God would have them guard. As to those women on whose part you fear disloyalty and ill conduct, first, admonish them, next, refuse to share their beds, and, last, beat them lightly. But if they return to obedience, do not seek means of annoyance against them, for God is most high, great.

And if you fear a breach between the two, appoint an arbiter from his people and arbiter from her people. If they both desire reconciliation, God will effect harmony between them. Surely God is ever knowing and aware.

4:34-35, *The Women.*

COMMENTARY

The Law of Islam

Islam, like Israel, centered the faith of the people in their active submission to the law of God. The Muslims, like the Jews, developed a large body of rules for living based on the Qur'an and the Hadith. The Qur'an lays down for the faithful the whole foundation and many of the details of Islam's way of life. As with the Jews in their relationship to the torah, this obedience to the law of Islam was to the faithful not an arduous duty but a righteous custom welcomed by the faithful. For the Muslim, the Islamic law provided the way to enjoy the promise and to find the goal of paradise. Similarly, for the Jew, the way to Israel's final redemption lay in the practice of the torah, while for the Christian the way lay in his active devotion to Jesus as the Messiah.

REFLECTION QUESTIONS

1. What was the attitude of the Muslim law toward the elders and children of the household?
2. If the claim were made that the readings in this part of Unit Eighteen constitute an example of didactic literature, would you agree or disagree? Why?
3. In a Muslim household, who, apparently, was the head of the family? Do you think this structure of authority was appropriate to the conditions of Arab life?
4. Develop a comparison of the status of women in Muhammad's Arabia with the status of (a) women in the typical American suburb, (b) women in rural America, (c) women in an American inner city.

Part 5:

THE QUR'AN ADVISES THE MUSLIM COMMUNITY CONCERNING ITS DEALINGS WITH OTHERS

The nations and states of Islam conducted their affairs with each other and with non-Muslim states and nations under principles set forth in the Qur'an. A large part of the Qur'an teaching in this area dealt with defining the enemy, and with the proper attitude and action of the Muslim group in dealing with an enemy.

SEARCH CUES
1. do not take them as friends
2. enmity and hatred forever
3. the good and bad example of Abraham
4. dealing kindly and justly

NOW READ BELOW: SURAH 60:1-8

THE RELATION OF A MUSLIM STATE TO A NON-MUSLIM STATE

O you who believe; do not take my enemies and yours as friends, offering them love, even though they have rejected the truth that has come to you, and have driven out the Prophet and yourselves because you believe in God, your Lord! If you have come out to strive in my way and to seek my good pleasure, do not take them as friends, holding secret converse of love with them, for I know full well all that you conceal and reveal. And any of you that does this has strayed from the straight path.

293

If they overcome you, they will be your enemies, and with evil will stretch forth their hands and their tongues towards you for they desire that you may disbelieve.

Of no avail to you will be your ties of kindred and your children on the day of judgment. He will judge between you. God sees what you do.

An excellent example exists for you in Abraham and those with him, when they said to their people: "We are clear of you and of whatever you worship besides God. We have rejected you, and there has arisen between us and you enmity and hatred forever—unless you believe in God and him alone." But not when Abraham said to his father: "I will pray for forgiveness for you, though I have no power to get anything on your behalf from God." They prayed, "Our Lord! In you do we trust, and to you do we turn in repentance. With you is our final goal. Our Lord! Do not subject us to trial in confronting the unbelievers, but forgive us, our Lord! For you are the exalted in might, the wise." Surely in them is a good example for you, for him who hopes for God and the last day. And whoever turns away, surely God is the self-sufficient, the praised.

It may be that God will ordain love between you and those with whom you are at enmity, for God is mighty, and God is forgiving and merciful.

God does not forbid you from dealing kindly and justly with regard to those who did not fight you over faith or drive you out of your homes, for God loves those who are just. God only forbids you from making friends with those who warred against you on account of religion and drove you out from your homes and helped to drive you out. Whoever makes friends with them is a wrongdoer.

60:1-8, *The Pleading Woman.*

REFLECTION QUESTIONS

1. What was the basic article of belief, which, if not held by a neighboring group, would tend to define it for Islam as an enemy?

2. What comment in this passage accents the responsibility of the individual Muslim regarding his own destiny?

3. How might this passage be used to justify patience and restraint in dealing with non-Muslims?

4. (a) How would you compare the general attitude toward "the enemy" that you find in each of the following: Hebrew Bible, Apocryphal and Rabbinic Writings, New Testament, Qur'an?

   (b) From your knowledge of history since the days when this literature was written, to what extent do you think those attitudes have changed, if at all, and in what directions? Can you cite examples?

6. How would you describe the influence of the sacred writings of Judaism, Christianity, and Islam on the subsequent development of Western literature and culture?

APPENDIX

AN HISTORICAL SKETCH OF JUDAISM, CHRISTIANITY, AND ISLAM

Introduction

This historical sketch is to provide an overview of the time sequence in which the development of Judaism, Christianity, and Islam took place. The period of history covered by the classical literature of the Jews, Christians, and Muslims stretches from approximately 2000 B.C. through about 900 A.D.—a span of almost 3000 years. Since all three are historical religions, you should have a general understanding of what was happening to these people and to the world around them during the development of their religion and, consequently, their literature.

The Hebrew Nomads of the Patriarchal Period

The historical memory of the Jewish people goes back to the patriarchal period, to a nomadic group of Semites who came out of the land of Mesopotamia, sometime between 2000 B.C. and 1800 B.C. These nomads migrated slowly out of Mesopotamia and down through Palestine, stopping where they could find water and good pasturage for their flocks. The leaders of these tribes were ruling fathers, or patriarchs, the chief of whom are known in the literature as Abraham, Isaac, and Jacob.

The ancient world where these nomads wandered was centered on two great civilizations, Mesopotamia to the east of Palestine, and Egypt to the southwest. Between the two, an arc of populated land, the Fertile Crescent, curved from Mesopotamia to Syria in the north and down through Palestine to Egypt. The Fertile Crescent provided a good living from the land for the people who settled there, and it was the route of trade and commerce between Egypt and Mesopotamia.

The Exodus from Egypt

The Semitic nomads, then, moved through the Fertile Crescent, and eventually some of them, who would later be known as the Israelites, came into Egypt about 1650 B.C. Egypt at that time was controlled by the Hyksos, a Semitic people like the Israelites, who had invaded Egypt in 1700 B.C. The nomads lived comfortably under the Hyksos rule. However, after the Hyksos were overthrown by the Egyptians, life became harder for the Israelites. They were subjected to conscription for slave labor. They were made to provide the manpower necessary for Egypt's intensified building programs during the reign of Ramses II, which began about 1300 B.C.

Finally, the Israelites rebelled against Egypt's harsh treatment and, under the leadership of Moses, they fled from Egypt into the desert wilderness to the east. This Exodus, which occurred about 1250 B.C., is when the Israelites became welded together as a nation with a sustaining sense of identity as God's chosen people. They saw the deliverance from Egypt as

God's divine intervention in history in behalf of his people. They felt his guidance in their wilderness wanderings as a demonstration of his willingness to care for his people. The Israelites accepted the laws given by Moses as the way by which the relationship between God and his people was to be expressed. And they received from their God the inheritance of the promised land.

Palestine Becomes a Home for the Israelites

After a period of wandering in the desert wilderness, the Israelites invaded Palestine and, over a span of several generations, took control of the land from its Canaanite inhabitants. There they settled, giving up their nomadic existence and developing communities with an agricultural and pastoral economy. From the initial entry into Palestine until about 1000 B.C., the Israelites were organized into twelve tribes, bound together by their common religious identity. They had a central sanctuary at Shiloh, at which all the tribes worshiped. But the Israelites had no central government. Each tribe was free to govern itself as it saw fit. Sometimes the tribes quarreled among themselves. Sometimes they would unite to repel invasions from outsiders who tried to take control of their land. At these times, heroic leaders, known as the judges, rose up from among the people and helped to organize a unified defense against the invaders.

During the last half of the 11th century B.C., a people called the Philistines took control of part of the southern coastal plain of Palestine and developed into a powerful military force. In 1020 B.C., the Philistines waged a decisive battle with the Israelites and destroyed their sanctuary at Shiloh. This became a stimulus to the development of a centralized national government among the Israelites. Through the leadership of David, the Philistines were defeated, and David was established as king over the twelve tribes.

The Kings and the Prophets

Under the kingship of David and his son, Solomon, the Israelites developed into a powerful nation exercising complete command over the Palestinian region. Jerusalem was established as the religious and governmental center, and a great temple was built there. Throughout the kingdom, there was intense building activity and economic development. But discontent arose among many Israelites concerning the ways of life their people were developing. Some had adopted the practices and beliefs of the Canaanite religions. The prophetic tradition developed under these conditions. The prophets were devout men who tried to guide their people back to the traditional religious beliefs and way of life of the earlier Israelites. This tradition of prophecy continued for more than 500 years.

The Divided Kingdom

There were other problems in the united kingdom of Solomon's time: military conscription, taxation, and forced labor placed heavy burdens on the people. After Solomon's death, the discontent of the people grew so strong that in 922 B.C. the kingdom split, and two separate kingdoms were established, Israel in the north and Judah in the south.

Israel and Judah quarrelled and fought with one another for the next two centuries. Judah continued under the rule of the Davidic dynasty, while Israel established its own series of kings. The temple in Jerusalem was maintained as Judah's central sanctuary, but Israel set up its own in the north at Bethel.

During the eighth century B.C., Israel and Judah came to the sober realization that they had more to worry about than just each other. A powerful force was developing in the north. The Assyrian Empire had grown and expanded its sphere of control over Mesopotamia in the east and Syria in the west. The kingdom of Israel tried to fight the Assyrian Empire and lost. In 721 B.C. many of the people of the northern kingdom were deported to Assyria, and eventually they became assimilated into the Assyrian culture. A handful of people, later known as the Samaritans, was all that remained of the northern kingdom. The kingdom of Judah decided it would be foolish to fight and, instead, submitted to the overlordship of the Assyrian Empire.

The power of the Assyrian Empire declined in the seventh century, and eventually Assyria was crushed by the rising Babylonian Empire in 605 B.C. Judah submitted to the control of this new overlord for a while, but finally the Israelites rebelled and in 587 B.C. were completely defeated. Judah was overrun by king Nebuchadnezzar's Babylonian army, Jerusalem was sacked, and the Temple was burned. The people were taken in captivity to Babylon, leaving none but the poorest in Judah.

The Babylonian Exile

During the exile in Babylonia, the Jewish people did not fare too badly. They were established in colonies. The Babylonians did not restrict their freedom, and the Jews became adjusted to life in Babylonia. The problem for the people was that of their faith. They had always thought of their faith in relation to the land of Palestine and the temple in Jerusalem, and they despaired over the loss of these. It was during these times of the Babylonian captivity that the prophets and the priests helped the people to find a new understanding of themselves as a settled worshiping community bound together by faith rather than by land.

Even with this understanding, many of the Jews still wished to return to Palestine. Their hope became a reality when the Persian empire, under the leadership of Cyrus, took control of Babylonia. Cyrus issued an edict of liberation to the Jewish people in 538 B.C., permitting them to return to Palestine. A number of Jews liked the life they had established for themselves in Babylonia and remained there, but many returned to their homeland.

The Jewish Community Is Reestablished in Palestine

In Palestine the people set about rebuilding the temple. They also sought to reestablish their community. This sense of community did not really become strong until about a century later when, through the work of Ezra and Nehemiah, two Babylonian Jews who came to Palestine, a religious revival came about. It was at this time that a very important event occurred. The Torah, or first five books of the Hebrew Bible, was made the basis of communal and private life for the Jewish people. The Jews remained under the nominal control of rulers appointed by the Persian empire, but direction and guidance for their day-to-day lives were provided by the high priests of the community.

Greek Influence on the Jewish Community

In 334 B.C., the Persian empire fell to the growing Greek empire of Alexander the Great, and Palestine came under Greek control. The conquest had little effect on the Jewish community politically, for the tolerant overlordship of the Persians was continued by the Greek empire. Culturally, though, many aspects of hellenization became diffused into the Jewish way of life, including Greek ways of thinking and the Greek language, as well as manners, styles of dress, and other social habits. Urbanization and commerce increased throughout the Greek empire, and the Jewish people became a part of the broadening system of international relations. But the Jewish community during this period was far from being completely receptive to hellenization. Many Jews adhered to their beliefs in the sacred history of their people and their laws, and felt that hellenization was a threat to the moral and religious order of Israel.

The tolerant rule of the Greeks was maintained through the third century B.C. But when Antiochus Epiphanes came to the throne in 175 B.C., the policy was changed. Antiochus tried to force the Jewish people to accept the Greek religion and to abandon completely their own ways of life. He abolished the Torah and desecrated the temple in Jerusalem. This act provoked the Jews to revolt, and what is known as the Maccabean rebellion ensued. The rebellion was successful, and in 164 B.C. Antiochus capitulated and allowed the Temple to be cleansed and rededicated. The Jews continued to press for their political and religious freedom, and they won their independence in 143 B.C.

Pharisees, Sadducees, and Rabbinic Scholars

From the time of the Maccabean revolt, the Jews were divided into two major groups, the Pharisees, who were more or less the popular party, and the Sadducees, who were made up of the priestly aristocracy and wealthy landowners. The control of Israel was in the hands of the high priest, and all through the period of independence, this control passed back and forth between the Pharisaic and Sadducean parties in a bitter struggle for power in which the political ambitions of both groups often overshadowed their religious responsibilities. A civil war broke out between the parties which was not quelled until 63 B.C., when the Jewish nation came under the rule of Rome. Rome at that time had succeeded the Greek empire in controlling the Mediterranean and Near Eastern World.

The loss of political freedom for the Jews, however, was accompanied by the development of various movements in religious thought and activity. During the period of struggle between the Pharisees and Sadducees, several other communities of believers were formed. They believed that by withdrawing into wilderness areas and separating themselves from the general Jewish population, they could maintain and develop the spirit of the true Israel. These separatist groups were called the Essenes. Other Jews, though, thought that the growth of the Jewish faith must take place within the Jewish nation as a whole. Through the work of rabbinic scholars such as Hillel and Shammai, schools of learning were established in Jerusalem in the latter part of the first century B.C. in which the Torah was studied as the central force of Judaism and the inspired source for all theological and moral beliefs.

The Christian Movement

It was into this atmosphere of political confusion, conflict, and diversified thought and teaching within the Jewish religious community that Jesus of Nazareth was born about 4 B.C., a Jewish child of a Jewish mother. During his career, Jesus gathered about him a small group of followers. His teaching concerned the immediate coming of the kingdom of God. Scholars believe that it reflected the religious beliefs of the Pharisaic line of rabbinic scholars. In many ways, they believe, Jesus was also influenced in his teachings by the Essene communities that had withdrawn into the wilderness areas.

After Jesus' death about 30 A.D., this Jewish sect, later to be called Christianity, continued to grow and develop. Its followers believed that Jesus had risen after his death and was alive as the spiritual head of the Christian movement. To them, this showed the power and presence of God and the coming of the kingdom on which Jesus had based his message. The followers, or disciples, spread their beliefs among their fellow Jews, and won new followers. Eventually the leaders of the group carried their message beyond the Jewish community and into the Greek and Roman cities of the Roman empire, winning great numbers of gentile adherents.

The disciples, however, faced opposition on two sides. The loyal believers of the Jewish community did not agree with the teachings of this new sect and felt it to be a heretical movement within their religion. Disputes developed between the Jewish community and the early Christian believers. It was at this point that the second force of opposition of Christianity made itself known. The Roman empire had had trouble periodically from the Jewish people, and this disturbing new movement was met with harsh treatment by the Roman government. Many of the early Christian leaders were put to death by the Romans, including Peter and Paul, who are believed to have been executed in Rome about 64 A.D.

Conflict with Rome

Paralleling the Empire's distrust of Christianity, during the first century A.D. the friction between the Jewish nation and the Roman Empire continued, culminating in the outbreak of the Jewish-Roman War in 66 A.D.

The Jewish military strength was no match for the Roman army, and the war ended in 70 A.D. with the fall of the temple and the complete destruction of Jerusalem. After this war, the Roman world tended to see the Christian and Jewish religions more and more as separate and hostile. By about the end of the first century A.D. the Romans considered Christianity a religion in its own right.

Both Christians and Jews continued to suffer periodic persecution under the Roman Empire. Order was maintained in Palestine for a while after the Jewish-Roman War. In other areas of the Empire, however, there were frequent rebellions by the Jews against Roman oppression. But these uprisings were always put down by Rome. In 132-135 A.D. another rebellion by the Jews occurred in Palestine when the Roman ruler attempted to rebuild Jerusalem and erect a temple to Zeus there. This rebellion also failed, and the city was reconstructed. This marked the last attempt of the Jewish people of the ancient world to reestablish their own nation in Palestine.

The aftermath of all these conflicts of the first and second centuries A.D. was that the Jewish people, instead of being concentrated in the Palestinian area, were dispersed throughout the Mediterranean and Near Eastern world, while the Christian influence spread geographically and established itself in a number of aggressive centers around the Eastern Mediterranean.

Rabbinic Scholarship Continues

Despite the suppression of the political and military power of the Jewish people, religious growth and activity developing from the scholarly rabbinic schools of the late first century B.C. continued. The rabbinic scholars of the first two centuries A.D. gathered to discuss and interpret the Torah and the oral laws under the influence of Hellenic and other Near Eastern thought. The intellectual activity of the first century A.D. also brought about the canonization, that is, the final authorized collection of the books to be included, of the Hebrew Bible, by the Council of Jamnia in 90 A.D.

The Growth of Christianity

The Christians meanwhile met with continued opposition from the Roman empire, and many followers suffered martyrdom in the second and third centuries A.D. But the number of people accepting the Christian beliefs continued to grow, and by the end of the third century the Roman empire had begun to treat the Christians more tolerantly than it had in the past. Perhaps one reason for this was that the empire had other problems with which to contend. Its vast sprawling organization had become unwieldy during the second and third centuries A.D. and was threatened with decay. For a while, there were two emperors, one in the eastern part of the empire and one in the west, at Rome.

In the beginning of the fourth century A.D. the Roman Empire was reunited and Constantinople, a new capital of the empire, was established in the East under the emperor Constantine. Constantine became a Christian. In 325 A.D. he proclaimed Christianity the official religion of the Roman empire. Under this new status the Christian church grew and expanded.

During the fourth century A.D. the canonization of the books of the New Testament took place. Many new ideas and doctrines developed, and various groups distinguished themselves within the Christian community of believers by their differing views of their religion. Much later, the differences in beliefs, coupled with regional power struggles, would lead to a general separation of the Christian church into rival Eastern and Western communions.

The Talmud

Among the Jewish people of the third and fourth centuries A.D. the rabbinic scholars continued their discussions and debates on the Torah and the oral laws, developing and refining their beliefs about their religion. Although the Jewish people were dispersed throughout the empire, two main centers of Jewish religious thought existed, one in Palestine and one in Babylonia. From these two centers, or schools of learning, came the scholarly writings of the Jewish thought known as talmudic literature. In Palestine, the Jerusalem Talmud was completed about the end of the third century A.D., and in Babylonia the rabbinic scholars completed the Babylonian Talmud about 500 A.D. Thereafter, through the rest of the centuries which this historical sketch covers, Jewish thought and study continued primarily in schools of learning known as the yeshibot, which were found throughout the areas in which the Jewish people were living. The scholars of the yeshibot were considered the religious leaders of their people and as such were the authorities for the regulation of Jewish religious, moral, and social relations.

The Fall of Rome and the Early Church

After the reign of Constantine, the Roman empire again became divided into the East and West, with each section having its own emperor. This was the final loss of political unity for the empire, for the western section declined in power and organization and finally collapsed following the invasion of Rome by the barbarians in 410 A.D. The Eastern, or Byzantine empire, however, continued to hold control over its area of influence after the fall of Rome.

The Christian church came through the disintegration of the Western Roman empire in better shape than did any other of the social and cultural institutions. As such, the church became the center of unity through which the Roman empire of the West was slowly rebuilt during the centuries that followed. The structure of the Western church was organized around the office of the pope, or bishop of Rome. Under the leadership of the pope, during the fifth and sixth centuries A.D., the social, economic, and political organization of the Western empire was reorganized. The monasteries of the Western church played an important part in the preservation of ancient culture and in the development of education during the centuries after the fall of the empire. The work of the church in these activities eventually was to lead to a formal coordination of powers between the church and the state when the Western Roman empire once again regained something of its former stature. This coordination between church and state was never fully free of tension, however, for at different times either the church or the state predominated in the control of power.

In the Byzantine empire, the Eastern Christian church developed along different lines from those of the church of the west. Instead of posing one papal authority, the Byzantine Christians were organized around several councils of bishops. There were also strong differences in belief between the Eastern and Western branches of Christianity, which became more and more distinct with the passing of time.

Byzantium and Persia

The Byzantine empire itself maintained its economic prosperity and its political and cultural influence throughout the fifth and sixth centuries A.D. In the late sixth century, however, it came into conflict with a renewed empire to the east. The Persian empire had been undergoing a political and religious revival for several hundred years, and it now emerged as a strong power under a sacred monarchy in the late part of the sixth century. The Persian empire sought to gain control over some of the territory which belonged to the Byzantine empire. In the early seventh century, the Persians conquered Syria and Egypt. The Byzantines were able to gather the forces necessary to retaliate against the Persians, and managed to force their withdrawal from Syria, Egypt, and Asia Minor. In 628 A.D. peace was made between the Byzantine empire and the Persians.

This, then, was the situation in the Mediterranean and Near Eastern world during the seventh century A.D. The Christian empire in the West had not yet recovered from the barbaric invasions of the fifth century, and the Christian and Persian empires in the East threatened one another's power across an uneasy peace. The stage was set for the rise of the Islamic empire.

The Land and People of Arabia

Arabia had been a rather isolated area. The harsh terrain of the Arabian desert had made it undesirable to the great empires that had grown and fallen around its borders. To be sure, there were some towns and cities around the oases, and trade routes intersected the area, but for the most part Arabia was a forgotten land, left alone by the empires which surrounded it.

The Arabian desert people, or bedouins, were organized into tribes. They led a nomadic existence, traveling from place to place in search of pasturage for their flocks. For the most part, these bedouins had a polytheistic religion. In the more settled towns and cities, particularly along the northern and western sides of Arabia, both Judaism and Christianity were known and accepted by some of the population.

Muhammad

Muhammad, the founder of Islam, was born in 570 A.D. in Mecca, one of the trade centers to be found along the western side of Arabia. He was a merchant in Mecca, and in the course of his travels and his business, he came into contact with both Jews and Christians. As time went on he became increasingly discontent with the polytheistic beliefs and the various moral practices of his fellow Arabians. In 610 A.D. Muhammad received what he believed to be a prophetic call from God, or Allah as he is called in the Arabian world. As a result of this revelation, Muhammad began to teach belief in only one God. He also taught that God's word had been revealed to the Jewish and Christian prophets in the past, and now he, Muhammad, was receiving this same revelation from God.

In the next few years in Mecca, Muhammad gathered a small following. But most of the polytheistic Meccan people disliked his teaching, and in 622 A.D. Muhammad and his followers were driven out of Mecca and took refuge in the neighboring town of Medina where they received a more friendly reception. This event, known as the Hegira, is really the starting point of Islamic history, for after this the group took form as a political society as well as a religious community. The new movement gained followers very rapidly over the next few years, and in 630 A.D. the strength of the movement was sufficient for Muhammad to reenter Mecca triumphantly and establish it as the center of Islam. By the time of Muhammad's death in 632 A.D., Islam was embraced by all of Arabia.

The Caliphate and the Divisions of Islam

During his lifetime, Muhammad had never established any pattern of succession for the leadership of the Muslim community. After his death the office of *caliphate* came into being in answer to this problem. The caliph was considered the head of the politico-religious Islamic empire, and as such was the guardian of Islamic beliefs and rules of life. In deciding who was to fill this office, party strife among the Muslims was rampant from the beginning. During the first thirty years after Muhammad's death, the two major divisions of the Islamic faith were formed. The first, and most widely accepted form, was Sunni Islam, in which the caliph was to be elected by a council. The second form, Shiah Islam, maintained that succession should remain in Muhammad's family. The clash between these two divisions of Islam was so strong that three of the first four caliphs died by violence.

Islamic Expansion

In spite of this problem, though, the Islamic empire expanded very rapidly in the first few centuries after it came into existence. The Muslims conquered large portions of the Byzantine and Persian empires, which had exhausted themselves through their previous encounters. Actually, many of the territories under the domain of these two empires submitted readily to Islamic control, for they had been subjected to oppressive taxation. Furthermore, the Jewish people and the various Christian sects who held different beliefs from those of the official religion of the Byzantine empire had suffered heavy persecution. The Muslims were tolerant of the followers of both the Christian and Jewish religions, for they shared many common beliefs with each.

By the end of the first century under caliphate rule, Islam had been carried successfully across the Mediterranean world to Spain in the West and to India in the East. The height of imperial power and control for Islam was attained during the ninth and early tenth centuries A.D. After this time, the expansion of the empire failed to continue, partly because its unity began to dissolve slowly as the office of the caliphate lost its power, and partly because the Islamic empire met with resistance from the Holy Roman empire of the West, which had regained much of its strength during the ninth and tenth centuries A.D.

Within this period of almost 3000 years, from Abraham to the tenth century A.D., the sacred literature of the Jews, Christians, and Muslims was written. In studying the selections from the literature, keep in mind the historical context out of which these writings came, remembering that the followers of Judaism, Christianity, and Islam believe that God has made himself known to them through these events which they recall in their history.

SUMMARY: HISTORICAL CHRONOLOGY

B.C.

2000-1800	1650	1250?	1200	1000	922	721	587	538	444
	Entry into Egypt	Exodus	Israelite Entry into Canaan			Fall of Samaria (Israel)	Fall of Jerusalem (Judah)	Restoration	Ezra-Nehemiah Reform—Torah Canonized
Patriarchal Period			Period of the Judges	United Kingdom	Divided Kingdom		Babylonian Exile	Persian Control of Israel	

332	175	168	167	165	164	143	63	late first century	6-4?
Alexander the Great	Antiochus Epiphanes	Temple Desecrated	Maccabean Revolt	Temple Rededicated		Independence Won	Pompey Captures Palestine	Schools of Hillel and Shammai	Birth of Jesus

Greek Control—Ptolemaic and Seleucid

Roman Empire

A.D.

28-30?	30?	64?	66	70	73	90	132-135	200	324
Jesus' Ministry	Cruci-fixion	Death of Peter and Paul		Fall of Temple		Council of Jamnia-Hebrew Bible Canonized	Jewish Rebellion	Final Mishnah Editing	Constantine Pro-claims Christianity the Official Religion
			Jewish War with Rome						

Roman Empire

4th century	400	410	500	570	610	622	632	655	7th-10th centuries
New Testament Canonized	Jerusalem Talmud	Fall of Rome	Babylonian Talmud	Birth of Muhammad	Muhammad's Call	Muhammad's Hegira	Death of Muhammad	Recension of Qur'an	Islamic Expansion

Roman Empire   Byzantine Empire

SELECTED REFERENCES

RELIGIOUS LITERATURE

While this text includes Rabbinic and Islamic readings, and you are free to use your own version of the Hebrew Bible and New Testament, it is suggested that you have access to the following basic texts for purposes of study and comparison:

The Bible, one of the newer translations such as the *New English Bible,* or *The New American Bible,* with footnotes, concordances, and other useful apparatus.

The Koran (one of the following)

Arberry, A. J. *The Holy Koran.* London: George Allen and Unwin, Ltd., 1953.

Dawood, N. J. *Koran.* Middlesex: Penguin Books.

Pickthall, M. M. *The Meaning of the Glorious Koran.* New York: Mentor Books.

Yusuf Ali, A. *The Holy Qur'an.* Cambridge: Hafner Publishing Co., 1938.

Pentateuch & Haftorahs. Hertz, J.H., ed. New York: Oxford U. Press (5 volumes).

BASIC REFERENCES

The following books are strongly recommended for inclusion in a school or classroom library. Annotation has been provided for those texts whose titles do not make their focus and value clear.

Aharoni, Yohanan and Michael Avi-Yonah. *The Macmillan Bible Atlas.* New York: The Macmillan Co., 1968.

Anderson, B. W. *Understanding the Old Testament.* 2d ed. Englewood Cliffs, N.J.: Prentice-Hall, Inc., 1966.

Baron, S. W., and Blau, J. L. eds. *Judaism: Postbiblical and Talmudic Period.* Indianapolis: Bobbs-Merrill Co., Inc., 1954. A representative selection of writings from what is called the second classical period of Judaism, which demonstrates that while there are differences in emphasis in Jewish religion before and after the Babylonian Exile there are no fundamental divergencies in approach, belief or ritual. An excellent historical summary of the period can be found in the introduction.

Grayzel, S. *History of the Jews.* Philadelphia: Jewish Publication Society of America. Revised edition, 1968.

Guillaume, A. *Islam.* London: Cassell, 1963; Pelican, Penguin pb.

Interpreter's Dictionary of the Bible. Nashville: Abingdon Press, 1962 (4 volumes). An indispensable reference to names, places, events, and themes in the Old and New Testaments. Clear, concise, and detailed articles, maps, and pictures. Longer articles are preceded by helpful outlines. Cross references and short bibliographies are provided.

Keller, W. *Bible as History.* New York: William Morrow & Co., Inc.

The World of the Bible. Yonkers, N.Y.: Educational Heritage, Inc., 1964. (5 volumes). Filled with useful color illustrations and commentary.

GENERAL REFERENCES

The Anchor Bible. New York: Doubleday, 1964. (37 volumes). Each volume contains text, explanatory notes on the text, and longer commentaries on problems and points of interest. Individual volumes from this series (e.g. Genesis, The Gospel According to John) may be purchased.

Coon, C. S. Caravan: Story of the Middle East. rev. ed. New York: Holt, Rinehart, & Winston, Inc., 1958.

Finegan, J. Light From the Ancient Past. 2d ed. Princeton: Princeton University Press, 1949.

The Interpreter's Bible. Nashville: Abingdon Press, 1952. (12 volumes). Much like The Anchor Bible in format. In addition to explanatory notes and commentary on the texts, useful general articles are found in the lead volumes to the Old and New Testaments, volumes I and VII. Individual volumes may be purchased.

Kraeling, Emil G., ed. Rand McNally Bible Atlas. rev. ed. New York: Rand McNally & Co., 1962.

Mould, E. W. K. Essentials of Bible History. 3d ed. New York: The Ronald Press Company, 1966.

Pritchard, J. B., ed. Ancient Near East: An Anthology of Texts and Pictures. Princeton: Princeton University Press, 1958.

HEBREW BIBLE

Ausubel, N. The Book of Jewish Knowledge. New York: Crown Publishers, 1964.

de Vaux, Roland. Ancient Israel, Its Life and Institutions. New York: McGraw Hill Book Co., Inc., 1961. 2 vols.

Finkelstein, L. ed. The Jews: Their History, Culture, and Religion. 3d ed. New York: Harper & Row. 2 vols.

Gordon, Cyrus H. The World of the Old Testament. Garden City, New York: Doubleday & Co., Inc., 1958 o.p.

Hunt, Ignatius, O.S.B. Understanding the Bible. New York: Sheed and Ward, 1962.

Orlinsky, H. M. Ancient Israel. Ithaca: Cornell University Press., 1954.

Rowley, H. H. The Growth of the Old Testament. New York: Harper and Row, 1963.

Sandmel, S. The Hebrew Scriptures: An Introduction to their Literature and Religious Ideas. New York: Knopf, 1963.

Sarna, N. M. Understanding Genesis: The Heritage of Biblical Israel. New York: Schocken, 1970

Westermann, Claus. Handbook to the Old Testament. Minneapolis: Augsburg, 1967.

APOCRYPHAL AND RABBINIC WRITINGS

Braude, W. G., trans. The Midrash on Psalms. New Haven: Yale University Press, 1959. (2 volumes)

Epstein, I., ed. The Babylonian Talmud. London: Soncino Press, 1948. (34 volumes)

Glatzer, N. N. Hillel the Elder. rev. ed. New York: Schocken Books, 1966.

Glatzer, N. N. The Judaic Tradition. Boston: Beacon Press, 1969.

Hertz, J. H., trans. Sayings of the Fathers. New York: Behrman House, Inc., 1945.

Kolatch, A. J. Who's Who in the Talmud. New York: Jonathan David, 1964. o.p.

Montefiore, C. G., and Loewe, H. A. A Rabbinic Anthology. New York: Meridian Books, Inc., 1960. o.p.

Moore, G. F. Judaism in the First Centuries of the Christian Era. Cambridge: Harvard University Press, 1927. 3 vols.

Silver, A. H. Where Judaism Differed. New York: MacMillan.

NEW TESTAMENT

Beare, F. W. *The Earliest Records of Jesus.* New York: Abingdon Press, 1962.

Kee, H. C., Young, F. W., and Froehlich, K. *Understanding the New Testament.* 2d ed. Englewood Cliffs, N.J.: Prentice-Hall, Inc. 1965.

McNeile, A. H. *An Introduction to the Study of the New Testament.* London: Oxford University Press, 1953.

Sandmel, S. *A Jewish Understanding of the New Testament.* New York: Ktav Publishing House, 1956.

Throckmorton, B. H., ed. *Gospel Parallels.* New York: Thomas Nelson and Sons, 1957.

Westermann, Claus. *Handbook to the New Testament.* Minneapolis: Augsburg, 1969.

Wikenhauser, A. *New Testament Introduction.* New York: Herder and Herder, 1963.

QUR'AN

Ali, Maulana Muhammad. *The Religion of Islam.* Mystic, Conn.: Lawrence Verry, Inc., 1950.

Guillaume, A. *New Light on the Life of Muhammad.* Manchester: Manchester University Press, 1959.

Hitti, P. K., *The Arabs: A Short History.* New York: Gateway Editions, Henry Regnery Co.

Khan, M. Z. *Islam.* New York: Harper and Row, 1962. o.p.

Kritzeck, J., ed. *Anthology of Islamic Literature.* New York: New American Library, Mentor Books.

Kritzeck, J. *Sons of Abraham: Jews, Christians, and Moslems.* Baltimore: Helicon Press, 1965.

Morgan, K. W., ed., *Islam—The Straight Path.* New York: Ronald Press Co., 1958.

Raham, F. *Islam.* New York: Holt, Rinehart and Winston, 1966. Also Anchor Books, Doubleday and Co.

INDEX

hope, 35, 101, 113, 114, 117, 119
Hosea, 103-105, 107
Hosea, Book of, 103-106
human sacrifice, 49, 76, 176
Hyksos, 35, 36, 87, 295

idolatry, 49, 104, 146, 246
immortality, 160, 161
incarnation, 218, 219
inspiration, 98, 99, 197
Isaac, 76, 78-82, 295
Isaiah, 107, 118-122, 137
Isaiah, Book of, 118-122
Ishmael, 75, 76, 246, 260, 262
Ishmaelites, 86
Islam, 244-246, 249, 251, 256, 262, 268, 280, 281, 292, 302-304
Israel, 31, 32, 36, 45-49, 52, 55, 57, 58, 63, 68, 73, 74, 85, 93, 105, 108, 120, 122, 137, 139, 150, 198-200, 216
Israelite, definition of, 140
Israelites, 35, 38, 43, 46, 54, 55, 81, 295

Jacob, 80, 81, 83, 84, 87, 295
James, Letter of, 230, 231
Jeremiah, 113, 114
Jeremiah, Book of, 113-115
Jeroboam II, 104
Jerusalem, 58, 107, 108, 113, 114, 117, 148, 296, 297, 300
Jesus, 198-219, 229, 233, 236, 270-273, 299
Jew, definition of, 140
Jewish-Roman War, 299
jinn, 281
Job, Book of, 128-130
John, 202, 220
John, Gospel of, 202, 204, 218-219
Joseph, 85-88
Joshua, 44-46, 49
Joshua, Book of, 45-47
Judah ha-Nasi, 169
Judas Maccabaeus, 136
judges, 48, 49, 52, 54, 55, 296
Judges, Book of, 48-53

Ka'ba, 246, 262, 290
kal vahomer, 192, 193
kerygma, 198, 201, 203, 207, 208

Khadeeja, 243, 245
King Herod, 148
kingdom of God, 209, 217, 226
Koheleth, 125, 126

Laban, 83
lament, 93, 94
Lamentations, Book of, 107-109
last judgment, 155, 165, 230
Last Supper, 210
Logos, 219, 273
Lord's Supper, 232
Lot, 76
Luke, Gospel of, 212-213

Maccabees, 148, 298
magi, 145, 215
Mark, Gospel of, 207-211
marriage, 103, 105, 114, 131, 132
Mary Magdalene, 204
Matthew, Gospel of, 214-217
maxims, 126, 176
Mecca, 243, 245, 287, 289, 290, 302, 303
mediation, 55
mediator, 32, 120
Medina, 246, 303
Megiddo, 50
Mekhilta Bahodesh, 189-193
mercy, 68, 93, 100, 117, 148, 281
Messiah, 137, 139, 155, 165, 176, 198-200, 204, 207-209, 211, 216, 226, 229
metaphor, 32, 34, 105, 122, 132
Micah, 107
Midianite, 52, 53, 55, 86
midrash, 174, 175, 180, 184, 189, 203
miracle, 187, 188
Mishnah, 169, 175, 176, 180, 182-184, 186, 188, 189, 203
Mishnah Pesahim, 178-180, 210
Moab, 43
Moabites, 76
monarchy, 54, 55, 57-59, 74, 94, 97, 99, 100, 107, 108
monotheism, 101, 120
moral retribution, 129, 146, 148, 165, 282, 284, 285
Moses, 33, 35-38, 43, 44, 48, 64, 69, 86, 173, 174, 264-267, 295
Mount Horeb, 36, 37

Mount Sinai, 32, 38
mountain, 32, 36, 43, 217
muezzin, 289
Muhammad, 243-246, 249-252, 256, 257, 268, 280, 302, 303
mystery religions, 126, 147

Nebuchadnezzar, 58, 108, 113, 114, 120, 138
Nehemiah, 136, 298
new age, 137-139, 176, 200, 216
new creation, 230, 233
New Israel, 213, 226
New Jerusalem, 220, 221
Nineveh, 114
Noah, 70, 71, 191, 193
nomads, 54, 68, 86, 244
northern kingdom (Israel), 58, 87, 97, 100, 101, 103-105, 108, 114, 119, 297

obedience, 32
oral tradition, 53, 64, 91, 149, 169, 174, 175, 180, 203, 217, 252
orders, 184
original identifying event, 44, 200

Pairs, 174-176, 184
pantheism, 161
parable, 189, 209, 212, 213
paragraphs, 176
parallelism, 50, 92
paschal lambs, 38, 180
Passover, 38, 44, 178-181, 210
patriarchs, 74, 80, 85
Paul, 200, 201, 208, 226, 228, 231, 232, 299
Pentateuch, 33, 69, 92, 173-175
Pentecost, 225, 226
Peter, 208, 299
pharaoh, 36, 85, 87, 265
Pharisees, 149, 150, 173, 175, 176, 199, 200, 207, 298
Philistines, 55, 296
Pirke Aboth, 169-173, 176, 177
plagues, 37, 38
Plato, 146, 161, 233, 235, 236
poetry, 50, 91, 92, 107, 108, 128, 129, 131, 132, 140
polygamy, 75

polytheism, 246
Pontius Pilate, 148
possession, 98, 99, 101
preexistence, 155, 161, 219, 253, 273
priestly writing tradition, 64
promised land, 33, 37, 38, 43, 47-49, 55, 74, 75, 79, 81, 83, 84, 87
prophecy, 97, 98, 101, 117, 180, 257, 268, 296
prophet, 36, 55, 97-101, 107, 148, 249, 256, 296
Proverbs, 126
Psalms, Book of, 91-94
pseudepigrapha, 163
pseudonym, 137
punishment, 32, 33, 46, 68, 70, 97, 100, 101, 104, 108, 113, 114, 138, 157

qiblah, 287, 289
Qumran community, 150
Qur'an, 245, 249, 251-253, 256-258, 268, 279, 281, 289, 291, 292

Rabbi Judah ha-Nasi, 175, 176
Rachel, 83, 114
Rahab, 46
Ramses II, 36, 295
Rebekah, 78, 80
recension, 257
reka, 193
remnant, 71, 76, 122, 136, 148, 150
restoration, 100, 107, 114, 118, 120, 135, 136, 148, 173
resurrection, 150, 155, 165, 199, 285
resurrection of Jesus, 200-204, 208, 211, 230, 272, 299
revelation, 32
Revelation, Book of, 220, 221
rhyme, 50
rhythm, 50, 92
riddles, 126
Roman Empire, 148, 213, 221, 228, 243, 299-301
Romans, Letter to, 228, 229

Sabbath, 65, 119
Sadducees, 149, 150, 173, 175, 176, 199, 298
Samuel, 54, 55, 58